The Laterite Road

My Life as an Engineer in Nigeria
1958-1982

by

Jack Muggeridge

Civil Engineer MBE CEng FICE FIHT

Dedication

This Memoir is dedicated to the many people of Nigeria who have identified with a life's cause of giving public service to their country, sustaining high moral values and a code of personal ethics that makes for a good society and a sound economy.

Only through their continued work and contribution will we see a united, strong and prosperous Nigeria that is federal, independent, free and democratic, promoting and protecting the rights, individual freedom and well-being of every Nigerian citizen.

"Words will not be adequate to thank you for your contributions to the development of Nigeria which you served so loyally the best part of your life."

Alhaji Shehu Shagari

Jack Muggeridge

Published by

Bound Biographies

Heyford Park House, Heyford Park, Bicester, Oxon OX25 5HD

www.boundbiographies.com

ISBN: 1-905178-00-X

Contents

Appendices

Illustrations Index

Preface

For very many years, my father's expatriate life in Nigeria remained clouded in mystery. During the formative growing up years of myself and my four brothers, he was largely an absent figure, but one regularly remitting back home to the UK each month all he could spare to support his family.

Occasionally, we did get to see him when he came back to England for periods of home leave, usually lasting three months but sometimes longer. He would normally rent a cottage somewhere in Sussex, either by the beach or in the country, so our visits to him in various holiday locations were very special and still remain rich in the memory.

So it was that, absent for most of the big family events, I did not really get to know my father well until he first retired from his work in Nigeria at the end of 1978 and returned home. Almost immediately, he threw himself with enthusiasm into a new project. With a colleague, Peter Guthrie, he set up a register of engineers who could be called on to assist in developing countries. With a vision based on long experience overseas, he saw not only the desperate and recurring need in the Third World for the assistance of qualified engineers, but also the possibilities of providing invaluable professional development to individuals whilst continuing to be employed by their companies. He particularly felt it important that engineers did not lose the ability to manage local labour and to help implement the low technology, sustainable solutions needed to provide basic amenities such as sanitation and water. He wanted engineers to be able to think on their feet, faced with practical problems such as restoring a missing river-crossing using locally available local materials and man-power.

Reading through this memoir, it will become clear that his value and expertise in Nigeria lay in finding solutions that were wholly practical for the environment and, importantly, also appropriate for the culture. Thus Jack Muggeridge became the first secretary of the charity RedR, and also one of the first engineers to go into the field on assignment, in his case to Malaysia at the age of 70.

Two years later found him back once more in Nigeria, coping valiantly with problems of incompetence and corruption in Abuja to achieve impossible deadlines. Returning home in late 1982 he was exhausted, yet barely a year later following Shehu Shagari's re-election he was more than ready to return yet again in a consultancy role. However, political events in Nigeria were to conspire against this.

As well as his assignments overseas, he still managed to serve some ten years in total with RedR, commuting daily by train to London. After this, he devoted himself completely to the care of his brother, Malcolm, and sister-in-law, Kitty, both in declining health. After Malcolm's death in 1990 and ever the efficient administrator, he undertook the difficult task of methodically sorting out his brother's papers and effects in preparation for their despatch to Wheaton College in the United States for archiving, and arranging the sale of *Park Cottage*, Malcolm's home in Robertsbridge.

And so it was that my father, now well into his eighties, finally turned to writing his 'Memoir', settled now in a small wardened flat in Mander Court, Caversham in Berkshire. It was a remarkable achievement – over 100,000 words, all produced on his small portable typewriter without the assistance of modern technology which he spurned. His greatest problem in an age of word processing was finding suitable cotton ink ribbons to replace the ones which he had worn out! The manuscript was painstakingly drafted and redrafted, typed, corrected with *Snopak* and then retyped, finally reaching completion in 1999 as a thick binder of A4 paper.

It was never entirely clear to whom the Memoir was directed. It was obviously not going to be of interest to a commercial publisher, the biography lacking the name of a recognised media celebrity or politician.

He sent copies out to a small number of close friends – Peter Guthrie, Nick Flynn (a journalist friend), Gerrit Jan Colenbrander (husband of Jack's niece), and Shehu Shagari – asking each for comments, and gave a copy to me.

Incidentally, this was not his only preoccupation in his later years. He also liaised extensively with Richard Ingrams over the publication of a biography on Malcolm Muggeridge and also completed a Memoir, started by his brother, covering his father's life. He loved writing and was a pedant for accuracy of detail. However, despite all his efforts, and mine, to get things right, no doubt this Memoir will carry some mistakes, omissions or inaccuracies for which I apologise on his behalf. I am also conscious that there may be remaining sensitivities, either personal or national, in some of the content but it is hoped that, with the passage of time, these will not detract from the enjoyment of the book as written by my father.

After a short illness Jack Muggeridge passed away on 30th March 2001 at the age of 91. Obituaries were carried by the *Independent,* the *Daily Telegraph* and the *Journal of the Royal Engineers* (see Appendices). After the well-attended funeral, my spare time became fully occupied with arranging, and then running, the centennial celebrations for his brother Malcolm in the US and in England. Sometime before my father's death, I had already started the planning of several events with him, endeavouring to keep his ever-active mind engaged, and also providing an important and significant event to which he could look forward.

Consequently, my father's Memoir was placed somewhat on the back burner whilst I decided what to do with it. I could not see all that considerable and laborious effort of several years come to nought and an opportunity came in 2004 when contact was made with Sally Gray of *Bound Biographies,* a company which specialises in small volume biographies for writers of personal memoirs.

The first task undertaken by Sally was to transform Jack's typewritten manuscript into a more manageable electronic format. Unapologetically, the decision was taken early on to edit, rearrange and supplement the work as felt necessary for ease of reading and understanding which, whilst easy to do in an age of computer technology, would have been impossible for my father to achieve. However, the manuscript largely retains his style of writing and content, and we have not attempted to edit for reasons of political or personal sensitivity.

It was always clear that the driving inspiration in the writing of these Memoirs was the great affection and respect my father felt for Shehu Shagari. In fact, on returning to the UK in 1982, my father had initially set himself a project of writing an intimate biography entitled *Shehu Shagari – the Man*. His planned return to Nigeria in 1984 would have been used to carry out the necessary local research. However, without access to information after the coup, and in the changed political climate, he felt he could not do full justice to his friend. And so he wrote his own account of life in Nigeria instead – one that is perhaps equal in love of the country and its people, and the wish that Nigeria would achieve through peace and democracy the prosperity it deserved as the largest and most highly populated country in Africa. It should be of no surprise that Shehu Shagari features prominently in the latter part of the memoir and fitting that the former President kindly consented to my request to write a Foreword to this Memoir. I am only sorry that it has been so long in coming to publication.

I do hope you will find interest in reading of a life spent giving honourable service to a developing country, often in harsh conditions away from the normal comforts and conveniences of home life. Whilst Jack Muggeridge did not achieve all the fame of his elder brother, he at least received recognition from the Queen and an invitation to Buckingham Palace! He deserves to have his life and contribution remembered and commemorated. That then is the purpose of this book.

Sally Muggeridge
The Old Farm House
Eythorne, Kent
England
April 2005

16

Introduction

Some years ago, I recall showing my name in the MBE Civil List to my last but one son, Richard. "What did you get that for Dad?" he asked.

Consequently, I did not set out to write an autobiography but rather a record of over twenty years' professional public service in Nigeria.

I ask those who may happen to come across this Memoir at some time, to study it in the understanding that I was motivated by my love for Nigeria and its diverse peoples, second only to my love of England and the English, and, more preciously, because I came by good fortune to know the remarkable Nigerian, Alhaji Shehu Shagari.

The biographical details of Shehu Shagari (I adopt that generally used appellation although I now claim him as 'my dearest friend') are well recorded in a number of books. One excellent example is *President and Power in Nigeria – The Life of Shehu Shagari* by David Williams, now sadly deceased, who edited with distinction the weekly publication *West Africa* for twenty years. Another is *Shehu Shagari – The Biography of Nigeria's First Executive President* by Okion Ojigbo. There is, too, a short official biography under the title *Meet Mr President* published by the information division of the Federal Ministry of Information soon after his election as Executive President in October 1979. Its introduction reads: "Where the greatness of Alhaji Shehu Shagari lies is in the truly remarkable preparation he has undergone for the great office which he has now taken up. But that is not all, it lies also in his transparent humility, his godliness, his purity of character and his self-effacement."

By the time we met in 1976, he had just concluded eighteen years in Federal Government either as a Minister or Commissioner before returning to his home town of Sokoto, resolved to be elected as a Senator

17

and thenceforth wishing to eschew active participation in Government. I, on the other hand, was an expatriate professional engineer originally engaged in 1958 by the then Colonial Power, but who had opted to remain after Independence in October 1960. I had been appointed Chief Executive and General Manager of Sokoto Urban Development Authority (SUDA) and it was there I met with its Chairman, Alhaji Shehu Shagari, who was to make my final years in Nigeria the most rewarding and professionally productive of all. Without him, my concept of the new Central Market of Sokoto would not be there in reality, nor indeed the other achievements of SUDA for the well being of the local people. His personal integrity was always to be unquestioned. He never asked me to favour a contractor, once only he recommended someone he knew who had suffered personal misfortune for consideration for a special SUDA bus service for school children, but I had already selected that person as eminently suitable for the role.

When the time came for me to leave SUDA in 1978, I felt sad that in reality this was to be the end of a friendship which had grown out of mutual respect and a confidence in achievement for the public good. Fortunately, it proved only to be a break, and the relationship was resumed a few years later but under very stressful and difficult circumstances at the Federal Capital Development Authority at Abuja. The new Federal Capital of all Nigeria had become, for Shehu Shagari, his greatest contribution to his beloved country. The defining moment for me was when I was able to honour my promise to him regarding the completion of the Presidential Lodge, but saw that there could be no further role for me with FCDA. It was time to bow out.

I was therefore spared being present when the Military took power again in 1984, deposing the President. Naturally, I was anxious as to the safety of Shehu Shagari whom I regarded as a close friend. It was impossible to communicate with him but I was confident that there would be a public outcry if the new Government harmed him in any way. He was in fact placed under house arrest.

Before regaining his unrestricted freedom in July 1987, I read with sadness a notice in *West Africa* that Shehu Shagari had lost four children in a motor accident on the Sokoto-Shagari road. I wrote to him but doubt if the letter reached him. Here then, I wish to honour Shehu Shagari, the man. His inspiration, his advice, his consistent support and understanding enabled me to give my professional services to their fullest throughout our association. A man of real modesty, integrity, a remarkable Nigerian I came to love and will never cease to admire. I cherish our friendship and the personal contact which endures to this day.

Nigeria has had to wait too long for its return to civilian rule, for the second time. It may seem ironical, but fully in keeping with the Nigerian way of doing things, its people have recently elected General Olusegun Obasanjo, an ex-Military Head of State, as its Executive President for the next four years. As I know General Obasanjo, however daunting the problems and difficulties, he will succeed in restoring Nigeria to its rightful place amongst the nations of the world.

The task ahead is awesome indeed. Perhaps he should try to persuade Alhaji Shehu Shagari to help in some non-political role. After all, it was General Obasanjo who, back in October 1979 as Military Head of State, ceremonially handed over to Alhaji Shehu Shagari as Executive President of the new, democratically elected civilian Government!

Sorrowfully, at 88 years of age, I am unable to make a repeat performance by offering to look after the drains at the Presidential Complex at the new Capital, Abuja. It is only a short distance from the infinitely preferable 'Lodge' now known, I understand, as *Aguda House*.

Jack Muggeridge
Mander Court
Caversham, England
May 1998

Editor's Note: Shehu Shagari later produced his autobiography *Beckoned to Serve* in 2001 published by *Heinemann Educational Books* (Nigeria) plc. This was received and read with great enjoyment by Jack just before his death.

Alhaji Shehu Shagari

Foreword

"All the world's a stage
And all the men and women,
Merely players."

William Shakespeare

To many people who knew Engineer Jack Muggeridge, especially in the United Kingdom, he lived his life in the shadow of his illustrious brother, Malcolm Muggeridge. To others who knew him, especially in Nigeria, West Africa, Jack Muggeridge lived his own life in his chosen way, and was always happy and proud of his achievements.

It is a pleasure and a great honour for me to be asked by the family of my Dear Friend, the late Jack Muggeridge, to write a Foreword to his Memoir of service in my country Nigeria. The Memoir is without a doubt a detailed account of his dedicated and selfless service sincerely and willingly rendered to a developing country in dire need of technical assistance at a critical stage of its history.

Jack Muggeridge arrived in Nigeria at the last lap of its transition from a British Colonial Territory towards National Sovereignty and Independence. He witnessed the task of nation building by a promising country with great potential but woefully embedded with multifarious problems of establishing Democracy, Unity in Diversity and the problems of Economic Development which called for foreign assistance in vital fields of human endeavour. It was a situation in which many Colonial officers and other professionals and experts were already on their way out of the country, that Jack Muggeridge joined the public service of Northern Nigeria and worked for a period spanning 25 years. He spent most of his time as a field officer working in the provinces under very difficult conditions which he faced with courage and determination.

His first posting was in the Middle Belt area of Nigeria just south of the great rivers Niger and Benue which traversed the country from west to east and at Lokoja Confluence flowed southwards into the Atlantic Ocean. Jack had at one time lived and worked in Lokoja and he was there as a Provincial Engineer when the Civil War broke out in 1967. He passed through the rigours and uncertainties of the war situation and saw it all from there and elsewhere in his subsequent Stations throughout Northern Nigeria. It happened that in most cases his postings to various places arose from crisis situations which had occurred in such places which urgently required his professional handling. He soon developed a reputation for handling difficult or delicate problems which he carried out with dedication and skill. In other cases his services were required because of the compelling desire to implement a new and important project efficiently within a limited period of time. It was generally accepted that there could be no better choice available for such an assignment than that of Engineer Jack Muggeridge because of his ability, integrity and enthusiasm to face challenges.

It was indeed within such a situation described above that I had the good fortune of coming across a wonderful man, Jack the gentleman workaholic; a man of conviction and integrity, a model civil servant and true professional who always regarded his job as a mission that must be accomplished.

I first heard about this rare gem among the remaining expatriate officers after Nigeria's Independence from Colonel Umaru Mohammed, the former Governor of the North-Western State of Nigeria, who came to my house in Sokoto one evening in order to persuade me to accept his offer of chairmanship of a newly established organisation known as the Sokoto Urban Development Authority (SUDA). While I welcomed the idea for the new organisation, I had previously declined the offer of chairmanship because it was announced publicly before I was consulted. The Governor, however, in his effort to convince me to change my mind first apologised and then spoke highly about the man he had chosen to be the General Manager of the new organisation. He told me about the new man's outstanding achievements elsewhere in Northern Nigeria including his success at Kaduna in planning and building a modern market. I eventually agreed to accept the offer, largely because I was attracted by the exemplary qualities of the person earmarked to manage the new authority.

My later experience of working with him in the SUDA confirmed in no uncertain terms his immense energy and reliability. Thenceforth we developed an everlasting mutual friendship, the type of which is difficult to envisage. The reason? Because we happened to discover ourselves with amazing similarities in our attitude to work and life in general, except that I cannot in all fairness claim to match him in his tenacity and devotion to work.

Perhaps the field in which we differed lies in his sense of vision which at times was forthcoming and accurate. I recall his insistence that I must prepare myself for the task of leading my country sooner or later. I neither agreed with him nor entertained any wish for such a position, and told him so. Later at the occasion of his retirement from service in October 1978 Jack Muggeridge promised to return to Nigeria if I became the President and jokingly offered to look after the State House if invited by me! In 1979 he was proved right, when I took over the reigns of government from the then military ruler of Nigeria as a democratically elected President.

In the end I did invite him in 1982, and at the age of 73, to assist in supervising the building of a Presidential Guest House at Abuja before our movement to the new Capital City of Nigeria. He was able to complete his assignment in good time, despite my interference in suggesting some modifications when building was in progress. For example, while inspecting the progress I noticed there was provision for a lift in the house which I thought was not necessary, since it was only a two-storey building. I stopped it. I came to regret it many years later when, as a guest of the then military government, I stayed in the house and had difficulty in climbing the stairs due to my old age!

I also remember that, in the course of my inspection of the newly completed building, I noticed some large framed murals all over the place. Jack had commissioned a Nigerian artist to paint them in order to depict Nigerian art. I was not very impressed and asked him to remove them. He explained that the murals were not necessarily intended for me alone but for visitors, especially foreign visitors who might one day stay there. He hoped that Her Majesty Queen Elizabeth II might stay in that house as a guest of the Federal Government and he was sure that she would be delighted to see the murals. Eventually, after a few years Her Majesty did indeed stay in that house for two or three days. Regrettably, she could not see the murals, however, because one of the outgoing Military Authorities who succeeded me had removed them!

I can go on and on *ad infinitum* writing about my Dear Friend Jack and his achievements, wisdom and vision, while hoping that I do not fall into the same trap that he had so unwittingly encountered in writing his Memoirs. Perhaps he was not aware that he spent a substantial part of his book speaking about me, which to me is rather embarrassing. Regrettably, he is no longer with us to be pleased or embarrassed by what is supposed to be a Foreword and certainly not another book about my Dear Jack Muggeridge of blessed memory.

May his soul rest in perfect peace. Amen.

Shehu U.A. Shagari
Turakin Sokoto
June 2004

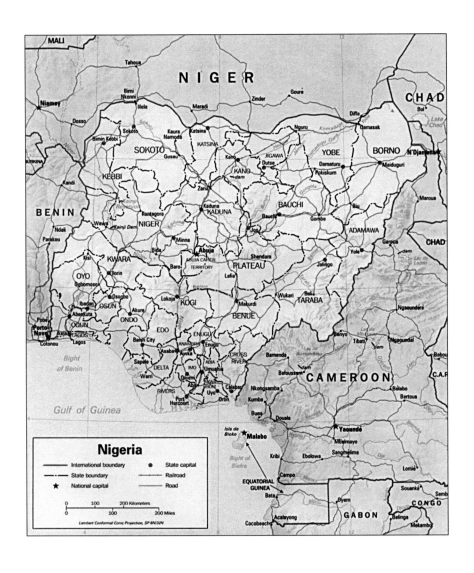

Map of Nigeria

25

Ilorin, Kabba and Benue Provinces

By the early 1950s I had reached the position of Deputy Borough Engineer with a North London Local Authority, and although content with the job professionally I had become concerned over two aspects. In the first place, the Government, then led by Edward Heath, would be implementing the policy to merge smaller Local Authorities with larger ones, inevitably leading to redundancies (or early retirements), especially amongst senior positions such as mine; secondly, with a family of three growing children, I needed to better myself financially since salaries in Local Government were below those of Government Service and certainly well below professionals in the business and commercial sectors.

Advertisements were appearing in technical journals, newspapers and the like by the Colonial Office/Crown Agents seeking professionals for service in Overseas Territories, even though there was increasing clamour for Independence from Colonial Rule. Contracts of service, salaries, allowances etc., were decidedly attractive.

In a mood of frustration, I applied for full information and received details of a Civil Engineering post in the Copperbelt of Northern Rhodesia (Zambia today), the Capital of which is Lusaka having earlier been moved from Livingstone to this more central area of the country. I submitted a completed application form and, after some weeks, I was called for interview. A long interval followed before I received an offer for the post, but by that time the children were four in number. We talked it over and decided against acceptance.

Two worried and stressful years later, having left Local Government for what transpired to be a short-lived managerial post with a small building and civil engineering firm, I renewed my application to the Colonial Office/Crown Agents. This time, presumably relying on my original

27

application and subsequent interview, I was offered a contract as an Executive Engineer with the Public Works Department of the Northern Region Government of Nigeria. The salary was almost double what I had been receiving with the Local Authority, and I understood that these contracts, of 12-18 months' duration depending on age, were normally renewable subject to satisfactory service, so I accepted the post. The family had grown again, and I now had five children who would stay at home in Hampstead, their education being of prime concern; the two elder boys were already attending University College School nearby.

Jacks' children

So, on 16th April 1958, I was at the start of a new beginning of my professional employment. At that time Nigeria where I would be living and working was little more than a name in a world atlas: known as 'the giant of Africa' it was seven times the area of the United Kingdom, had a population at the time uncertain but any figure over 50 million, and a tropical climate which I had no idea how would I react to, considering I was nearing 50 years of age. Certainly, I had no inkling that, henceforth, my professional working life would be centred on that overseas country called Nigeria until it finally came to an end, almost 25 years later, in October 1982.

By 1958, the long customary means of 14 days' sea passage for Government personnel of all grades using the *Elder Dempster Shipping Line* out of Liverpool for West Africa, had recently been superseded by air travel. The flight by *BOAC* piston-engined aircraft called *Stratocruisers*, took a mere six hours from London Heathrow to Lagos at the southern tip of Nigeria, its then Capital. I was about to learn that these *Boeing 377* aircraft were referred to by the name 'Stratoboozers'!

Most passengers mustered at the *BOAC* Headquarters in Buckingham Palace Road, London Victoria for coaches to Heathrow Airport Terminal. In those days, because of the likelihood of violent turbulence to the aircraft when flying over the desert areas of North Africa during daylight hours, due to heat and air pockets, schedules were arranged for the cooler night time hours. Thus was my flight on 16th April 1958 scheduled to touch down at Tripoli (Libya) for passengers and then continue on to Kano in Northern Nigeria to arrive early in the morning of 17th April 1958. However, we were informed at Tripoli that there was trouble with one of the engines and the aircraft must go to Barcelona for overnight stay to await a replacement engine being flown in from London. At Barcelona all passengers would be accommodated for the night in an hotel – at *BOAC's* expense, of course.

By this time, we passengers and crew – numbering about sixty – had been together for long enough to be fairly relaxed, exchanging names and general talk. I had gathered that most were seasoned Government officers of mixed ranks returning from leave or *en route* to a fresh posting. As first class passengers, all drinks were free at the understandably popular

29

bar, a long narrow space seemingly underslung three steps down from the floor of the aircraft. I had noticed this had been tightly packed almost from take-off, so the news at Tripoli and the prospect of the overnight stay at Barcelona – late as it might be – was generally greeted as a mildly exciting diversion.

My name, Muggeridge, attracted the by now usual question regarding Malcolm Muggeridge – remember this was 1958. The furore and aftermath of my brother Malcolm's long and outspoken article about the Monarchy published in the American *Saturday Evening Post* in October 1957 still lingered on, also his editorship of *Punch* from 1953-1957. When asked, I explained that I was a contract Executive Engineer on my first tour of duty in Nigeria with the then Public Works Department. I was to report to PWD Northern Headquarters at Kaduna for posting to a Provincial Engineer's Organisation in a Northern Province. I sensed a slight withdrawal of interest. Quite how the gradings within Departmental Establishments determined social contacts and particularly at the focal point of 'The Club', I had yet to experience.

Jack's elder brother Malcolm

30

Arriving at Barcelona after midnight, it took some time to sort out the allocation of bedrooms at the five-star hotel, some sharing being inevitable. We were told to be at breakfast not later than 6.00am for take-off to Kano as would be announced.

For me, this delay provided an opportunity to glean quite an amount of useful information – as well as, I am sure, some kindly leg-pulling! There had been more drinking at the hotel after some argument with the *BOAC* local representative about payment, so many passengers were rather bleary eyed at breakfast. I had yet to acquire the drinking habits of the tropics; whisky, brandy, gin, cocktails etc., and, of course, long beers.

We were packed and waiting for the move to the Airport when came talk of more delay. I cannot recall now whether it was that the replacement engine had not yet arrived or that it had turned out to be the wrong type, but certainly we would not now leave until early morning of the next day, 18th April 1958, and we were to return to the rooms we had just vacated! The additional delay was no problem to the drinkers. The *BOAC* representative was resigned to a huge bill for our stay to include accommodation, all meals, drinks almost *ad lib*, cables etc. etc., the only argument being the bar hours. Because we were passengers in transit no-one could leave the hotel to go into Barcelona – our passports were ineffective.

An even earlier call for breakfast the next day and we were off to the Airport without further incident. There was a general air of "…we've had enough let's get on with it now." We took off just as the sun was about to rise into a cloudless sky. The sunrise was quite overwhelmingly beautiful, all the colours imaginable. As the aircraft circled for landing at Kano – the Northern International Airport – there below was one of the largest native cities of Africa, built almost entirely of brown mud (laterite) with the dominant feature of the four towers of the great Central Mosque, a scene I was to see again many times, but, at this moment, I saw with wonder and a sense of excitement tinged with apprehension as to what lay ahead for me as I set foot in Nigeria. As a number of us parted from the passengers staying on for Lagos and filed down to the tarmac, two things impressed me: the traditional welcome as the long horn sounded (which I believe has now ceased) and the overpowering scent in the atmosphere

31

which I was later to come to recognise as 'Kano night-soil smell'. The City, said to have a native population of a million, has its soil buckets emptied each night into trucks by 'night soil gangs' and taken to sites outside the City for disposal on open ground. The wind seems always to be in the same direction bringing the odour given off back to the City. I believe, however, there has since been change!

My passport was duly stamped 'Kano Airport Immigration Office, Arrival 18th April 1958' but I was still 'in transit' to Kaduna, the then Capital of Northern Nigeria. Internal flights to a number of principal Cities in the Country were run by *Nigerian Airways* which operated single-engined aircraft, and I was put on a flight to Kaduna an hour or so later. Most of the passengers were new to me. I think we had had one quick stopover on a grass airstrip at Zaria. There was no checking etc. on landing at Kaduna as passport and customs had been done at Kano.

All the other passengers were met and driven off quickly. I was left to wonder what to do when a small car drove up at speed, the driver alighted and hurried in to find me with a broad smile saying, "Captain Mace of PWD you must be Muggeridge – sorry I was late but we've only just heard about your coming and know nothing about you but come along… my job to meet and look after newcomers…" or words to that effect. His non-stop talk and joviality continued as we drove off at speed explaining that he had booked me in at the Government Rest House but really nothing could be done to sort out the situation until Monday as it was now Friday afternoon and all offices were closed down for the Muslim Holiday ending the period of Fasting called Ramadan. He had left a jolly party to come and meet me and everyone would be pleased if I returned to it with him after dropping my baggage at the room at the Rest House.

I was able to show him a copy of my signed contract. He glanced at it but was more interested in making it back to the party. For this, he drove into an area of detached houses and bungalows all with large gardens – he called them (correctly) 'compounds' – and the area 'the GRA' (Government Residential Area). There was no mistaking the party, cars of all descriptions were blocking the road and the drive-in to one of the larger houses and there was a hubbub of voices and laughter. We parked where we could and inside Mace forced us into a large room through a mass of people who made various jovial remarks to him until we reached the hostess. Somehow he managed to effect an introduction and then went off to get drinks. A coherent conversation with the hostess was quite impossible as people, clearly well 'lit up', kept interrupting with remarks to her such as "... a damn shame you've got to go back to England just now, we'll miss you terribly, but never mind we'll look forward to seeing you here again next tour..."

Eventually the party began to break up and Mace took me back to the Rest House. Was it going to be like this most of the time I wondered? Apparently, as explained to me later, I had arrived at the point which was reached by the hostess some time during each tour. Her husband was one of the senior Administrative Officers in Kaduna and as a couple they were very popular. But somehow by about the middle of each tour a number of 'incidents' had built up – no doubt arising from drink – which came to the notice of the Governor causing his displeasure and he had to ask for her to be sent home. It was all very sad but she always managed to come back at the start of her husband's next tour.

Now I had to fill in time until Monday morning when Mace would send a car for me after breakfast, at about 10.00am, to take me to Headquarters so I wrote letters home. The meals at the Rest House were quite good. In the evening, the lounge with a bar at one end would fill up with expatriates and their wives. We talked and all seemed friendly and interested. During the day, although hot, I could walk round the area of tarred roads lined with trees for shade, passing the hotel, the Club with its tennis courts, Government House and so on. I did not then reach the commercial and business area where there would be banks and offices and shops.

Everyone explained that the first priority should be to get a car. My first priority, however, was to establish my existence at Headquarters so that I could arrange about transfer of money for the family at home. This, and a car, to my great surprise and relief proved all too easy!

I was to see the Chief Civil Engineer of the Department, Mr Scott (inevitably known as 'Scottie'). He, presumably, had been told by Captain Mace that I was in possession of a signed contract from The

Crown Agents in London. Affable and welcoming, Mr Scott explained that the Provincial Engineer of Ilorin Province, Mr Philip Temple, was considering the appointment of an Executive Engineer to establish a District covering Ilorin Township – an area of the Province. He would post me to Ilorin informing Mr Temple to expect me in a few days' time. Being in the Middle Belt of Nigeria, Ilorin would enable me to adjust to the climatic conditions without undue difficulty. We talked briefly about my background and my three years' service in the Corps of Royal Engineers during the Second World War. He then passed me to an expatriate accountant who would take care of my personal matters.

The accountant, although rather dour looking, was a great help. A cursory glance through my signed contract seemed to suffice. That I was unlikely to receive any salary for about three months "...the system, you know," should, however, be no deterrent. He rang his friend, the Manager of *Barclays Bank* Kaduna, who said he would be happy to see me during the morning if I would call at the bank. For me, as a touring officer, he advised a Vauxhall pick-up. His friend at the local Agent at *UAC* (*United Africa Company*) would co-operate. Another telephone call confirmed that there were several in stock and one could be made ready for me during the morning – I suggested light grey.

First to *Barclays Bank,* an imposing building, employing expatriate staff mostly. I was soon in the Manager's office being warmly greeted. Certainly he was interested to study my contract document. As we talked, he made a few notes and said he would be pleased to open an account for me. I offered two £10 travellers cheques I had with me. (Sterling was still the currency in Nigeria.) So to my particular problem. I informed the Manager that the accountant had told me I was unlikely to receive any salary for about three months. I had a wife and five children at home, and the money I had left to tide them over would not last that long. "Would an overdraft be at all possible?" I asked. "How much did you have in mind?" Very tentatively I suggested £300. "Yes, of course, and I am grateful to you for asking. Most Government officers do not bother to ask but take overdrafts for granted." As near as I can recall, that is the exchange which took place. He then agreed to start, with immediate effect, a monthly transfer of £100 to my bank in England. He called a member of staff to take me over and complete the relevant documents.

I left the bank with a cheque book, to my great relief, and feeling buoyed up. Lesson No.1 for my future in Nigeria: how to deal with new officers who might be posted to me; ensure that priority has been given to their personal problems. I was to experience instances of engineers, particularly young ones, who were quite incapable of attending to their duties because of failure somewhere to settle them in properly.

To *UAC* where I was ushered in to see the Manager, the accountant's 'friend'. The telephone call had sufficed, and he took me outside to a waiting light grey Vauxhall pick-up, already licensed for one year, with a month's cover-note for full insurance with the British Insurers, *Employers Mutual* with a Representative in Kaduna but, of course, I could go elsewhere if I wished. In fact, I continued with *Employers Mutual* and remain with them to this day, although the name has been changed several times since. I had no occasion to make a claim in Nigeria and only once at home when my car was broken into and the radio stolen. I cannot recall the documents I signed regarding payment, but it was by monthly instalments in some form. Within half-an-hour I was driving away from *UAC* in the pick-up with a full tank of petrol!

I had brought a minimum of suitable 'working' clothes for the tropics taking the advice of the Crown Agents to buy articles such as shorts and shirts in the local markets in Nigeria. These should be 100% cotton avoiding nylon or mixtures which did not absorb sweat. In any case, such items, which needed to be replaced quite often, were much cheaper in the markets. I reported progress to the Chief Civil Engineer and when I told him about the pick-up he advised me to try it out on the road from Kaduna to Kachia before setting out on the long journey to Ilorin.

The first few miles out of Kaduna had a 'black top' (bitumen) surface, but then this gave way to a loose dry reddish surface (which I later came to know as 'laterite') creating a fine dust which penetrated into the car and all over the person's eyes, nose etc. Moreover the car tended to 'skid' as on a frosty surface – an entirely new experience for me. However, I kept going until I reached a village – Kujama, I think – where I decided to go back to Kaduna. Turning and reversing the car on the narrow rough road added another experience. I was, indeed, grateful to Mr Scott for his advice. I was now warned what I should expect on my journey to Ilorin which I realised was likely to be on 'dirt' roads.

Helpful enquiries at Headquarters had told me that to reach Ilorin 400 miles away I should proceed through Zaria, Samaru, Funtua, Birnin Gwari, Tegina, Mokwa, crossing the mighty River Niger using the railway bridge (single line) at Jebba to finish at Ilorin. Certain sections of the Funtua to Birnin Gwari road were steep and rocky and great care was necessary. (A few years later, a new road was constructed from Birnin Gwari direct to Kaduna avoiding the long loop through Funtua and Zaria). I survived the journey fully appreciating the excellent advice to select the Vauxhall pick-up.

So at the end of April 1958 began my first tour of duty in Nigeria at Ilorin under the Provincial Engineer of Niger Province, Philip Temple. He and his wife Hilary (also a qualified engineer) did everything possible to help me 'learn the ropes' and be introduced into the general social life of the Station. Initially, I was District Engineer Ilorin and then District Engineer Bussa, a northern area of the Province which included the site of the proposed Kainji Dam on the River Niger, a major project to supply electricity.

While at Ilorin, I was put in charge of a number of Polling Stations for the 1959 Federal Elections because as a Local Government officer in the UK I was familiar with the procedures. I found that the local personnel detailed to act as polling clerks at my Stations had no idea of the duties. To instruct them, I set up a mock Polling Station acting myself as a voter requiring a ballot paper etc. They took to it with zest and amusement but it worked well in the event. I had to learn too that the candidates of the various parties were identified on the ballot papers by well known symbols ('logos') such as a spade, duck etc., since literacy in the North was about 10%. At Bussa I had to be self-reliant. In fact, Bussa itself and much of the surrounding area would disappear under water once the dam was constructed. The population affected would be moved to other areas and already were very apprehensive as to their future.

36

The first indigenous Works Superintendent (senior grade) of the Ministry of Works, Northern Nigeria, posted to me in Ilorin Province, 1958

I was, however, before long, to provide them with an exciting diversion. After all this time, it is impossible to recall the actual sequence of events. I had no telephone at Bussa but the District Officer (DO), also based in Bussa, had a radio link. Through this I received an instruction to proceed to Headquarters in Kaduna at once for a top priority assignment – no details given. I had to send a reply that, due to the recent rains, the only road out of Bussa was under closure as might, indeed, be other roads on the route to Kaduna. Reply came that a *Piper* aircraft would pick me up the following morning and fly me to Kaduna.

There was a grass/laterite airstrip at Bussa and somehow news of the plane's coming had been circulated in the Township and there was an animated gathering at the airstrip to see me off. (I learned later that many of the local people had never seen an aeroplane.) The *Piper*, a 4/6 seater was piloted by a British expatriate. We flew at about 5,000 feet so it was fascinating to see the variety of animals, particularly elephants, on the move, in the 'deep bush' far from any roads or footpaths.

At Kaduna I was seen by both the Chief Civil Engineer and the Permanent Secretary of the Department. The former explained the top priority for PWD. United Nations Representatives and accredited observers were presently engaged in preparations for a plebiscite in the then Northern Cameroon, an area to the east of Nigeria, to determine whether the people there chose to become part of Nigeria. Already, two other areas of Cameroon had become Sardauna Province to the east of the existing Province of Adamawa of Nigeria, Capital Yola.

The plebiscite personnel were based in Yola, situated only a few miles back from the existing international boundary, and journeyed each day in their white-painted UN Landrovers on the road from Yola into Northern Cameroon. Virtually on the boundary was the River Benue. Annually, during the rains, the river would become swollen and fast flowing, the water spreading into a wide flood plain. A long causeway, several feet high, existed to carry the road across this flood plain and included, at about midway of its length, a bridged opening. This released the flood water on the upstream side of the causeway in order to prevent it becoming in any sense a dam with obvious danger to its survival. Just at this critical moment, the bridge, of timber construction, had been swept away by the flood water and already the opening in the causeway had been enlarged to about 100 feet.

It was now a matter of extreme urgency to provide a temporary bridge to span the gap so that UN personnel could continue with their activities in time for the plebiscite date. PWD had been instructed to take immediate steps to overcome the crisis and had decided to use Bailey Bridge components (which had become available for general use after the Second World War) to span the gap using stocks which were held in Kaduna against such emergencies. Based on the somewhat sketchy details from the site, the Chief Civil Engineer had already seen to the despatch of quantities of Bailey components to Yola and assembly was being undertaken through the supervision of an Army officer who claimed to have some experience of Bailey Bridge. However, the great concern at present was that progress had come to a standstill.

Mr Scott remembered seeing in my CV and hearing during our talk that, while in the Corps of Royal Engineers during the Second World War, I had been an instructor at Newark in Bailey Bridge and later one of the small number of uniformed officers serving under the designer of the Bridge, Donald Bailey, at the Experimental Bridging Establishment at Christchurch, Hants, developing the uses of the Bridge for wartime needs. Because of this background he had sent for me to go to Yola at once and overcome the difficulties. The information from the site which he gave me led me to conclude that, apart from the inexperience of the Army officer, vitally essential Bailey components were not present for the launching of what had been assembled over the gap. To be technical, these were base plates, plain and rocking rollers, panels for the 'launching nose' including its special links etc. Without these the operation could not possibly succeed over the water gap of 100 feet. Fortunately, I had with me in Kaduna my Royal Engineers Handbook regarding Bailey Bridge specially designed for 'field' use. From this it was fairly certain that the quantity of components required for a Bailey Bridge over a 100-foot gap capable of taking up to 10-ton vehicles (the then nationwide restriction on all roads but, of course, widely ignored!) would not be available on site. I explained this to Mr Scott and we agreed that, for the moment at least, to meet the dire urgency even a bridge capable of taking Landrovers would be acceptable. Thereafter, the bridge must either be replaced or load restrictions rigorously enforced – but that was probably impossible!

With Mr Scott's approval I went to the Depot in Kaduna where Bailey equipment was held and found most of the essential items just mentioned together with additional panels etc. and arranged for their immediate despatch to Yola and onwards to the bridge site. I may have left a schedule with the Chief Civil Engineer who would at once find out where all the items were held and take all necessary action for them to be delivered. Finally, I saw the Permanent Secretary – not an engineer. (The Administrative Class in the Civil Service still held sway regarding these top appointments.) He emphasised the great urgency to restore road access to Northern Cameroon for the UN personnel and thanked me for my co-operation and wished me success.

The next morning I joined the *Piper*, with the same pilot as before – a very responsible and likeable man. Later I understood he was "i/c *Pipers*". Already aboard were the UN Representative "i/c the plebiscite" and an observer. My place was alongside the pilot. Fortunately, little conversation was possible during the flight. We flew to the east for Yola and again I watched the fascinating scene below.

An amusing incident happened as we landed: I was dressed for 'work', in shorts and shirt. I had to get out first and as I did so a whole posse of formally dressed expatriates surged forward, obviously expecting to greet the UN Representative. I quickly said, "You don't want me," and made for a waiting PWD Landrover. This took me to the Rest House and then to the bridge site on the causeway where I found the work stalled and the labour doing nothing. The British Army officer – a tall guardsman whose name eludes me – was clearly relieved at my arrival and I took to him at once. He frankly admitted that he was 'stuck' with the exercise being beyond his limited experience of Bailey Bridging. We went over the situation including the motley collection of local mechanics, labourers and so on. I explained about the essential items due to arrive which he did not have at present. We agreed that I should take over and he left on good terms.

Before returning to Yola that evening I had made a quick inventory of what was on site and what I was expecting, I hoped the next day. I also checked the bridge span. Already the flood water was subsiding but the rains elsewhere were not yet over and the river could still rise again. Allowing for the bridge base plates on each side of the gap to be not less than 10 feet back from the faces of the causeway, the bridge should be 120 feet long. Now I could determine what 'class' of Bailey Bridge could be provided at least to take loaded Landrovers safely which was the immediate requirement using the equipment now on site and expected. I told those in charge of the labour to leave and be sure to return early the next morning. At the Rest House that evening I would prepare the work programme to bring a bridge to completion.

I calculated that it would just be feasible – taking a few chances – to assembly a bridge for the safe passage of cars, light vans, Landrovers and the like provided vehicles did not cross in close convoy.

Tired as I was, I needed some relaxation so I went to the Club. There I met some of the UN personnel and told them about what I was planning and that I hoped the bridge would be completed within two days. Some PWD officers were curious to see the work and would visit the site the next day. Overnight the essential items had arrived at Yola and were on site by the time the labour force arrived. Now it was possible to organise the assembly of the bridge in the correct sequence. By the close of the following day, it was complete, decked down and tested using my PWD Landrover fully loaded with labourers, highly excited, as the test 'load'. Several trials and all seemed well. I would have to insist that lorries, loaded or otherwise, must be prohibited and guards must be in place at all times to give this effect. I knew, of course, that the enforcement would not be 100%, some lorry drivers would 'get at' the guards, but the flexibility of the Bailey Bridge was its great strength under occasions of wartime overload which commanders in the field had to take from time to time. Now the scene at the causeway was beginning to change. I gathered from the local people that lorries etc. would soon resume their 'dry' season crossing of the flood plain without using the causeway. Even before I left Yola I saw some sign of that because of the guards put on

41

the Bailey Bridge. However, the Bailey Bridge had enabled the UN personnel to resume their activities at the critical moment.

I was able to report completion to Headquarters and requested the *Piper* to return me to Bussa. I cannot now be sure whether we returned via Kaduna so that I could report in to Headquarters but certainly almost the whole population of Bussa were at the airstrip, more, perhaps, to see the aircraft than to welcome me back!

It was some years before the Yola Bailey was replaced by a permanent bridge. Some people I later happened to meet who had come from the area told me that the Bailey was still there although it had acquired rather a 'sag'! This was the first of around 16 Bailey Bridges I dealt with during my 20 years in Northern Nigeria. One or two assignments involved dismantling a Bailey at a tricky site following its replacement by a permanent bridge of concrete/steel. There was one unusual case which called for the span to be 'broken' in its middle on a pier constructed of Bailey panels founded on the river bed. There were many anxious moments when using unskilled labour!

I was about halfway through my second tour at Bussa in Ilorin Province which had begun following three months' UK leave from 16th May to 25th August 1959, when I received a posting as Acting Provincial Engineer, Kabba Province. The Provincial Capital, Lokoja, was situated at the confluence of the Rivers Niger and Benue and quite near the border between Northern and Eastern Nigeria. This was promotion giving me the status of Local Head of Department amongst other Heads in the Province. However, because I was a Contract Officer fulfilling an Establishment Post in the Civil Service, I had to be classed as 'Acting'.

Lokoja was a comparatively small Township but of historical importance, particularly regarding the country's early trading activities and indirect rule under Sir Frederick, later Lord, Lugard. The history is well described in *The Story of Nigeria* by Michael Crowder.

Climatically, there was little relief from humidity so close to the two rivers. The 'official' residential area was on the high ground overlooking the Township. Storms were really violent, their imminent arrival being visible by an advancing bank of brown dust. One had to rush to close

42

windows and outside doors within seconds to prevent the dust coming in and spreading over everything, dust so fine that it would penetrate every nook and cranny and be most difficult to remove.

Igala, part of the Province, was on the far side of the River Benue. A vehicle ferry – a lumbering flat boat affair – went from Lokoja to Shintaku from where the road led to Enugu the Capital City of Eastern Nigeria (Ibo land). As I was responsible for the development of boreholes for water in Igala I toured there regularly. The people were delightful: most of the work in the fields was done by the women, many of whom, while working, carried their latest baby close against their back by means of a wide loin cloth round their waist. They would stop work, put the baby to the breast for a feed, and then resume work. I was told, but would not accept, that there were those who just stopped work for long enough to give birth and then went on working. Everything came so naturally to them. In the villages, the men could be seen asleep under the trees or sitting around gossiping. To the stranger, from the so-called 'civilised' world, it seemed an idyllic life. But, of course, there was disease, failure of crops and rain, village rivalry and so on. I could not know that I would be returning to Lokoja and the Province in just a few years' time under wholly changed and very stressful circumstances.

The other principal Townships in the Province were Kabba, an important road junction, Idah, again on the River Benue with a ferry crossing, and Okene with its College. It was clear, so near the border with Eastern Nigeria (Ibo land), that there had been long established inter-marriage and a better literacy spreading through educational facilities available at Catholic or Baptist schools and Missions. So much of this was to break down and lead to tragedy later.

The focal point of trading and commerce at Lokoja was along the river front which was lined with spacious two storey buildings of the major trading companies such as *UAC* (*United Africa Company*) and *Holts*. The paddle steamers called regularly to be loaded with groundnuts etc., collected in from a wide area of the country's farms etc. Any day one could watch the paddleboats being loaded for their long journey down the river to Lagos for the cargo to be shipped to Europe and so on for processing. Men ran carrying one hundredweight (50kgs) sacks of

43

groundnuts across their back encouraged by the beat of drums, the drummers being specially engaged for the purpose. This rhythm of work would go on for hours with only very short breaks, sweat pouring off the men's bodies. The reward was one penny per sack. Their shoulders were permanently bent by years of this work and all they had to eat during the times they were working might be a dry crust of bread.

Also along this river front were the Waterworks (MOW), a small electric generating plant (Company) with a limited overhead distribution system, and a one million gallon circular storage tank for petrol and some diesel which was refilled periodically from tankers which came in by river. These vital facilities were to come under my direct control later.

By the end of September 1960 – on the eve of Independence for Nigeria – I would complete my second tour. I was granted leave from 24th September 1960 to resume by 9th January 1961. On 1st October 1960 Nigeria gained its Independence and became the Federal Republic of Nigeria and a Member of the Commonwealth with the Queen as its Head. Consequently, from now onwards in this Memoir, the term Ministry of Works (MOW) replaces Public Works Department (PWD).

The grounding I had experienced in Ilorin Province as District Engineer and now as Acting Provincial Engineer in Kabba Province should prove invaluable for the future particularly the latter which implied promotion to Local Head of Department. I was confident that I would be able to hold that level from then onwards.

In practical terms, the family position at home had stabilised. Support for them was easier including education for the older boys. Physically, I seemed to accept – certainly to withstand – the change of environment. Mentally and workwise the challenges were stimulating and the frustrations felt in Local Government at home had effectively disappeared. The social nuances amongst the layers or gradings of public servants – and their wives – which made up what might be called 'the social rounds', were mostly amusing, sometimes irritating. Club Night, by tradition on the last Saturday of the month (and after salaries had been paid on the 23rd!) could be guaranteed to produce at least one scandal or mis-demeanour which led gossip for days. There were also some bizarre attempts at evening dress which, supposedly, was *de rigueur* for Club Nights.

I am unable to say whether contracts had formally to be renewed tour by tour, but I received a posting notice during leave to Acting Provincial Engineer Benue Province, Capital Makurdi, situated on the River Benue and, like Kabba Province, it had a long southern boundary with Eastern Nigeria. I would be taking over from a substantive British Provincial Engineer whom I had met from time to time. I had also heard of J.S. Tarka, the leader of the Tiv tribe in Benue Province who was involved in national politics.

There was no set rule, but postings were expected to be arranged so that the incoming Provincial Engineer would arrive a few days before the outgoing Provincial Engineer was due to finish, giving time for a face-to-face handover in addition to obligatory Handing Over Notes. The latter would also introduce the former to other local Heads of Departments and, if possible, to The Resident and the Senior District Officer Administration. At Makurdi I was welcomed at a monthly meeting of Heads of Departments called by The Resident to review matters of general concern and interest. During these first years I had become conversant with one of the important responsibilities of the Ministry of Works – road maintenance. My touring alone had provided direct experience!

This is not the place to explain in detail the technicalities involved but some general outline is worthwhile. Provincial Engineers were given considerable funds for the maintenance (as distinct from improvements or new roads) of 'A' (Federal) and 'B' (Regional) roads, unclassified roads (rural areas) being the responsibility of the Native Authorities.

In Northern Nigeria, in 1960, the great majority of 'A' and 'B' roads had laterite surfaces – generally described as 'dirt' roads to distinguish them from 'black' (bitumen) hard surfaces. Each Northern Province had hundreds of miles of dirt roads which by their very nature, required constant maintenance – one vehicle alone could disturb the surface creating the 'corrugations' which caused so much discomfort to travellers. During the rains and spells of heavy downpour, the dirt roads would become impassable unless barred to traffic for long periods to dry out.

The enforcers of closures at the barriers were road labourers who, sadly, were subject to intimidation by important travellers or bullying lorry drivers to let them through, resulting in the soaked surface disintegrating into deep ruts. The outcome was that later vehicles would get stuck in the ruts and in no time there would be a long line of virtually abandoned vehicles bringing all traffic to a standstill. The road took days to recover and in the meanwhile frustrated drivers vented their anger on the unfortunate labourers in torrents of abusive language.

Apart from maintaining the 'running surface', grass which grew on the road verges had to be kept low or close cut so that run-off rainwater could quickly reach the open drains (ditches) provided on each side of the road. These ditches and the 'turn-offs' into the bush were of prime necessity. Also culverts of concrete rings or of 'box' construction under the road to relieve possible surcharge in the side drain on the higher side to the lower side were introduced at strategic places and added to as experience determined.

Finally, unremitting maintenance by manual labour to the roads was paramount. However, appropriate machinery had to be put to the road from time to time to restore lengths of a road where quick rehabilitation was essential for traffic considerations.

The labour force lived (with its families) in round-house camps provided about every five miles. Each 'gang', on average, consisted of five labourers under a headman (with bicycle). There would also be one or more supervisors (possibly with motorcycles) depending on the length of a road. Wages were paid monthly along the road by the Road Engineer in charge who was held responsible to the Provincial Engineer for the road and was required regularly to inspect and submit a written report.

There was a tendency for headmen to adopt a daily-task attitude to road maintenance. For example, he would tell his gang that the day's task was to carry out maintenance on a given length of road which when completed they could finish for the day. This was bad practice and had to be condemned, as it led, inevitably, to gangs finishing before the prescribed closing time. Wherever I found this in operation in any Province under my control I stopped it at once. It undermined discipline and the travelling public would comment that no-one was working on the roads quite early in the day, and that they found the condition of roads below expectation. I was quite insistent that the roads in any Province where I was Provincial Engineer should be maintained at all times to an acceptable standard.

I toured regularly and made surprise visits to roads. Sometimes, to the surprise of the men I would take a rake or a shovel and work with them for a short time. This was not just to 'show off' but to demonstrate that the work was very important to the general well-being.

I was based at Makurdi as Acting Provincial Engineer Benue Province from January 1961. My house was close to The Residency and almost opposite The Club! By now I had found that working hours were fully taken up with Departmental meetings, interviews, administrative matters and, most vital, keeping the books i.e. accountancy. Funds – which were considerable – were issued by Headquarters annually – 'Revenue' allocations against specific Heads of Departments like maintenance of roads and so on. Already I had experienced a 'bad' accountant and sent him away. So I was keeping the accounts myself – after all I was responsible for the proper use of funds.

It was then that I formed the habit of going to my office after tea when I could concentrate on reports, accounts and staffing matters without being interrupted. I was no longer a regular at The Club.

I think that the year at Makurdi consolidated my confidence as a Provincial Engineer, a posting which I hoped would follow elsewhere from then onwards. I should record several incidents worthy of comment during the year. Water for the treatment works was drawn through a pipe intake from the River Benue. One morning the Works Superintendent in charge reported to me that the intake seemed to be blocked – no water could be drawn by the pumps. He had investigated and found what he thought was a long snake – probably a python – stuck in the intake pipe. What could be done? By sheer chance, I remembered one of the touring District Officers relating in the Club an occasion when he was in the bush with his gun and suddenly found he was about to be attacked by a large snake and shot it just in time. Fortunately, he happened to be in Station. I offered him the thanks of everyone if he would shoot the large snake now blocking the water intake. He came suitably attired and, with his gun, did the deed, and the body was pulled out. It was about 20 feet long as I recall. Another – and true – story for The Club!

Then there was the official visit to Makurdi of the first British High Commissioner Lagos after Nigeria's Independence who was making a tour of Regions. He was Antony Head, recently made a Viscount, who would be well remembered as having resigned from the Anthony Eden Government at the time of the Suez crisis in 1956. He, with his wife, would stay at The Residency where there would be a Reception to meet him. Invitations to be present would be limited to a certain level of the Civil Service Establishment, local commercial interests etc. Who had, or had not, received invitations would be the main topic of gossip at The Club, particularly amongst the wives, and agonizing moments for husbands left out.

Guests would assemble on time, and stand in a ring round the large Drawing Room of The Residency, cleared of most of its furniture, to await the VIPs. The Senior District Officer, as unobtrusively as possible, would ensure that all Administration staff, with their wives, would be the first to be introduced as the Resident led in the High Commissioner and his wife – but there was no wife. Slowly the small group moved round the circle, stopping to have a few appropriate words with those introduced. Feeling hot dressed in a suit while standing waiting my turn to make small talk, knowing that the VIP would be as bored as I was, I suddenly spotted a lady standing alone in the wide open space in the ring, obviously expecting to be noticed. Her coiffure of black hair was startling but more spectacular was her figure, almost obscured by dangling beads and personal adornments quite impossible to describe at a distance. There were glimpses of a long dress of many colours. As she moved into the centre of the Drawing Room to join the small group nearing the end of its round, there was a noticeable hush – Lady Head had put in a belated appearance. I can still picture the moment after all these years.

In all fairness, I should include the following from the Directory of Notable Biographies 1901-1985:

48

"HEAD, Antony Baron. Born 19/12/1906 died 29/3/1983. Only son and younger child of Geoffrey Head a *Lloyds* Broker who was one of eleven children. One uncle was drowned in the *Titanic* and another, Sir Henry Head, was an eminent neurologist. Antony was educated at Eton and Sandhurst.

"Appointed Minister of Defence in succession to Sir Walter Monckton. When Macmillan succeeded Eden as PM in January 1957 he declined an offer to remain Minister of Defence – inadequate budget for armed forces – and he retired to back benches. Created Viscount in 1960. lst. British High Commissioner in Lagos Nigeria. Close relationship with PM. Great success in Nigeria travelling widely in the country – 3 years tenure. Went on to be HC in Malaysia. Again success.

"In July 1935 he married Lady Dorothea Louise, daughter of Antony Ashley Cooper, ninth Earl of Shaftesbury. She was a portrait painter of outstanding ability and like her husband witty and artistic. Considerable help to her husband throughout his career. Red Cross and the Order of St John his charm never failed and he had a way of expressing himself which delighted his friends and amused the staff of the office he held, consistently devoted to him. A keen and expert ornithologist and entomologist he loved butterflies. In Lagos he would rise early and set forth in pursuit of rare varieties."

The Permanent Secretary Ministry of Works, Headquarters Kaduna, Mr E. Jones, who, in 1959 had become the first professional engineer to occupy this position of Head of Department – came to Makurdi early in August 1961 for a tour of the Province for three days. I knew how much he delighted in getting away from Headquarters so I had arranged a full round of touring by Landrover. In fact, one day he wanted to go further than I had planned, so much so that the ferry at the last river crossing on the way back had closed and I had to round-up the ferry man. Finally, the last 100 miles was in the dark – we had covered 500 miles in the day – and he was still full of beans!

Later, his letter of 20 August 1961:

Dear Muggeridge,

Since my return from Benue Province I have been tied up with meetings and arrears of work which inevitably accumulate. Hence my belated letter of appreciation for a most delightful tour. For my own part, I must admit I have never enjoyed myself better. The success of my visit I attribute to your excellent arrangements for which I thank you.

It may interest you to know that never before have I visited a Provincial Organisation so well run. Indeed, I have no criticism to make.

Yours sincerely
E. Jones
Permanent Secretary

A brief profile of Eifion Jones:

"Executive Engineer, Nigeria 1942. Senior Executive Engineer, 1951. Chief Engineer 1954. Then Deputy Director of Public Works, Lagos 1958. Pulled back to Kaduna Ministry of Works by Sir Ahmadu Bello, Premier of Northern Nigeria after Independence in October 1960, to be the Permanent Secretary Ministry of Works. He was still in this post, close to the Government of Northern Nigeria, when the first military coup took place in Kaduna in the early hours of 15th January 1966, quickly spreading to the other Regions. The Premier was assassinated in his house, top military officers were killed while others took over."

'Jonah' (as he was called within the Ministry), now nearing 55 years old, saw no future for himself, quickly took retirement and left Nigeria. A man of strong – even overbearing – personality, perhaps a bullying type, and in age three years my junior, I had occasion to stand up to him when, not long after his tour to Benue Province, he wanted to move me to Ministry of Works Kano. He had decided, because of the importance and status of the Ministry, that apart from the Provincial Engineer, there should be a Chief Engineer in charge and one other, purpose undefined at the moment. I was to be the 'one other'. He called me to Kaduna. There, before I saw him, without going into personalities at Headquarters, I was able to find out the background to his proposal and firmly decided against being drawn into the position. When I saw him, I emphasised that my usefulness in the Ministry was best at the level of a Provincial Engineer. He complained at my attitude but grudgingly accepted my refusal of his proposal. I heard no more and, to be fair, I am sure he did not act against my future postings. In any case, as events turned out, he left the Ministry and Nigeria in 1966. We were to meet several times between 1961 and 1966 memorably at Bida in Niger Province in November 1964 which I will describe in a later Chapter.

Next the Chief Civil Engineer, Ministry of Works Headquarters Kaduna, Mr Gordon Manners, came to Makurdi in October 1961 for a tour of the Province for three days. His wife, Estelle, accompanied him. Extracts from her letter to me of 10th October 1961:

"This is to tell you how much we enjoyed our tour of Benue, and to thank you for all your hospitality and for the most efficient arrangements you made for our comfort, and to ensure that we came to no harm on river crossings..." Later, "He (Gordon) wishes me to congratulate you on a tidy and well-organised Province, which we are sure you will be most reluctant to leave because of the beautiful scenery."

Certainly, Mrs Manners was right. I should miss touring to the beautiful area north of Makurdi and the towns of Nasarawa and Keffi. But I felt the call for a new challenge. I did not then know that it would come so dramatically within a few years.

During UK leave from 12th April 1962 to resume on 30th July 1962, I received a posting notice to Niger Province, Capital Minna, in the Middle Belt. Would this be the challenge I hoped for?

Niger Province – Two Tours

Before leaving Kano International Airport early in April 1962 for three months' UK leave, I had decided that the Vauxhall pick-up, acquired on my arrival in Nigeria in April 1958, was due for replacement. For most practical purposes, including mechanical, it had served me well, but with space in the cab for only one passenger it was too restrictive for social use. Now I needed a dual-purpose car which normally could take up to four persons but, by quick adjustment of the back seats, could be converted into a large 'boot' space to take folded camp-bed, cooking equipment etc., when touring to rural areas.

On these trips I was accompanied by a cook/steward and stayed in the delightfully cool bush Rest Houses with thick mud walls and grass roofs which were usually situated on the outskirts of villages. Sitting outside a bush Rest House on the wide verandah which circled the inner house, looking into the deep darkness or, by contrast, the brilliance of a full moon almost as bright as day, heightened one's awareness of the vast immensity of the African bush. Add the buzzing of cicadas and other night-flyers, the distant howling of hyenas, the repetitive drumming from the village, probably for some local ceremony or ritual, induced a humbling experience never to be forgotten. On these tours I made sure I had with me my cassette player and some of my favourite music; listening to a Beethoven concerto or a Donizetti opera, for example, in that hypersensitive atmosphere was a greatly enriched experience. Certainly, there was no fear of disturbing the neighbours!

Peugeot cars had become increasingly popular in Nigeria and, for me, the Peugeot 403 Estate car was ideal, so I had placed an order with *SCOA,* the Agency for Peugeot in Kano, to await my return from leave in July 1962. The car cost £1,000, including one year's licence, and was ready for me at

SCOA. After a night in the *Central Hotel* Kano, I set off for Kaduna to call at Headquarters on my way to Minna, Niger Province to take over as Provincial Engineer. By this time, I knew a number of the senior staff at Headquarters so inevitably I was invited to dinner, drinks at The Club, and offered a bed for the night. Actually, it turned into quite a party!

In the morning, in spite of a slight hangover, I moved off as soon as possible. By now, most of the way was familiar up to Tegina where the route turned for Zungeru and Minna. I reached the Government Rest House, where I had booked a room for several days, about 5.00pm, the Peugeot 403 having proved its excellent qualities. The Head Steward took me to my chalet room and I parked the car right outside as, being a new Station, I suspected the security might not be all it should, as events in the next 24 hours were to show!

I made a courtesy call on the outgoing Provincial Engineer, at a well situated house in the Government Residential Area, and noted the glass doors which folded back giving access to a spacious *stoep* (terraced veranda). I knew him slightly; he was a young man, one of the last cadets recruited just before the end of Colonial rule who, after Independence, had decided to stay on for a few years. I excused myself from accepting his invitation to drinks and dinner as we would meet at the office in the morning.

I had already complained to the Head Steward that the lock on the door to my chalet was defective, but he had assured me that the night watchman regularly patrolled all round the chalets during the night – which, of course, I did not believe. Preparing for bed, I brought my large, light-blue fabric suitcase and a white holdall into the chalet from the car. In Nigeria, from the start, I had slept nude, except for a small towel drawn round my waist just adequate to cover private parts, as I had noticed that stewards bringing in morning tea were oddly embarrassed about full exposure! I had to switch off the noisy hole-in-the-wall air-conditioner as it would have made sleep impossible, but luckily the double bed had a mosquito net. For safety, I put my wallet containing Nigerian notes and some loose change in the locking suitcase which already contained £30 UK notes, travellers cheques, a cheque book, my passport and other personal papers, and an unopened bottle of whisky etc. Inside the net I took a key ring holding the car keys and those of the suitcase, and my wristwatch to lay by the pillow.

I don't know how long I had slept before I suddenly woke up, and instantly knew something was wrong. Switching on the table lamp just outside the net, I saw at once that my suitcase and holdall had gone, and so had the clothes I had taken off when preparing for bed. All I had left were the small towel round my middle, my wristwatch, key ring and sandals. I sat on a chair completely dazed by this appalling situation. It was 2.30am and without clothes, money, or passport what could I do? The situation would still be the same at 6.30am when morning tea came, and upon that thought despair changed to rage against the Head Steward. He had obviously told some friends of his about the chalet, its occupant and what was available.

Forgetful of my near nakedness I rushed out of the chalet to the Stewards' Quarters shouting for the Head Steward and saying that all my belongings had been stolen during the night. This caused a great stirring of the staff who assembled quickly while I raged at the Head Steward. I remembered listening at dinner parties or at The Club to dramatic stories of how thieves, hastily examining stolen belongings as they fled, would throw away personal papers etc. which were of no use to them and might even incriminate them if rounded up by the police. So I ordered all the staff to bring torches and lamps to search the immediate area round the chalet looking for papers, clothing and baggage, although I had little hope of recovering that. Quite soon, they were bringing me my passport, travellers' cheques, cheque book, sundry papers etc., but not, of course, my £30, my clothes or the bottle of whisky, and there was no sign of my baggage.

During all this excitement I heard the unmistakable sound of a train in the distance and guessed it would be stopping at Minna Station. The Rest House was on high ground and I could see the moving light of the carriages in the valley. To this day, I cannot account for the immediate inspiration which came to me – what safer way of making off with the loot than by train! Calling out to the staff to carry on searching, I told them I was going to the Railway Station and why. Then without a thought as to my near nakedness, I drove off in the car and reached the station in a few minutes. The whole place was a seething mass of people, goods etc., waiting for the train. My small towel still holding up, I forced my way through to the Railway Police office. There I rather rapidly explained my position to the Officer in charge who showed no surprise at being confronted with a white man in a state of nakedness in the middle of the night. I asked him to come with me to search for my suitcase and holdall on the platform as I was convinced the thieves would be trying to escape with my baggage on the train. We were battling our way towards the top end of the platform when ahead I just caught a glimpse of my light-blue suitcase and white holdall. The police rushed forward pushing people out of their way which, of course, alerted the thieves, who abandoned the baggage and fled into the darkness of the bush. Had the police moved forward slowly and then sprung on the thieves, my £30 etc. might have been recovered but I was overjoyed to have the baggage.

Thanking them and promising to return in the morning to thank them again, I drove back with the baggage to the Rest House where more papers etc., had been found. I was so relieved that I told them to stop searching and return to their quarters. It had been easy for the thieves to force the two locks on the suitcase so my £30 and the bottle of whisky had been taken, but none of the clothes were missing. At least that nightmare was over.

In the morning, I went to the Railway Police to thank everyone concerned in the night's incident, leaving a modest contribution to the Police Welfare fund. But of course, that was not the end of the story – I should have known what was coming! Already the bush telegraph had been busy around the Station putting out this sort of story: "Have you heard about the new Provincial Engineer who arrived yesterday afternoon? Well, he drives around in the night almost naked, he was seen on the platform at the Railway Station with just a small towel round his middle…!" I dined out for nights on this story and expected a query from Headquarters – but nothing materialised. No doubt there were enough eccentrics in Kaduna to keep gossip going. I still have that suitcase and when I look at it I marvel how I was galvanised into action which led to its recovery. This Memoir will record other occasions during my years in Nigeria which verge on the unbelievable!

My contracts after October 1960 were with the Northern Nigerian Government. Basically, the conditions did not change but, tacitly, the arrangements regarding leave for expatriates were amended. Entitlement was reduced from 7 days to 5 days for each month of service, and the length of tours against age – for example, in my case, it had been twelve months – quietly lapsed or became 'upwardly flexible'. In other words, leave was granted at a time to suit the exigencies of the service, the exigencies being negotiable between officer and employer. Within a few years, leave was to be caught up in the general instability of Nigeria.

It might be helpful to give some information about Niger Province of which Bida, Minna, Abuja and Kontagora were the principal Townships. In 1962 there were 900 miles of classified (A and B) roads, mostly of laterite surfaces, which were the responsibility of the Provincial Engineer to maintain. Historically, Bida, situated near the confluence of the Rivers Niger and Kaduna, lay claim as the Capital City. Climatically, however, it was hot and humid and the Administration had moved to Minna where conditions generally were better.

It is worth recording here a fascinating description of Bida from Elspeth Huxley's *Four Guineas – A Journey Through West Africa* (The Reprint Society, London 1955) Chapter IV *In Nigeria*:

"Bida is the capital of Nupeland; an ancient and alluring walled city of round clay houses with pargeted walls, sometimes painted in bold red or black designs, and arranged in quarters according to their owners' crafts. For Bida is a nest of craftsmen, still organised into hereditary guilds. The houses stand in clusters, their small farms round them; although the soil looks light and sandy, everything grows: groundnuts, guinea corn, rice, cotton, beans, tomatoes, maize. The guildsmen, however, do not cultivate; they are too busy. Every day except Friday, for Bida is a Muslim city, they start at dawn and ply their craft with speed and skill until about four o'clock. No Trade Unions here, no regulated hours, no shop stewards, no five-day weeks; and those who work for wages draw about twopence a day. And yet they manage, and do not seem in the least oppressed or exploited. On the

57

contrary, these glass-workers, bead-makers, weavers, brass and silver smiths are honoured citizens of Bida, burghers as it were, ranking only below the Fulani aristocracy.

"The glass-workers are perhaps the most spectacular. In the hut's centre is a sunken furnace, its clay walls built up about a foot above the ground. A boy feeds it continually with logs; it is a Moloch of timber. (Moloch was a Canaanite idol to which children were sacrificed by fire in Biblical times, the term here referring to its insatiable appetite). Another, or an apprentice, works a leather bellows by means of two sticks. He pumps these two sticks up and down with a rhythm fast and regular, and seems to continue for hours without a break. The work must be very exhausting, but the boy or youth never falters, for the red-hot furnace must not for an instant cease to roar and glow. Some of the raw material derives from melted-down bottles, of which the dark-blue and amber medicine bottles are the most popular. There is also a kind of black, opaque, home-made glass, still fused in the traditional manner from earth rich in silica and from soda which comes (once by camel, now by lorry) all the way from Lake Chad.

"Four men sit round the furnace, each with a long iron rod in his hand. One has a lump of molten glass on the end of his rod. Each of the other three pokes off a bit of the glowing stuff and, with the aid of a pair of tongs, holding it over the flames, shapes it roughly into a bangle or ring. Then, with marvellous dexterity, each man twirls his bangle round on his rod and taps it into shape as it cools, finally sliding it off on to the ground beside him. All day long he keeps this up in the heat of the fire, the pile of bangles growing by his side. The workers in each hut belong, as a rule, to one family, whose head is the guild-master. He arranges the supply of material, the work and the sales, and pays the men a fixed share of the profits.

"In another quarter are the brass-smiths, who make spoons widely used as market measures, and the silversmiths, who have fallen on evil days because they cannot get the raw material. I saw one smith breaking up an old touch-case to make ear-rings, another transforming an abandoned aluminium kettle into bracelets. The results, as could only be expected, were ugly and crude. The soaring cost of metal has hit the smiths all over West Africa so severely that, in the next generation, their craft can scarcely survive.

"The glass-workers have a tradition that they came from Egypt, bringing their craft with them. The whole declining art of the bead-workers is to re-grind, polish and refine beads, some perhaps derived from the graves of ancient Libyan or Egyptian kings, brought across the desert by Hausa and Arab merchants..." so it goes on.

I would tour regularly to Bida and my stay always included a visit to the craftsmen. The palace of the traditional Ruler of Nupeland known as The Etsu, was in Bida and I made certain of a courtesy call. Minna Township, by contrast, was much smaller and offered nothing of cultural or historical interest compared to Bida. Its importance, however, related to the early days of the railways: for example, to quote from Chapter XIV *The Unification of Nigeria* of Michael Crowder's book, *The Story of Nigeria,* published in 1962, in 1914 "...there were two competing systems, the Minna–Baro-Niger system rivalling the Minna-Jebba-Lagos system and a new line was envisaged from Port Harcourt through Enugu to the North..."

On the high ground of Minna quite substantial houses had been built for the senior staff of the railways, using quantities of the high quality red bricks which lined the railway tunnels. The Administration, at some time, had been able to acquire some of these houses for their senior staff when the transfer from Bida took place, but for the majority of expatriates in other Departments, more conventional houses and bungalows had been located on the outskirts of the Township which constituted the GRA, including the house designated for the Provincial Engineer.

Senior Nigerian Staff and families at Minna

A few miles out of the Township was Bosso Dam impounding up to 50 million gallons of water. This dam had been constructed using earth and stone some time earlier by the Native Authority and supplied water to the Township and the immediate area. It was fed by the run-off from the surrounding high ground during the rains and from some small streams and springs. As I arrived a Water Treatment Works at a suitable location near the Township was nearing completion and its commissioning and testing would fall to me to arrange. I gathered that its designed output capacity would not meet the current demand, which included a large farm with hundreds of pigs, each of which needed a minimum of 5 gallons of water a day!

The data used in the design specifications of the Works had been determined some years previously for the then population of the area to be served, and had not been re-assessed when it was decided to construct the Works. Moreover, during the last few years, many people living in adjacent areas where water was always a problem, hearing of the new Works and better supply in Minna, had moved into the Township area. In short, I was the fall-guy with the looming problem. I think I did see the owner of the pig farm to warn him that his supply might have to be restricted. I had to consider all the demands which could be made on the system. This problem, however, was nothing compared to what was to confront me after just a few weeks as the Provincial Engineer of Niger Province – a real disaster in the making.

It was early September 1962 and the rains were increasing. This was real Middle Belt Nigeria with six months' dry season November to May, June to October constituting the wet season when a number of the dirt roads had to be closed to traffic for periods of up to eight hours to dry out. A report from the Bida road said that the embankment at one end of a bridge had been partly washed away due to rising floodwater in the river below, bringing all traffic to a halt. At once, I went to inspect. Vehicles had begun to build up at each end of the bridge and there was some agreement amongst car drivers to help travellers on urgent business in each direction by going back the way they had come and warning others not to travel, or to find another way. It was here that, by pure chance, I first met Alhaji Aliyu, Makama of Bida, the Minister of Finance in the Northern Nigerian

Government, who would act as Premier in the absence of the charismatic Sir Ahmadu Bello, Sardauna of Sokoto. After a brief discussion, we led him across the bridge to where another car was waiting for him as arranged so that he could reach Kaduna for urgent meetings. I assured him that the bridge would be fully open by the time he was due to return to Bida the next day. Before returning to Minna I settled with the road headmen the nature of the repair work to be carried out using stones and other material from the nearby bush, engaging additional local labour as necessary. Full overtime would be paid to all workers but it had to be completed by early the following day – and it was.

Within hours came a confusing and very worrying report of damage at Bosso Dam. Certainly there had been hours of heavy rain over the whole area; I was to learn later that five and a half inches had fallen in five hours. I went at once to the dam to find the maintenance men looking at a point at the outside base of the dam where water was gushing through and into the overflow channel. Stones and earth were gradually being dislodged along the fault, and the effect was of a 'bite' being taken at the body of the dam which, if not halted, would eventually breach it. Within a short time, most of the 50 million gallons of water would have been released with disastrous consequences as it flooded the surrounding area, possibly into Minna itself. The eventual outcome was impossible to foresee if immediate action was not taken to repair the 'bite'.

Although I had only been in Minna for a few weeks, the dam was one of the first places I had visited. With its lake-like appearance in a rural setting it was attractive to visitors, and several times I had taken a walk round its perimeter in the late afternoon as the sun went down, so I was quite familiar with its surroundings. Now I had to be there to confront a really dire situation. In simple terms, this is what had happened. The recent heavy downpour had fallen on the catchment area already saturated by earlier rain, resulting in most of the run-off quickly reaching the dam already nearing, if not actually at, its top water level. This situation can arise at all dams so to prevent surcharge an overflow spillway is provided with its sill at or near the top water level of the dam. Water spilling over the sill is directed to the overflow channel at ground level so arranged to take the water away from the dam to a nearby stream, river or to spread onto a suitable area of the bush. At Bosso, however, for some reason this channel at ground level had been located close to and along the outside base of the dam creating the 'bite' where I had found the men anxiously watching the base of the earth dam being eroded away.

Firstly, I sent some men to check the length of the surcharged overflow channel and the stream or river or the bush for obstructions which must be removed at once – all sorts of debris could have been washed into this channel during the heavy rain. My top priority was to find stone and other material with which to fill the bite. My afternoon walks around the dam were about to pay off. I remembered quantities of scattered stone at the quarry, which clearly had been the source of material for the initial construction of the dam by the Native Authority years earlier, and at once I went to the quarry with the Headman. Much of the stone scattered around could be picked up by hand, and head or head-pan carried to the bite. The Headman was to send some of the local maintenance men to their areas with instructions to round up men, women and even children to come at once to the quarry for paid work to save the dam from failure which might destroy their homes etc., bringing torches and lamps, hand tools and head-pans with them. They would have to stay during the night until the work was finished, and those left behind should prepare food etc. to bring to the site. Success would be rewarded by adding three hours' paid overtime to whatever overtime had to be done to complete the task. I also sent a messenger to my Mechanical Superintendent at Minna to round up some Landrovers or cars to come to the dam to provide light at the working areas with their headlights. This was top priority and several drivers responded and placed their vehicles where they could be most help.

As I recall, a work force of about 700 came, more women than men and some children. They formed lines of unceasing labour each carrying a stone on the head or in a head-pan throwing the stone into the bite as directed by the Headman. Gradually, I could gauge that we were succeeding. Luckily the rain had ceased, the level of water flowing over the sill of the spillway was falling and the condition of the overflow channel was improving, so by daybreak only a trickle of water was seeping through the bite.

Now I could tell the Resident and the other Heads of Departments what had happened and that the crisis had been averted – it had been a near thing though. In fact, during the following dry season, my anxiety was that the dam would run out of water, particularly as its low level disclosed several feet of silt on the bottom reducing its water capacity – another dam problem!

Bida, too, was being provided with a Water Treatment Works and a piped supply. The Project was under the control and supervision of the Chief Water Engineer at Headquarters at Kaduna, Mr Brian Brough, whom I had met several times, and with a water engineer, Mr Proctor, in charge of the work at Bida. The Works were sited at Badeggi and drew water from the River Kaduna with a pumping main to a storage reservoir at Bida, some twelve miles away. Although the Project was not under me as Provincial Engineer, I naturally took an interest in its progress. The last few miles of the road to the Works at Badeggi were a typical narrow causeway across a wide *fadama* (swamp) area, part of the extensive flood plain of the River Kaduna. The pumping main leaving the Works had to be laid during the dry season for some miles through this *fadama* until it continued as normal under the roadway to the reservoir at Bida.

The laying of this pumping main was, of course, a crucial element of the responsibility in the hands of the Water Engineer in charge. So far as I was aware, progress on the Project, including the main, was satisfactory. However, a visit to the Province by Mr Brian Brough accompanied by one of his senior staff at Headquarters, Mr Crosby Hunter, revealed that the Premier had directed that he intended formally to inaugurate the Bida Water Scheme on Saturday 2nd March 1963 at 5.00pm just a few weeks away. The Works, including the pumps etc., were virtually complete as were the reservoir and distribution pipes at Bida. The concern was the rate of progress in laying the pumping main through the *fadama* to close the gap, although Mr Proctor was insistent that it would be closed in time. Here let me quote from the programme for the Formal Inauguration at Badeggi:

The Scheme

"The Waterworks have a basic output of 10,000 gallons per hour increasing, if required, to 25,000 gallons per hour. Raw water from the river, before being pumped through nearly twelve miles of pipes to the 200,000 gallon Storage Reservoir near Bida, is subjected to rigorous chemical treatment and filtration through layers of specially graded sand and stone aimed at complete removal of suspended impurities and dangerous bacteria.

"From the Storage Reservoir water is distributed, by gravity, to 96 standpipes, these being supplied from a pipe layout which is almost 20 miles in length. Three balancing tanks and a Repumping Station to serve the higher areas complete the scheme.

"Generally, Bida as bounded by the City Walls and embracing an estimated population of 50,000 is the area served. The future has been cared for by designing the Works for an ultimate output of 51,000 gallons per hour with the addition of more settling tanks and filters."

By now, I had become closely involved in the Project, being responsible for the Ceremony. As 2nd March drew near, it was only too obvious that the *fadama* section of the pumping main would not be completed in time for water to be pumped to the Storage Reservoir in Bida. Fortunately, I think the Chief Water Engineer was relying on me as Provincial Engineer to keep him informed, which I did. We would arrange for the Premier to start one of the pumps to put water into the beginning of the pumping main and this would agitate a fountain in the ground outside as an indication of supply. We would cajole local contractors with Water Bowsers (mobile tanks) to fill them from rivers or streams and position them at some of the most prominent stand-pipes in Bida Township to indicate what would soon be readily available via the pipe layout.

The Ceremony was my personal responsibility. In addition to the Premier, the Minister of Finance (Makama Bida), the Minister of Works, the Hon. Provincial Commissioner, the Etsu Nupe, the Provincial

Secretary (Successor to the Resident), the Chief Water Engineer and other local dignitaries would be present. There was no space in the Works for such an assembly so I decided to have a large *rumfa* in a suitable area outside. A *rumfa* is an open-sided temporary shelter built with upright poles (usually founded in old oil drums filled with sand or earth for stability) with a traditional-style grass roof which would at least protect them from the sun. A platform would be erected and a few seats provided for the dignitaries for the short ceremony and then the assembled guests would proceed to the Works for the starting of the pump. The *rumfa* was completed by the afternoon of 1st March.

During the preparations I had the use of a vacant quarter in the GRA at Bida, and the Chief Water Engineer who would arrive during 1st March would be my guest for his stay. After dinner that evening we were sitting talking when, to our surprise, we distinctly heard thunder in the distance, most unusual for the time of year. It came closer and within minutes we were experiencing near hurricane winds and heavy rain – a typical tropical storm which did not last very long. We looked at each other in dismay thinking of the *rumfa*! As soon as it was daylight I went out and found the *rumfa* had suffered from the high wind. I sent for the men who had erected it, and offered them double overtime if it was put right by midday. Thankfully, it was!

The Ceremony went well: the fountain impressed the dignitaries and later I heard that four Water Bowsers had turned out to serve the public in Bida as planned. I will quote from Brian Brough's letter of 6th March 1963:

> "You will be amused to know that I painted your Bida efforts (including the road from the Zaria boundary) so successfully at a propitious moment, that Jonah (Permanent Secretary) has talked of nothing else ever since! He is tickled to bits especially as the Minister has reinforced my painting. I'm drafting letters to all concerned for Jonah to sign."

The treatment at the Works at Minna was similar to that at Badeggi. I had found time to commission this Scheme satisfactorily although the staff were occasionally negligent about back-washing the layers of graded sand and stone of the filters, resulting in interruptions to the flow of water into supply. The raw water from the dam sometimes brought with it some of the silt from the bottom particularly during dry periods. As mentioned earlier, demand could exceed output through the Works and some areas had to be shut off for specified periods. High areas supplied from elevated storage tanks had to be replenished, which could only be done during the night when demand generally was low, otherwise they might run dry during the day. Similarly with storage tanks at the large pig farm, but it did manage to have all the supply it required.

Despite having to give much time to urgent water problems, I was determined to raise the overall standard of road maintenance of the 900 miles of classified roads in the Province. Regular tours stopping to talk with headmen and labourers during working hours had begun to take effect, and I was able to encourage them by passing on favourable comments made to me by a wide variety of travellers, such as: "I know I'm in Niger Province because the roads are in good condition."

I had found the general standard of the Superintendents' grade was higher than I had experienced elsewhere, and two of these men showed excellent reliability: George Metherell (expatriate), who was Yard Superintendent responsible for building maintenance; and Felix Thwanko (Ibo), who was a loyal and efficient Mechanical Superintendent.

It was nearing the end of 1963, and I had been in Niger Province since July 1962. I was hoping to apply for about four months' UK leave starting early in 1964 and began to wonder about my posting on return. The Federal elections were due in December 1964, four years since those in late 1960 in preparation for Independence. Politicians were showing obvious signs of close attention to the electorate, not least amongst them the Premier of Northern Nigeria, Sir Ahmadu Bello, Sardauna of Sokoto. Starting from Kaduna, his tours would bring him into Niger Province, and the occasions being well publicised, I would make sure that the roads were in good order. Moreover, in case of mechanical breakdown, Felix and some mechanics would be at the Provincial boundary to await the arrival of the Premier's entourage. It would stop to dust down after the long drive on dirt roads before moving on, and from then onwards Felix and his mechanics would tail the entourage until it left the Province. Felix always reported to me after each visit; sometimes a vehicle needed attention, tyres changed and so on, all of which he could deal with and for which he was personally thanked by the Premier. On one occasion, he told me with great amusement, as he moved forward to greet the entourage, the Security Police tried to hold him back, but the Premier saw what was happening and called out: "Don't you stop that man, he always waits to follow me when I come this way," or words to that effect.

My UK leave was approved beginning on 8th February 1964 to conclude on 17th July 1964. During the leave I received a posting notice to Acting Provincial Engineer Bauchi Province Headquarters at Bauchi, to the north of Niger Province bordering on Kano and Bornu Provinces. I had handed over at Minna to one of the recently qualified indigenous engineers whose family was well connected. Then almost at the last moment the posting was changed and I was to resume as Acting Provincial Engineer Niger Province for a second tour at Minna. The Nigerian engineer was to take the post at Bauchi.

On arrival at Minna I reported to the office where I found the Nigerian engineer far from pleased at the change, and he left within a few minutes without Handover or Notes. In the circumstances, however, this did not really matter. Sometime later I heard that the Makama Bida had intervened for my return to the Province. Before dealing with this second tour in Niger Province – which, incidentally, well outdid the first – I must insert the following odd assignment. Headquarters Kaduna informed me that Alhaji Sir Ahmadu Bello, the Premier, was intending to visit the grave of Umaru Nogwamatse of Kontagora who died about the turn of the century and whose grave is in the remote village of Mamba, said to be some thirty miles from Kontagora in the Province. (Umaru Nogwamatse was the founder of Kontagora and a famous Fulani Warrior Prince of Sokoto who carved a Kingdom for himself to what is now Kontagora Emirate in Niger State. He is a distant uncle of Sardauna Ahmadu Bello.) I was to check at once what Landrover access there might be to this village and, in any case, to take all necessary steps to ensure access.

I assembled assistance in Kontagora and set off in a Landrover along what seemed to be a road of sorts. The going was very rough and slow, cutting away the overgrown bush to clear a passage, and doing some crude repairs to such surface as existed as we went forward. I was dependent on the guide as to direction. After several hours without meeting anyone we reached the village. Our arrival created some excitement; the village Chief was summoned together with his elders and as best I could I told him why we had come. He took me to the grave in a small white building like a tomb. Eventually we had to leave and the Chief gave me the customary scrawny chickens with lots of handshaking, chatter and smiles.

We had only gone a few miles on the way back when from both sides of the road emerged numbers of people waving and crying out and running alongside the Landrover looking at me! This continued almost all the way back to Kontagora, with more and more people emerging from the bush, causing us to stop repeatedly to be looked at and greeted. Reaching Kontagora at last, I was able to ask for some explanation of the obvious interest and excitement. Somehow the news had been spread from the village that there was a white man in the area, and as many had never seen one before everyone rushed to take a look! I reported what I had done to Headquarters and heard no more.

The instantaneous departure of the outgoing Provincial Engineer left the house in the GRA immediately available so I moved in – no drama at the Rest House this time! Everyone seemed very pleased at my return. Again, I was resuming duty during the rainy season so it was not long before troubles began. A quick tour gave the impression that whilst the standard of road maintenance generally had not fallen away, there would have to be closures for eight hours on some roads as the rains intensified.

One evening I was sitting in the darkness on the open verandah outside the folding doors of the lounge taking a drink before a light meal and watching the skyline which resembled a grand fireworks display. There must have been several storms competing with each other. Then the wind began and I just had time to get into the lounge and, with the steward's help, close the folding doors before a ferocious gale struck the house. Dust and debris lashed against the glass followed by intense rain. At once we sought protection in the narrow passage leading to the bedrooms, in case the glass shattered, but fortunately it held. It was nearly thirty minutes before the fierceness of the storm (or storms) abated. My car in the carport at the side of the house had survived so I was able to move out to inspect the damage. Large tree branches and general debris were strewn over the roads but I managed to get by and reach the Township where I arranged a call out of labour and transport to start the clear up. By daylight the real damage could be seen – roofs blown off at schools and missions etc. I was able to get to the dam where there was no damage immediately noticeable. Meteorological information was that there had been a line storm with wind up to 105 miles an hour on Minna. A 'line storm', by definition, is one that concentrates on a 'line', sometimes no wider than 100 yards, but, of course, it is devastating as it rushes through. This effect could certainly be seen where the worst damage had taken place.

Next, in early October before the rains had finished, came a report that the long causeway carrying the road through the flood plain of the River Kaduna to Badeggi had been breached in one place by a build-up of flood water on one side with a 20 feet gap, but that, as could only be expected, in a short time, this had extended up to 100 feet. I was reminded of the earlier incident at Yola which I recounted in the previous chapter! At once I drove for inspection at the breach. More serious, perhaps, was the fact that the pumping main to Bida was now suspended unsupported across the gap and might fracture or joints open up. This was another case for a Bailey Bridge to restore road access and provide support for the main. Checking the gap, I decided that 120 feet of double-single Bailey Bridge was the minimum needed.

Based on previous knowledge, I knew that there were considerable stocks of Bailey equipment at Kaduna, so I arranged top priority collection of all that I required. Then I designed an arm or extension piece which could be bolted to the bottom of a Bailey panel with a hoop to go round the main. These arms were to be spaced near the pipe joints along the length of the suspended main. The hoops bolted to the arms would take care of any thrust of the main during pumping. Fortunately, the skilled mechanics in Bida were able to make the arms and the hoops with the nuts and bolts. When the equipment arrived, labour was gathered for the bridge construction.

As at Yola, I found the labour quickly acquired the routine of construction of a Bailey Bridge under direction and, in fact, had to be restrained from pushing the assembled length of bridge on the rollers too far over the gap and therefore beyond the point of balance with disastrous outcome – the front part in the drink! Any RE officer who allowed this to happen would be shamed for life! Within a week, all was completed and everyone was very pleased.

Eager workers building the Bailey Bridge at Badeggi Water Works

I do not know how long there had been a ferry crossing of the River Kaduna at Wuya, on the road from Bida to Mokwa, the junction with the A1 route from the South to the North, but the maintenance of the ferry boat machinery etc. lay with the Ministry of Works, Niger Province. The ferryman in charge, an Ibo mechanic, was remarkable for his ingenuity in keeping the ferry operational. I am sure, on one occasion, I saw string had replaced a belt. Other staff to guide vehicles on and off the pontoon were equally reliable. Now the ferry was to be replaced by a splendid bridge which the Northern Government was financing.

71

The bridge had been designed by the international firm of Consulting Engineers, *Scott Wilson Kirkpatrick & Partners* of London and Basingstoke. Its location at Wuya over the River Kaduna with its wide flood plain and only a few miles from the confluence with the River Niger, had prudently led the Consulting Engineers to investigate the likely effect of seasonal currents, flood water etc., by creating a model of the site. This would be used for simulating the influence of those factors, determining not only the best location of the bridge proper in the flood plain but also the embankment approaches and any necessary protection to them. This would have been carried out at their office in the UK.

Now, after 34 years, with no written or photographic records, I can only envisage a bridge of, say, ten spans, each of 60-70 feet in length, with a long embankment approach on the Bida side with its protective apron. It was a concrete and steel structure, comparable to any on highways in Europe at that time, strikingly graceful to the eye in every way. The inclusive contract for its construction was with *Costain Ltd.*, again an international firm of contractors well established in Nigeria and Africa generally.

During my regular tours to Bida, although I had no direct responsibility for the Project, I always visited the site. I saw the great efforts being made by everyone concerned to bring about completion despite a number of hazards, particularly the seasonal behaviour of the river.

Then, as happened in the case of the Bida Treatment Works, early in October the Premier directed that he would formally open the bridge at Wuya on the 22nd November 1964 – the Federal Elections were due countrywide on 31st December 1964! Certainly, the bridge itself was virtually completed but major earthworks etc., so vital to the whole concept, were still in progress. As Provincial Engineer I would be responsible for the Opening Ceremony. I was called to Kaduna to see the Minister of Works and was informed that the Premier wanted an impressive Ceremony. At the meeting with the Minister and the Deputy Permanent Secretary (expatriate), without thinking of the implications I suggested traditional fireworks to be let off over the bridge. Before leaving Kaduna I was told the Premier was enthusiastic about the idea, but I was to discover that because of growing countrywide tensions, the import of fireworks into Nigeria had been banned. By sheer luck I was going to see the Deputy Permanent Secretary about the programme which Headquarters would send out once I had settled timing etc., and mentioned the problem of the fireworks. He thought some fireworks had been left over from the Independence Day Celebrations in Kaduna on 1st October 1960, and if I would stay a little longer he would find out. He made a few enquiries and learned that in the store were a quantity of rocket exploding fireworks, apparently in good condition, and he agreed to release them and, to my great relief, send them with the expert (another expatriate) to let them off!

Driving back I thought about the programme, part of which would take place in the afternoon – the speeches, cutting the tape etc. – with the fireworks display after dark. I estimated that if the formalities took place at 4.00pm, people could return to Bida for evening prayers etc. and be back at Wuya by 8.00pm for the fireworks. The latter meant that the whole site must be lighted. Another problem was the twelve miles of dirt road from Bida to the site. It would be impossible to water it to keep down the dust, but the road gangs must be out and mechanics at the ready for any possible breakdowns. Because of the long embankment approach to the bridge, the only place for car parking was the final section of the road itself which must be lighted, and strict control would be essential. But where could we build a *rumfa* for the speeches? There was no area at the start of the bridge proper except the top of the apron (shaped like a blunted triangle) on the right hand side of the bridge abutment. Levelled off with some fine gravel, this ought to be able to take a *rumfa* for about 200 guests including the VIPs. Any members of the public would have to squeeze in at the back or, for the fireworks, line the riverbank on each side of the bridge. For those returning for the fireworks, there would be another *rumfa* on the far side of the bridge from which to view the display.

By now I was really going all out to make a success of the Ceremony, and to be honest I was enjoying the challenge! Through contacts at Kaduna, two large generators came to provide light at the site including the parking on the road. I conceived the idea of symbolically 'constructing' the bridge by floodlighting the spans of the bridge each pair in sequence starting with the two outer spans simultaneously, until they joined up in the centre. When I explained what I had in mind the expatriate Mechanical Superintendent who came with some mechanics joined in with enthusiasm. We decided that this symbolic lighting display should take place before the fireworks and be repeated three times. So he went ahead with the arrangements.

The day arrived and early in the afternoon Jonah (Permanent Secretary) and some senior staff from Headquarters came to look around. He expressed his satisfaction and then went off to the Camp of the Consultants and the Contractors saying, "I'll be back later." The proceedings in the late afternoon followed tradition. After the speeches the Premier; VIPs and other guests, moved to the start of the bridge where he cut the tape. The party then walked across the bridge stopping at the middle where the Premier unveiled a plaque on the parapet to mark the Opening Ceremony. At the far end cars were waiting to drive the party back through the bridge and on to Bida.

One rather sad ritual had been expressly asked for by the ferryman and his men. As the Premier and the VIPs started to walk across the bridge, the ferry with the men dressed in white (the mourning dress for Muslims in contrast to the Christian black) made its last crossing of the river. I remembered to ask the party to look over the parapet and signal to the ferrymen that their farewell had been noticed.

Soon after dark, before the crowds had returned after evening prayers, we tested the lighting display and it worked well. At 8.00pm the Premier, VIPs and guests gathered in the *rumfa* on the far side. The floodlighting of the bridge was perfect and about 50 rockets exploding overhead brought the usual exclamations from the surprising number of the public who had somehow managed to come and line the river bank on both sides. The bush telegraph had been operating! Concerned there might be some congestion I had stayed on the Bida side with one of the Superintendents I had brought from Minna to help generally, so as to ensure that after the fireworks the cars of the Premier, the VIPs and invited guests coming from the far side would get clear to return to Bida ahead of the cars parked in the road. The one VIP car which did stop for a few seconds was that of the British High Commissioner Lagos who said a few kind words to me – a characteristic gesture much appreciated.

Returning to my quarters at Bida, tired as I was, there had to be a party. I was delighted to be able to thank all those who had helped – not forgetting the fireworks expert from Kaduna. Jonah came and showed around the expensive watch the Premier had given him in the *rumfa* at the fireworks with these words, overheard by George Metherell and reported to me later: "Thank you Mr Jones you must be very tired after seeing to all these arrangements...!"

Unashamed, I include these two letters which I received later at Minna:

> December 1964
>
> Dear Mr Muggeridge, I write to offer you my congratulations on the outstanding success of the opening ceremony at the Wuya Bridge. The conception of the details of the ceremony and the execution of all the arrangements could not have been surpassed, and it should be a matter of great satisfaction and pride to you that everything went off so smoothly and so well.
>
> I fully appreciate the tremendous amount of work to which you and your staff must have been put in the very short time which was available to prepare for the opening. That such an impressive ceremony was organised in the limited time and with the limited space available at the site reflects great credit on you personally and on all your staff.
>
> Thank you very much for an excellent show. Please pass on my thanks to all members of your staff who contributed in any way to the success of the occasion.
>
> Yours sincerely,
> Usman Maska
> Minister of Works

And this:

10th December 1964

My dear Mr Muggeridge, I very much regret not having written to you before to express my appreciation and very sincere thanks for the magnificent arrangements you made for the opening of the Wuya Bridge on 22nd November 1964. Everything worked like clockwork, and it was quite obvious a great deal of hard work and careful planning had been carried out previously to make the actual opening such a success which was so much enjoyed and appreciated by our many visitors and all present.

2. I realise the initiative, drive and planning came from you, for which I am very grateful and realise also how you so well moulded your team to produce such a wonderful result, will you please convey to them all my grateful thanks.

3. We are very proud of our new bridge and very thrilled, you and your excellent staff made the occasion of the opening such a memorable one.

Yours sincerely,
Jakubu Lame
(Hon. Alhaji Yakubu Lame)
Provincial Commissioner Niger Province

There were several other appreciative letters including one from the Deputy Permanent Secretary who had been present and seen the fireworks display.

Now before I move on to the last two incidents of this tour in Niger Province, I must refer to the developing ethnic tensions and political turbulence nationwide as the Federal Elections drew near at the end of December 1964. I have mentioned these factors in influencing the Premier's decision regarding the Ceremonies of the Badeggi Treatment Works and the prodigious Wuya Bridge. It was impossible not to be aware of the tensions building up everywhere. The talk at any gathering of expatriates was that during those four years of indigenous Government Rule corruption, abuse of privilege, political intrigue and so on had openly emerged throughout the whole country, and the consensus was that something had to give. What that was to be came barely a year later.

I quote from Chapter 21 of *The First Dance of Freedom – Black Africa in the Post War Era* by Martin Meredith, published by *Hamish Hamilton* in 1984:

"The sense of optimism about Nigeria's future, so much in evidence when the country was launched as an independent state in 1960, remained buoyant in the early years of Independence. As the most populous nation in Africa, led by politicians widely applauded for their long experience of government, endowed with a strong, diversified economy and possessing an efficient civil service, Nigeria was clearly marked out as one of Africa's emerging powers. Whatever disputes between the country's three regions had occurred during the closing stages of British rule seemed largely resolved with the advent of Independence. The federal constitution, over which there had been such fierce argument, in its final form was regarded as a sensible compromise, effectively balancing the country's rival political interests and well able to contain the strains and stresses which the hurly-burly of Nigerian politics invariably produced. At the helm of the Federal Government was a coalition of Northern and Eastern politicians from the conservative Northern People's Congress (NPC) and the more radical National Council of Nigerian Citizens (NONO), providing a broadly-based administration that avoided the danger of either the North or the two regions of the South holding power exclusively. It was led by a moderate Northerner, Sir Abubakar Tafawa Balewa. Western politicians in the Action Group meanwhile settled for the role of parliamentary opposition in the traditional British manner. At a regional level, each of the three major parties remained in control of regional government. By outward appearances, therefore, Nigeria provided a promising example of a carefully balanced and stable parliamentary democracy.

"Behind this reassuring facade, however, politicians on all sides were engaged in a scramble for power and profit, conducted with such reckless abandon that it led finally to the downfall of civilian rule within six years. The advantages of political office were used at every opportunity by Nigeria's leaders to accumulate empires of wealth and patronage with which to improve both their personal and their party's fortunes. In return for political support, party and government bosses were able to provide their followers and friends with jobs, contracts, loans, scholarships, public amenities; indeed with any favour that came within their purview. Public funds were regularly commandeered for political and sometimes personal gain. At every level, from the Federal Government to Regional Government down to local districts and towns, the system was worked by politicians in office to ensure that their own areas and members of their own tribe benefited, while opposition areas suffered from neglect. Politics thus degenerated into a corrupt and bitter struggle for the spoils of office. Each region was locked in competition, for a larger share of federal revenue, for the location of industries, for appointments to public office, for political advantage, often in an atmosphere of such cut-throat antagonism that tribal fears and mistrust inevitably became more deeply rooted. By nature, Nigerian politics tended to be mercenary and violent. Political debate was routinely conducted in acrimonious and abusive language, and tribal loyalties were constantly exploited. The tactics employed were often those of the rough-house variety. The eventual consequence of these rash and profligate years, however, was that Nigeria was led into sudden upheaval and, ultimately, towards a tragedy of monumental proportions."

This tragedy began some months before I went on leave from Minna and was still there on my return. First, however, came the Federal Elections on 31st December 1964. There were two Constituencies in Niger

Province, one based in Minna, the other in Abuja. I found myself appointed Deputy Returning Officer for Minna. The Returning Officer was the Chief Veterinary Officer, an elderly, bearded and devout Muslim. He had no idea of the duties and was greatly relieved when I agreed to take charge of the count – in any case, he said, the appointment would interfere with his prayers.

The count was to take place at a school in Minna. The poll closed at 8.00pm and the ballot boxes had to come in from a wide area with the Polling Station Officers and their returns. Most of these were incomplete but I had to accept them. I alone held the key for opening the boxes and I poured out the contents on to the tables for the counting staff to get to work. I expected that most ballot papers would be for the ruling Party in the North, the Northern Peoples Congress (NPC) and the opposition, the Nigerian Council for Nigerian Citizens (NCNC). It took only the opening of a few random ballot boxes to reveal what I had feared had been taking place, the rigging of the result in favour of the NPC. I will try to describe the evidence. Clearly, after the poll had closed, the staff at a number of the Polling Stations had filled the boxes with unused ballot papers which they marked in favour of NPC, taking care to reconcile the number used by ticking unticked names on the relevant electoral list. In effect, this could bring about almost a 100% voting turnout at the Stations concerned. So keen were they, in some cases, that even the 'tendered' ballot papers had been used! In their haste or, perhaps, in their indifference to responsibility, many ballot papers had not been folded properly, and others were in number sequence as one might sometimes receive new banknotes at a bank. Other boxes were almost empty except for ballot papers in favour of NCNC – probably indicating intimidation outside the Stations of those thought to favour NPC.

I put my evidence to the young Nigerian Electoral Officer in charge of Minna Constituency but he just laughed. That was more than enough for me; I would get the count over now as quickly as possible. I sent for the Returning Officer to come to declare the result. When he came I gave him the form I had filled in giving the result, massively in favour of NPC, but without comment about the rigging. There followed the customary speeches of congratulation and thanks to all concerned etc. etc., and I just had time to reach The Club for Auld Lang Syne at midnight for the New Year 1965. Most expatriates were there with their wives and families who had come out for Christmas and the holiday period. I told those I knew well of my experience at the count and learned that events were much the same at Abuja Constituency.

To quote from Martin Meredith's book again, after describing the political manoeuvrings leading up to 31st December 1964 he writes: "No proper election was held..., electoral malpractices had occurred..." and gives the example of 61 constituencies in the North where the NPC candidates were declared 'returned unopposed' despite opposition nominations having been put forward. Certainly something had to give.

The constitutional crisis continued throughout 1965 until – Meredith again:

> "...the end of civilian rule came with sudden and violent finality. On 15th January 1966, after three months of chaos in the Western Region and mounting disgust with the flagrantly corrupt and avaricious manoeuvres of the country's politicians, a group of young Army majors attempted to mount a revolution, overthrowing the entire order. In the early hours of the morning, rebel officers in Lagos seized the Federal Prime Minister, Sir Abubakar Balewa, took him outside the city and executed him by the side of the road, dumping his body in a ditch; in Ibadan, the capital of the Western Region, Akintola was killed by rebel troops after a brief gun battle; and in Kaduna, the Sardauna of Sokoto, Premier of the Northern Region, was shot dead at his residence. Senior Army officers, also on the death list, were killed."

My radio was always tuned to the *BBC* Overseas Service (later World Service) so I was hearing the dramatic news of the events in the early hours of that day as I drank my morning tea. Incidentally, during the whole of my time in Nigeria I was in and out of many offices of top and senior civil servants, ministers and so on. In the background the radio would be on tuned to the *BBC* so when the news came on our business would be halted until it was over!

Reacting immediately, I made for the Provincial Office, the operations room of the Administration, to consult the Officer in charge, Brigadier Macdonald who was inevitably known as Mac. These 're-treads', as they were known, were found in that role at most Provinces in the North. Already other expatriates had mustered and it was interesting to see how Mac had assumed command of the situation. He advised us not to leave the Station and to assemble again in the late afternoon, meanwhile keeping a low profile in our dealings with local people and staff.

By the afternoon Mac was suggesting that we should go about our business as normally as possible, and he would call us together when it seemed necessary. I heard some with families expressing concern as to their safety, and Mac advised that, for the present, they should not leave their houses. That evening a messenger arrived at my house with a handwritten note on a flimsy page torn from a small lined notebook signed by the Provincial Commissioner, Alhaji Muhammadu Sokoto. In view of what had been taking place he was asking for my help in providing a lorry so that he and his family could leave under cover of darkness for his home in the North. I sent the messenger back with a note saying that transport would be sent within an hour or so. Then I sent my steward on his bicycle to the Township with instructions to find my Landrover driver, Usman, wherever he was – probably at one of his brothers in the Town – and tell him to come with his Landrover at once. He had my authority to keep his Landrover with him at all times out of working hours – in any case, I knew he would do this, but if he was found outside the Township with it he would be in much trouble! Usman, a tall imposing figure always traditionally clothed as a Muslim, was an excellent driver, reliable and loyal. I had chosen him myself and when touring, at prayer times without a word to me he would draw into the side of the road, get out his kettle of water (during the rains he would even fill it from the road puddles), unobtrusively carry out the routine cleansing, say his prayers, return to the Landrover and, again without a word to me, we would resume our journey.

When Usman came I told him to find a lorry driver he could rely upon, tell him to get his lorry, check the fuel and then go to the house of the Provincial Commissioner with a note I gave him. Once the Commissioner and his family had left Usman should come and tell me. Late the next day, the lorry driver came to me with a note, again on a flimsy page. I have it still, dated 16th January 1966, the words and the signature shakily written, the ink now faded and not always clear:

> PE,
>
> I am almost certain that you will feel very happy to know of my safe arrival at home. My family and I are indeed grateful for your very kind assistance you have done to my family. This will ever remain indelible in my memory. If not for your mercy to give a transport for my sake at this juncture is not necessary. I thank you very much indeed. I know Allah will redouble the reward of this assistance to you.
>
> signed very truly,
> Alhaji Muhammadu Sokoto
> Provincial Commissioner

I feel sure he was the Provincial Commissioner who attended the Ceremonies at Badeggi Water Works and Wuya Bridge and afterwards wrote appreciatively. I certified a generous number of hours' overtime in the lorry driver's log but I am sure he had been well rewarded by the grateful Commissioner.

In 1966, I believe there were still about 10,000 expatriates – dominantly British – actively engaged in public service, contracting, commerce and general business in Nigeria. There had been no noticeable antagonism to these who had agreed, or decided, to stay on after Independence. Now, of course, the overthrow of indigenous Governments would create uncertainty as to the future. In Niger Province, however, after the initial shock of the events of 15th January, it seemed we should continue life and work as normally as possible.

It had been a strenuous tour of duty and I badly needed leave. I applied and was granted leave from 24th April 1966 with a return date of 8th October. I would be leaving amid great uncertainty with Nigeria in turmoil and violent unrest under military rule. In fact, I wondered if it would be wise, or even feasible, for me to return?

Nigerian staff with Jack at his farewell party before going on leave

In the background is Brigadier Macdonald,
British Resident of Niger Province

Staff at MOW HQ Minna

With expatriate and Nigerian staff at Minna

During leave, when I was in two minds whether to return, the following article appeared in *The Times* on 29th September 1966 which I felt strove, with considerable clarity, to describe the current situation in Nigeria and led me to decide, despite the alarming press reports, to return on my due date. Also my posting notice had come; believe it or not I was to go back to Kabba Province, to be based at Lokoja at the confluence of the Rivers Niger and Benue. Kabba the most southerly of the Northern States and has a boundary with Eastern Nigeria (Ibo land). Had someone at Headquarters got it in for me, I wondered, or, perhaps, having decided what, in fact, was soon to happen, regarded me as the right person to be in the right place – poor fellow! Anyway, here is the article in full from the *London Times* of 29th September 1966 by Bridget Bloom:

Nigeria Seeks New Framework for its Future

"In Ibadan recently I was sitting in with Nigerian friends on the perennial Nigerian argument – to be or not to be one nation. After all the difficulties had been churned over, one man of goodwill said in despair: 'I honestly do not see how we can live together.' Another silenced him with the impassioned plea: 'But don't you see – if we in Nigeria fail, Africa itself is finished!' He was right. Nigeria today is the epitome of the African problem of creating nations from races, tribes and creeds. In Lagos the problem is faced by 28 civilians from Nigeria's four regions and the federal capital. The issue is stark. Is Nigeria, once considered one of Africa's most stable and promising states, to remain one country? Or is the Commonwealth soon to be enlarged by three more independent states?

"Ironically, Nigeria's reputation abroad has taken more from its size, wealth, and economic policies than from its political performance. In the first two years of Independence the party system seemed to western eyes to be working calmly. But later, tribal and political conflicts could not be contained. When the Army took over in January, the politicians, parties, and the British-inspired constitution were totally discredited. General Ironsi's regime, which took over from young majors

85

who attempted the coup, produced the temporary feeling that Nigeria was reborn. Indeed, I found in Nigeria at the time, after the initial shock was over, a marked euphoria. The old politicians had been sent packing. It was felt that a salutary period of military rule could restore to civilian Government a Nigeria purged of tribalism, with corruption under control, and with hopes for social justice restored. When I returned four months ago for a prolonged stay some of the euphoria persisted. Even the massacre of eastern civilians in the North had failed to bring home the gravity of the crisis. It took the Northern coup in July (1966 JM) to do it. General Ironsi's tragedy was that he failed to see that Nigeria's problems would not easily succumb to a few orders and a decree centralising government in Lagos. A bluff, urbane soldier, he was not equipped to be a national leader. Initially he seemed at pains to avoid tribal pressures. But by May it was clear that he leant heavily on a small group of unrepresentative and blinkered Ibo advisers. When his regime was overthrown it was obvious that, instead of being able to cure the country's ills, the Army itself had succumbed to them. The old tribal distrust, now most acute in the Army, has once more infected Nigerian society. Traditional rivalry of the North and East in Nigerian politics has left these two regions deeply estranged. Many ordinary Nigerians are fearful of the Army, yet apprehensive of a return to civilian rule if it means a return to the stresses and cynicism of the old regime.

"The main obstacle to peace is the crisis of confidence within the Army. Today it is split down the middle. In January probably a dozen senior officers, mostly from the North were killed. The July coup was activated largely by revenge. Some Ibo officers were killed, and many more escaped or were repatriated to the East. About 120 officers are there now and it is doubtful if there are any eastern men in the five battalions in the rest of the country. There are increasing retorts of lawlessness among troops.

"The first task of the supreme Commander who succeeded General Ironsi, Lieutenant Colonel Gowon, is to control the Army and restore its confidence and efficiency, though he has had to assume as well all the burdens of the head of government. Unmarried and a Christian Colonel Gowon comes from one of the smallest tribes in the North. Sandhurst trained and only 51, he keeps in much closer touch with the Army than did General Ironsi, under whom he was Chief of Staff. He has stayed in barracks instead of living and working in State House. He has the traditional British soldier's distaste for politics. He has declared that he will keep the Army out of politics as far as possible, though other politically minded officers may disagree. Various solutions, including overseas training missions, have been suggested to deal with the Army problem. Even the impractical step of disarming it has been suggested. But the Army cannot withdraw from politics until a basis can be agreed for civilian government.

"Constitutional steps alone, unfortunately, cannot solve Nigeria's problems. No conference can find solutions for fear and suspicion. Colonel Gowon himself has ruled out both a complete break-up and a unitary state. He suggested four possible alternatives: a federal system with a strong or with a weak central government: confederation: or '...an entirely new arrangement peculiar to Nigeria.'

"There is no precedent for the partial break-up of an existing political sovereignty into a confederation. But such a solution is clutched at by many Nigerians, particularly in the East, where the current mood is strongly isolationist. Confederalists envisage existing regions as quasi-independent nations, each with its own Police Force, Army and even Air Force. A non-political central council would organise common services, apparently on the lines of East Africa. Advocates of this solution see it as temporary. But the danger is that a loose association would not endure. Such a degree of separation would lead not to closer association but to divorce. It would be a decree nisi. And regional autonomy leaves each region with its own tribal minorities, mirroring the federation's problems in miniature.

"Leaders of small tribes think creation of new regions for minority tribes would enable them to live with the bigger tribes. Other Nigerians argue that, provided economic viability is also taken into account, creation of more regions could produce a balanced federation. But at present oil (exports were worth £70 million last year) is produced in minority areas in the East. Northern Nigeria has previously resisted all attempts to split the region. Two factors modify this stand now. Joseph Tarka, long an advocate of a Middle Belt region, is a respected member of the Northern delegation at the conference, and many northern Army officers come from minority areas. Some do not share in the belief of 'one north'. But this is an emotional time. The difficulties of creating a new kind of federation with many new regions may prove so great that Nigerians will choose confederation as an apparently easy way out.

"Nigerians are conservative. They may be able to retreat from the confederate precipice, and yet be unable to find that 'peculiarly Nigerian' solution. A decision to maintain the status quo is then possible. This could have nominal safeguards such as regional recruitment and stationing of Army units and a constitutional clause making secession possible. This would keep the country together for a time. But it will not cure the deep tribal problem, or produce a radical change of heart, particularly in the political classes. One or two central institutions still stand: the Nigeria Police is intact and so far it maintains law and order and discipline. Neither have the year's events yet affected the efficiency of either the regional or the federal Civil Services. The resilience of the federal service in particular has been remarkable.

"For businessmen it is, so far, business as usual. In the North some essential services have been depleted. But in the other regions conditions are fairly normal. The foreign business community undoubtedly feels apprehensive, but just before I left Lagos two British businessmen told me they were going ahead with investment planned months earlier.

"These are the problems. What of the men? The Lagos conference is less unwieldy than might have been feared – 14 delegates with 14 advisers. Whatever may be thought of individuals, the choice has been careful. It excludes politicians discredited by office in the old regime. Chief Owolowo, pardoned the day after Colonel Gowon took office for his conviction of treasonable felony, leads the delegation from the West. A man of great stature, he helped build the first federation. Although he has personally suggested a federation of 18 regions, in the conference he has been highly flexible. But it is not clear if he can now emerge as a national leader. Chief Owolowo's colleague, Chief Enahoro, who is so well known in Britain, and who wishes to maintain the federation with additional regions, leads the delegation from the mid-West. The Northern delegation is led by Sir Kashim Ibrahim, a man respected even in the East for his objectivity. The East is led by Dr Njoku, the scientist Vice-Chancellor of the East based University of Nigeria, who was a competent federal Minister in the early '50s. Dr Elias, the many-sided former Attorney General, leads the Lagos contingent. But in this crucial debate no delegation speaks for the federation.

"The Lagos conference, if it is successful, can only recommend a framework within which Nigerians, collectively, can live together. Ultimately, what every Nigerian does and says will determine whether Africa's greatest country remains one nation."

That very perceptive article filled me in regarding what had been taking place in Nigeria while I had been away as well as analysing the efforts which might be made to settle the country down in the short term and decide on the future return to civilian rule. At least, it helped to prepare me for joining in the fray.

I reached Kano international airport in the early evening and went to the *Central Hotel* half expecting to find that my booking had been overtaken by events, but my reservation was still valid. So on to Kabba Province, soon to become Kwara State.

Kabba Province Again

I was back in early October 1966 and about to resume duty as Acting Provincial Engineer at Lokoja Kabba Province. Henceforth, I would be able to assess the developing situation myself.

However, writing this in 1998, I must be mindful that this Memoir is primarily about my long period of professional service in Nigeria and not a running history of that country. There were moments, of course, when my service became inextricably tied up with crucial events and happenings taking place nationwide, as well as occasions when personal feelings and impressions were uppermost, which may be revealed in quotes from letters I wrote to my brother Malcolm and others.

I will be quoting from two books: Martin Meredith's book already mentioned, and *My Command,* an account of the Nigerian Civil War 1967-1970 by General Olusegun Obasanjo published by *Heinemann Education Books (Nigeria) Ltd.* in 1980. I ought, however, to point out that there are other books about the Civil War, with or without bias, for example: *The Biafra Story* by Frederick Forsyth, from which I will also quote, and *Faith in a United Nigeria – Yakubu Gowon* by John Clarke.

First, then, this letter of 9th October 1966 to my brother addressed from the *Central Hotel* Kano:

> "We left London on schedule, touched down at Rome for half-an-hour and reached here about 6.30pm. At one time the Captain announced that we might have to overfly Kano as he could get no weather reports from Control there, but later all was well. This would have meant going on to Lagos and hoping to come back on the London flight! There were only about 20 passengers from London but a number got on at

Rome, presumably Italians making for Kainji Dam where the Contractors are an Italian Consortium. All was calm at the airport, and at customs, largely manned by inexperienced staff, I got the tape recorder through without any duty! My baggage was searched which was unusual; they were probably looking for firearms. The normal staff being Ibos had either fled or been killed during the previous weekend's troubles.

"At the hotel, several expatriate staff, previously with me and now stationed in Kano who had seen my name in the passengers' list, were waiting for me, so it was grand to get a friendly welcome. The hotel is functioning with a depleted staff, again the result of people fleeing to the East or being killed. The previous weekend had certainly been really grim: the English Press figure of 600 here was less than the actual, which is regarded as 1000, and bodies are still being found. I thought the trouble had been in the City but it was at the Airport first, then the Trading Area around the hotel where the Ibos live and work. On the Saturday evening it was the soldiers who broke out, filled up with drink and Indian hemp. Then on the Sunday the mob took over and went around flushing out Ibos from houses, including the GRA, and also outside the hotel.

"Fortunately, the Police have not joined in. I gather they have been really very good but, of course, they cannot cope with the soldiers. All internal flights have been stopped and the planes are being used for the two-way exodus – Ibos to the East, Northerners in the East to the North. This is the intention now to return as many to their place of origin as possible. Few trains are operating (most railway staff were Ibos) and most of these are being used for the exodus. I am told very little commercial transport is moving from the South to the North so supplies will become difficult soon. Other tribes of Southern origin do not appear to be affected but it is thought they will also get on the move rather than face the anxiety of staying on in the North. This would bring even greater difficulties in commerce and public services, telephone, rail and the like. I have just had a drink with the expatriate Assistant Commissioner of Police in charge here whom I know – one of the very few Britishers left in the service. He thinks the blood lust has now largely spent itself and that the people being returned to the East will be able to go quietly on the planes and trains. Apparently, what really brought the violence to such a degree was a broadcast from Cotonnu in Dahomey that the Ibos in the East were killing off the Northerners there who were trying to get away to the North. This is supposed to be untrue but the harm was already done. The killings in other places, Zaria, Jos (a mining area) and Kaduna, have been in hundreds, and in Minna my last Station the figure is given as 100, which is very heavy for a small place – there were a lot of Ibos there. All is quiet here as I write.

"Tuesday 11th October 1966 at Kaduna. Fortunately, the instructions I sent regarding my car had been received before things became bad, and the majority of the work had been completed. The Manager told me that most of his good mechanics (Ibos) had been killed in the disturbances or had gone off. Bribery was necessary to get outstanding jobs completed, and I was able to get on the move by midday Monday. Petrol was difficult to come by but I managed to get sufficient and reached Kaduna by 5.00pm Monday.

"Kaduna had had their killings on the Thursday before the Saturday/Sunday troubles at Kano. There are many stories of plots and counterplots regarding the 29th July coup going the rounds. It seems pretty clear that at that time the Ibos of the Army had planned to kill off Permanent Secretaries here in Kaduna but were forestalled by Gowon's chaps going for the Ibos a few hours before. The idea was for the East to take over the whole country.

93

"My Headquarters are functioning apparently more or less normally and everyone I have seen has given me a very pleasant welcome. Lokoja is reported quiet but telephone and mails to that area have more or less come to a stop for the time being. Kaduna Town shops have an air of normality but business is obviously much reduced. Banks are only open from 8.00am to 9.00am and are recruiting European wives for staff.

"What may yet happen is anyone's guess. It is thought that blood shedding may be over, unless something vitally affecting Ibos and Hausas occurs. There is no doubt that events since 29th July have rocked the whole set-up and more recent events, particularly commerce and public services. Recovery or reorganisation to meet the disappearance of Ibos from the North will take a long time. If the other Southern tribes go too then everything will sink still lower because without these more intelligent, experienced people many services both, public and private, cannot function.

"On Thursday I start off on my journey to Lokoja via Minna, Ilorin, a long way round because a ferry is closed. Getting away from Kano and Kaduna I expect to find the tension reduced but normal facilities probably poorer. These are all first impressions and, of course, I have listened to many stories, explanations and theories.

"I am hoping to send this by someone flying to London on Wednesday which should be more reliable than the post. I do hope you receive it. I will write again when I can, although it may take time to reach you."

I reached Lokoja on 13th October 1966, which, being a much smaller Town than Kano or Kaduna, seemed quiet and calm by comparison much as I had known it some years earlier.

The outgoing Provincial Engineer was, I believe, a youngish British expatriate on his final tour having decided not to return, largely for family reasons but also influenced by the prevailing uncertainty. There were several other British expatriates at Lokoja, a British Water Engineer and three Works Superintendents whom I had yet to meet. The office staff had barely changed, and the same Chief Clerk whom I remembered as a capable and, I think, loyal worker was still there.

I was soon to find an atmosphere of increasing apprehension which later, sadly, turned to panic. I was pleased to hear that the Provincial Secretary (successor to The Resident) was Alhaji Abubakar Mashegu whom I had known elsewhere when he was a Senior District Officer clearly destined for promotion. We would soon find ourselves co-operating on crucial matters. His Nigerian wife was a charming hostess. As I recall, Federal Officers of the Inland Waterways Department were still in post from its Headquarters in Lagos. They were responsible for the Rivers Niger and Benue, together with an Officer in charge of the public vehicle ferry across the River Niger from Lokoja to Shintaku. This crossing was on the route through Igala Division of Kabba Province to the Regional boundary at Ankpa and onwards to Enugu, the Regional Capital. Two-storey houses had been built for these personnel who bitterly resented having been posted away from the bright lights of Lagos – more of that later.

Extracts from my first letter from Lokoja dated 20th December 1966 to my brother:

"... the mails are pretty hopeless. I don't suppose you can possibly get this by Christmas, and in any case I'm late in writing. I thought I'd like to send you and the children cables for Christmas but on enquiring at the Post Office it's no good. There is no-one there now who can work the telegraph for cables...

"With the inappropriate weather and the almost non-existent social life (which really doesn't worry me) I have three days' break in which to catch up on many jobs, and have been pegging away at the Departmental shambles. I will write again about the situation here over Christmas when I will know more than at present. I can't write with any reliability as I'm too cut off and too far away from Lagos and Kaduna, but I'll give my impressions and the 'feel' of things. Crudely, I should say there's a fifty-fifty chance of Civil War breaking out. Whether the East or the North will start it is anyone's guess, if it starts. But more when I write again."

There were no cables again, doubtless the Ibo staff had been called home. As for the national situation, I will quote Meredith:

"By the end of the year 1966 more than a million refugees, many of them wounded, exhausted or in a state of shock, had sought safety in the East. And amid a sense of outrage and bitterness at the fearful sequence of events that had occurred – the downfall of Ironsi, the return of Northerners to power, the murder of Eastern officers the months of persecution and the massacres of September and October – Eastern leaders made plans for secession."

I made a point of day touring to other towns in the Province which meant that I saw that road maintenance needed attention, although traffic was noticeably reduced. At Idah I visited the local hospital, the town market and the ferry. Despite the growing tension with the East, trading by ferry and local boats was still active across the River Niger. As with all border areas inter-tribal marriage was common but might yet cause difficulties.

At Kabba it seemed 'business as usual' while at Okene a new College was nearing completion by Italian Contractors who characteristically grinned and shrugged their shoulders at the idea of 'real trouble'. My visit happened on a Friday, Mosque Day, and I thought the Township seemed over-excited and very noisy. There were crowds of people on the move making it difficult to drive through to reach the office of the District Officer to pay a courtesy call. He was astounded to see me, as apparently he had just returned from trying to quell a highly charged demonstration, or, as he put it, "You've just come through a riot over who should be the Imam at the Mosque today!" I'd had a lucky escape from being embroiled.

In an earlier chapter I described the general bustle of activities at the waterfront, the loading of sacks of groundnuts and other produce into the paddleboats, the Waterworks, the Electricity Company and the one million gallon fuel storage tank. Now, at the beginning of 1967, loading had almost ceased, truck drivers from the North were fearful of coming so close to the border with the East as, should fighting break out, they might not get away, and the paddleboats were not coming in. The Managers of the various trading companies were becoming apprehensive and had made plans for evacuation. The Manager of the fuel company explained that he had good stocks of petrol and particularly diesel at present, but he was concerned that replenishment from the East by river tankers could be severely interrupted, or even cease, if conditions changed for the worse. We were to meet the worst before very long. First I made contact with the Electricity Company which adjoined the Waterworks, as fuel would be necessary to maintain the power supply. The personnel in charge were local and we agreed to co-operate in the event of a crisis.

As I mentioned earlier, one of the key persons with whom I had made contact on my return to Lokoja was the local Head of Police, a Nigerian, who showed ready understanding of our respective roles. He was anxious to know about help with transport should he find it imperative to move police at short notice. I was able to reassure him that I would always give top priority to any request for emergency transport from him, but said he should apply to me personally. I did not tell him that I had already set up a 'stand-by lorry' with driver for all non-working hours, weekends and so on, and that my Landrover driver kept his vehicle with him at all times – I had seen where he lived in the Township – just as I knew Usman at Minna had done! I then asked him kindly to discourage his officers from hijacking MOW lorries on the spot, which police felt they had a right to do.

Another advance preparation foreseeing difficulties was that during my first tour in Kabba Province I had found several local contractors on whom I could rely to supply laterite for road maintenance. After satisfactorily carrying out various small contracts, I decided to put two of them who always responded quickly on 'stand-by' for any eventuality which might arise should the crunch come. Hassan, my cook/steward, would know where they lived in the Township and could go for them on his bicycle. There was none more loyal than Hassan – of whom more later.

My next letter to my brother, 26th February 1967:

"I'm afraid it's been a long time since I last wrote to you. Having felt I must try to pull my work out of chaos, it meant travelling quite a lot, a great deal of work and much swearing. However, some order and results are slowly emerging… Last weekend ten Russians were here – the first I've met I think – technicians investigating the feasibility of setting up an iron and steel industry in Nigeria. The hills round here are mostly ironstone and there are similar places elsewhere in the country. Coal is also known to be not far away but not thought to be of the grade required for smelting. Actually, this Province is reputed to be one of the richest in raw materials – gold, diamonds, talc (magnesium silicate in crystalline form), iron ore, and limestone (for cement), but little so far has been done to exploit them. I had to talk to them through an interpreter, a tedious business. Oddly enough they did not appear to know that Kosygin was, or had just been, in England. The fact that he had been to a football match aroused their interest more than anything else!

"What may blow here is anyone's guess. There is virtually no Government at all. Commissions are set up to investigate this, that or the other, but mainly they result in exposing what was well known in any case, the gross inefficiency and corruption of Public Corporations, Marketing Boards and the like. So far those exposed still seem to be around and, in fact, in some instances have been selected as Representatives on a strange body called 'Leaders of Thought' which is supposed to be composed of the best people from all walks of life to advise the Military Government on the feelings, reactions and wishes of the people.

"Meanwhile the general economy is taking a knock. In the North, one of the main sources of income is groundnuts. The evacuation season started almost without any trains, much reduced road transport, and only one outlet, Lagos, Port Harcourt in the East being barred. I'm told there are many thousands of tons in the far North, the main growing area, awaiting removal, including some left over from last year.

"The 'Get Together' at Aburi in Ghana was so much eyewash. Certainly, the stalemate seems just as bad if not worse. Meanwhile the Civil Service becomes more entrenched as 'The Government' as power moves into their hands. No doubt they like the feel of it and the longer they have it the more reluctant they will be to surrender it, if and when some political form of Government is set up. The ordinary soldier thinks of himself as 'The Government' too with authority to do what he thinks fit and feels like doing. I have had several instances of my drivers or labourers being beaten up by soldiers without any reason at all. Indiscipline is quite apparent amongst the soldiers.

"To what the Country is drifting (drifting is the operative word) I cannot say. I'm too far away from any real contact with what may be going on or contemplated. One feels some change is inevitable, bursting out of the lethargy, turmoil and violence as there is too strong an air of temporariness about everything. When, in what way and where something will happen is anyone's guess. For myself the only thing to do is to push on with the many things that want doing until it becomes too difficult or even impossible to do them..."

At this point a quote from Meredith sets the scene, ending with Ojukwu's declaration of the Independent State of Biafra:

"The key figure in the East was now Ojukwu. Until the Northerners' coup in July 1966, he had been unpopular as military governor of the Eastern Region, but afterwards he came to be acclaimed as the saviour of the Ibo people.

"An ambitious and clever man, 34 years old, the son of a wealthy Ibo business man, with an Oxford degree and training in Britain as an Army officer, he relished the exercise of political power and skilfully rallied the Ibos behind him.

"Spurred on by an inner circle of Ibo advisers, mostly displaced civil servants and academics who had become fervent Ibo nationalists, Ojukwu began to sever the remaining links with the Federation. Though there were still possibilities for conciliation that would have given Easterners the security they sought, he made little effort at compromise. In October 1966 he ordered the expulsion of all non-Easterners from the Region on the grounds that he could no longer assure their safety. He refused to send back Eastern delegates to the constitutional conference which had resumed in Lagos, or to travel there himself for negotiations, saying that he feared for his life, and he called on Easterners still living in other parts of the Federation to return home.

"In January 1967, at a conference in Ghana, Ojukwu and Gowon met face to face, but their discussions proved abortive. In April 1967, Ojukwu issued decrees appropriating all Federal revenues collected in the East and giving the East control of Federal corporations, railways, schools and courts. While this process of gradual withdrawal was underway, the government radio and press kept popular opinion at fever pitch with a constant stream of propaganda, stressing details of the atrocities that had taken place and warning of the threat of genocide... the effect of the propaganda, as well as binding Ibos together against the Northern threat, produced a momentum of its own towards secession."

Meredith then went on to explain how, for the East, secession was a far more viable proposition than for the landlocked North:

"As Ojukwu made his final moves before breaking away, Gowon, determined to hold the Federation together struck decisively at this weakness in the East's position. Having first obtained the agreement of the North and the West, he issued a decree on 27th May 1967 abolishing the four Regions and creating in their place twelve new states. The North was divided into six and the East into three separate states. Thus, in one fell swoop, the old power blocs dominated so long by the Hausa-Fulani, the Yoruba and the Ibo were broken apart, giving minority tribes a voice of their own and placating Southern fears of Northern hegemony. Gowon's measures came too late to affect the launching of Biafra, but by offering the Eastern minorities new states of their own freed from Ibo rule he gave them new cause to remain loyal to the Federation, thus undermining Ojukwu's strategy for survival. Three days later, on 31st May 1967 a year after the first riots against Ibo in the North, Ojukwu proclaimed amid high jubilation the Independence of the new state of Biafra."

Now extracts from my letter of 31st May 1967 to my brother which implies that already I might have been aware of Ojukwu's declaration:

"It's a terribly long time since I wrote to you. I've been absurdly involved in so much work that by the time the day is over it's bed for me.

"Possibly you've been wondering how things are with me. I suppose really the general atmosphere has been one of bewilderment for some time. The North Government – such as it is or has been – has been floundering. I've been asked to do quite fantastic things, such as, extending an airstrip in about six days to take larger planes – where they might have been coming from no-one seemed to know. Now I have to put up a pretty large Bailey Bridge in another Province on the only road northwards, because the existing bridge is likely to fall down at any moment. Everyone knows it's been likely to fall down for years but nothing was done and now there's a scare about it. Whether I'll get it done or not I just don't know. The fact that it's 200 miles away, in a place where there are a lot of indolent Pakistanis who should do much of the preparatory work, doesn't exactly give me much encouragement. If I'm to do it at all I'll just have to move over there for some time and commute. It's an interesting job on a nasty site over a deepish gap with the river about to rise at any moment. I'd enjoy it if it weren't for the drawbacks.

"Now the period of phoney edicts, decrees and the like seems to be over the crunch has come. Here, being off the beaten track, one wouldn't know about general mobilization, economic blockade and all the general stir which is apparently going on. There's one road in and out at present as the mighty Niger is so low that all the ferries are at a standstill. Although I'm not really in a position to judge, I'd say the fighting is almost bound to start at any moment. Where or to what degree it's impossible to say, and whether it would come this way again can't be forecast. As it is, naturally one would expect the so-called 'Federal forces' to go to the East to crush the rebels, but it's anyone's guess really. All I'm doing is to keep things going as usual. There's nothing else to be done. The mails are no more erratic than usual at the moment so I'm hoping you will get this..."

Ojukwu's declaration coincided with the arrival of a letter of 2nd June, the first of several from the British Deputy High Commissioner in Kaduna, Mr E.O. Laird, from which I quote extracts:

"By the time you receive this you will no doubt have already heard from the office of the Provincial Secretary that the Northern authorities have decided to advise the dependants of all expatriates to leave the area of Benue and Kabba Provinces south of the River Benue and east of the River Niger. This action has our full support and while I have no doubt that the Provincial authorities will ensure that their advice is made known to all expatriates concerned, I would be grateful if you would pass the word round through your associates. An important consideration is that it will be in everybody's interest not to arouse alarm. The Northern authorities are watching the situation very closely indeed, as we ourselves are, and if there is any need for further advice this will be given promptly. Dependants need not, of course, accept this advice but we expect that most will and that while some will no doubt want to leave the country altogether, for example anticipating leave, others may simply wish to move temporarily to another part of the North.

"All is quiet throughout the rest of the North and it is not considered that there is any need to give any particular advice to expatriates living elsewhere in the Northern States. As you have no doubt heard, dependants of expatriates in the East are also being advised to leave their area.

Yours sincerely,
Michael Laird
(E.O. Laird)"

Our correspondence had started because I had accepted the role of 'Operations Officer' for the evacuation of British expatriates in the Province, should this become imperative. I would then make contact with as many as possible telling them where to muster etc. It struck me as an odd arrangement, since I was asked not to give any advance details, but to locate as many as I could against the eventuality of the evacuation plan having to be activated. I did what I could by discreet enquiry and was surprised at the number of British expatriates 'hidden away' in the Province, including some who had served during the colonial regime and then decided to retire in the bush, and others who were long-standing missionaries living in remote corners. It was obvious that nothing would persuade these sorts of people to leave.

Further correspondence ensued with Mr Laird and some points are worth recording. For example, my point regarding possible conflict of loyalty between my two roles about which in my letter to Mr Laird of 20th June I said:

> "I have never been easy in my mind about this matter and I am sorry I have not written you before. I know you will realise that, as a Government officer and in particular as a local Head of Department, my position *vis-à-vis* the evacuation problem can cause a conflict of loyalty.

> "Moreover, my Department bears a not inconsiderable dependence in relation to other Departments, particularly perhaps to the Administration in times of stress when roads, water supply and the need for transport (drivers, fuel, and the like) to mention only a few things, are likely to be very vital. To some extent this dependence is my own fault as I have tried to put the Department where I think it belongs; I thought it was at a very low ebb when I came. This also means that I must be available to take decisions and give the required authority to use lorries and other things which I need not detail. There is then no question for me but that my loyalty, my services and my time must be at the complete disposal of Government as represented by the local Administration and its attendant services whenever required."

Possibly, I rather over-emphasised this aspect, but I continued:

> "Most fortunately, the Provincial Secretary, Alhaji Abubakar Washegu, whom I have known for some time, is an intelligent, broad-minded man with whom I can be entirely frank and open over almost anything and I feel sure he reciprocates. I have talked with him about this responsibility which, please understand, I by no means shrink from on behalf of my own Country's Representative, as symbolised by you, and have explained my views as outlined above. I am glad to say that he is very much alive to the question and, in fact, fully accepts that if evacuation becomes necessary under conditions of real disturbance, he (being the

Government on the spot) is fully involved and should give help in every way. I feel there is an understanding there which is very valuable and sufficiently reliable and clear to enable the whole matter to be handled in a joint way. I would ask you then to regard my participation as being possible only on that basis which I feel is, in fact, preferable and, in the event, probably more effective. I feel I need say no more and that you will completely understand."

Later I said:

"I have been quite unable because of other duties to get to know people in Igala at all well. I do know that mostly they are there in strength under the general term of 'missionaries'. These are not the sort of people surely who will leave readily, since it is in times of trouble that they come into their own when there are the sick, the aged, the destitute and the injured to be cared for. Finally I can tell you that Lokoja is quiet. It has an extraordinary beauty only marred by the climate (for the expatriate) and the people give out a sense of timelessness probably due to the river."

Mr Laird replied on 20th June:

"Many thanks for your letter of 20th June. I would like to say straightaway that I have never, in cases like your own, seen any conflict between loyalty towards the Nigerian Government and loyalty towards your fellow countrymen. The aims of the Nigerian authorities are precisely the same as ours and you will be glad to hear that this is fully accepted at the highest level here in Kaduna. I am personally in close touch with Ali Akilu about the situation in Kabba and Benue, and it is our joint determination to work together as closely as possible should it ever be necessary to consider further evacuation from your area."

He then gave me some names of people at Idah and in Igala Division who were in touch with missionaries and others there. Then:

"We have, of course, been thinking of the desirability of sending somebody down to your part of the country, but after talking it over with Ali Akilu I have decided that it would be better if we were to keep away from the area, at any rate for the time being, as our motives might be misunderstood, not here but elsewhere."

Mr Laird wrote again on 28th June 1967:

"I would like you to know that we do appreciate very much what you are doing and that we hope you will be able to exert a steadying influence in your local community. In particular it would, I believe, be helpful if you could make it known to expatriates in the Province that there are most comprehensive plans to deal with any eventuality, and that, although it may seem to you in Lokoja that nobody is interested in your welfare, we here in Kaduna, both Nigerian and British, are watching the situation very closely indeed and will issue advice and take action immediately if it is necessary. For the present we are advising a policy of heads down in Igala Division and the withdrawal to the main centres of any missionaries still left in exposed situations near the border."

On 6th July 1967 came the 'defining moment', the start of the Nigerian Civil War. General Obasanjo described it in his book *My Command*:

"The month of June was used by both sides to prepare for war. Each side increased its military arsenal and moved troops to the border watching and waiting until the crack of the first bullet at the dawn of 6th July 1967. No self-respecting leader would take Ojukwu's bluff and treasonable act of secession without reacting with all the force at his disposal. Hence the first bullet was from the Federal side. The war had started."

In a way, the 'defining moment' released much of the tension of the uncertainties of recent weeks. Now, if we wanted, I and my expatriate staff could just pack up and leave for home. There were no heroics in my decision to stay; I think what followed bears that out. A quote from Meredith:

> "The Nigerian Civil War began in fits and starts in July 1967, with bizarre and confusing episodes, fought haphazardly by two Armies with raw and inexperienced troops. Gowon looked on it at the time merely as a 'police action'. Ojukwu too was confident that the fighting would be resolved in a matter of weeks. But it grew into a terrible war of attrition that lasted two and a half years, arousing passionate argument and controversy around the world, and in the end cost nearly a million lives."

I have mentioned Gowon's Decree of 27th May 1967 setting up twelve States each with a Military Governor. Ilorin Province and Kabba Province became Central West State but retained their separate administrative status. Major D.L. Bamigboye was posted as Military Governor of Central West State with Headquarters at Ilorin. Soon after 6th July 1967 he made an official visit to Kabba Province starting at Lokoja. The programme included a visit to the Waterworks at Okene (under MOW), one of the earliest installations in the North. Its supply was drawn from a borehole by a real 'museum-piece' engine and pump with its great fly-wheel, the pride and joy of the foreman in charge for many years. He still found time, however, to cultivate a vegetable garden and he presented Major Bamigboye with various items of produce from his garden. The Military Governor wrote this charming letter of 19th July to me:

> "You would have received my letter before this time but for my State duties. However, it is better late than never. I would like to take this opportunity to thank you for the excellent services rendered to the vehicles which accompanied me during my tour of the Province. My visit to the Waterworks will always be fresh in my memory.

> "Lest I forget, please give my fondest regards to the foreman at the Waterworks and my thanks to him for the beautiful

vegetables from his garden! It is my sincere wish that he will continue to look after his proud garden.

Well, it is goodbye from me.
Bamigboye Major
Major D.L. Bamigboye
Military Governor Central-West State Ilorin

I believe the whole installation at Okene was destined to be retained as a Museum when it was replaced by a new Waterworks elsewhere in order to meet the ever-increasing demand for water.

My next letter to Mr Laird dated 13th August is full of happenings at Lokoja. But before giving it I should mention the incident at Idah Hospital, details of which only reached me after the bombing at Lokoja on 10th August. Apparently, two persons had been killed and superficial damage done to two wards. When I found time to visit, I was told that an aeroplane had appeared low over Idah during the afternoon of 6th August and dropped two explosives which went off in the grounds of the hospital. These had fragmented into small pieces of metal, some of which struck two persons passing through the grounds who later died. Other pieces had peppered the roofs of two wards making numerous small holes in the galvanised sheeting. I searched around and found several small slivers of cast iron, which certainly would penetrate the body, and a round piece with screw thread. I had heard that the ingenious Ibos were devising home-made anti-personnel bombs using Calor gas or similar containers filled with explosive material and some form of detonator. The round piece with thread would be part of the screw top of a cast-iron container. However, the bombs dropped at Lokoja were identified as 50lb bombs no doubt acquired with the B26.

Here is my letter to Mr Laird:

"I imagine you will have been told of the two bomb raids on Lokoja. One about 5.00pm on the 10th, and the other about 11.00am on the 12th. Six or so explosives were dropped on each occasion, a mixture of HE anti-personnel and oil bombs. Only superficial damage was done but some people were killed and others injured. On the 12th the bombs were nearer the possible objectives which I feel are the Mobil Oil Depot (which has very large stocks of diesel and quite an amount of petrol), the Lokoja-Shintaku Ferry and the VBF Station. On each occasion, the heavily populated areas of the town were affected, and on the first occasion some bombs fell in the GRA, one about 30 yards from my house interrupting my afternoon cup of tea.

"Predictably, amongst the local people morale suffered a considerable setback and a quick gangster-like incursion by a few rebel soldiers in Okene the day following the first raid worsened fears and a large exodus is going on. There are only a few expatriate wives and children in Lokoja, a mixed bag of Anglo-Indian, Italian, Pakistani and British. Most are Federal staff and the husbands have decided to take their families to Lagos where they will stay or make for their home countries. Mrs Davies, the wife of my Water Engineer is the only British Northern States person in the Station and I think she will wish to go very soon, in which case she will come to Kaduna for Kano. All my British staff (Messrs Davies, Hoyle, Hewitt and Robison) are staying and are in good fettle.

"Inevitably we regard the bombing in a very different way from the local people. It is virtually impossible to project oneself into the minds of the indigenes and the devastating effect which bombing must leave with them. One has to remember that probably most of them have only seen an aeroplane for the first time during recent years, and then not close to. I well remember the look of absolute wonder in my steward's eyes when he saw the *BOAC* plane at Kano which was to take me to the UK some years ago, and in 1959 the wild excitement and awe of the local people when Treverton came in a *Piper* to collect me at Bussa to fly to Yola for some Bailey Bridging. Whether with the takeover in the Mid-West the ground situation will develop towards this area I have no means of knowing. At present, British families in those areas are still there and I have heard of no suggestion that they intend to go, nor would it seem necessary at this stage. In any case, should events take place as quickly as in the Mid-West there is little one can do except face the situation when it happens.

"Finally, I do feel that our presence – and I am fortunate in having a mature expatriate staff – is of real value. Water and electricity are being kept going which frankly I doubt would have been so had we not been here. Naturally we value these amenities for ourselves, but nonetheless I am sure that their continuation is some support to the general morale.

"I hope the general atmosphere here will recover rather than deteriorate further, but only events will decide."

Mr Laird replied on 4th September:

"I am sorry you have not had an earlier reply to your letter of 13th August. I have been waiting for someone to take the letter to Lokoja, but as there are so few people going in that direction at the moment I have decided to send my reply through the post.

"I am very grateful for the picture of life in Lokoja which you gave me, and I am filled with admiration about the sturdy way in which you and the other expatriates have reacted. I don't think that I can usefully comment on the present situation because events in your area seem to change so quickly. I would like to say, however, that we are very grateful for any news about expatriates which you can send us."

Now I shall describe in greater detail some of the incidents mentioned in my letter of 13th August. The bombing on 10th August changed the prevailing apprehension in Lokoja into fear and near panic. Within a few hours columns of lorries, cars, handcarts etc. loaded with possessions and people were on the move out of Lokoja to the 'safety' of the forest and the bush along the road out. This movement was in darkness, as the limited street lighting had either failed or had been intentionally turned off. By the early morning of 11th August I found the Township deserted, a ghost town. I doubt if there were more than a few hundred people left, and at my office there was no-one except for my Chief Clerk who explained that all others had gone with their families to the forest and bush several miles out on the road to Kabba. I discussed possible action with him but first I had to see the Provincial Secretary Alhaji Abubakar Mashegu.

I found him calm and very ready to see me. I reported the general position as of the morning, and that electricity and water were still operating, but he already knew that overnight there had been a large exodus. I raised the vital question of maintaining fuel supplies for essential services, and suggested that it might be advisable if stocks at the storage tank were requisitioned. He agreed and asked me to go and do the necessary requisitioning! I went and told the Manager that I had come on the authority of the Provincial Secretary to requisition his stocks for the use of the State Government and those associated with it, in view of the present emergency conditions. He seemed greatly relieved at this action and would inform his Head Office accordingly. I gave him nothing in writing then or later! I think this was the 'control' we agreed: LPOs (Local Purchase Orders) for fuel from the pump issued by Lokoja based Government Departments should be accepted and payment made in the usual way. I would be informing local Heads of Department of the action taken to requisition and asked them to ration as much as possible. All individuals seeking fuel at the pump, including public service officers, would be told to see me for a signed chit for so many gallons at prices he gave me and payment would be made to me. I would have to decide whether supply was justified. He and I would reconcile money collected by me against details on the chits at convenient moments. I know that, at one time, I had as much as £2,000 in my safe! Traders, commerce and business in general would not be served at the pump and should seek other sources of fuel. The Manager would press his Headquarters to seek a river tanker to replenish his stock. That was just one of the rather extraordinary actions I had to take!

It was a day or so before I discovered that the local bank (*Barclays*) was closed. Enquiries showed that the Nigerian Manager had locked up and departed with his family in the general exodus as, in fact, had most of his staff. Any junior staff living in Lokoja could do nothing. With great difficulty I was able to get a message to *Barclays,* Lagos, about the situation. Meanwhile I urgently needed money for wages for road gangs and so on.

I now knew that Major Bamigboye, the Military Governor, intended to visit Lokoja as a morale booster for the Province following the bombing. I decided to send my Landrover – the driver had not joined the staff in the bush – with a confidential letter to the Governor explaining my problem and asking him to bring £3,000 with him! He duly came with the money which I put in my safe for wages and other expenses.

I had to deal with the matter of my office staff who were still in the bush with their families. I discussed with my Chief Clerk and we drove out to see them. They had put together make-shift shelters but already some of the woman and children were ill, some had been bitten by snakes and all were miserable. I had to accept their real fear of the bombing, something completely strange to them. Eventually, we agreed that some of the staff would come in each day – I would come myself or send transport – and they would be returned by the evening. They could also collect food for everyone.

A few days later, I was quietly working in my office when a stranger knocked on the door. He introduced himself as a representative of *Barclays Bank* from Lagos and said that my message about the absence of the local bank Manager had been received. He explained that his role was as the 'roving solver of problems', and he had left Lagos for Lokoja stopping off at various towns on the way. At each place he had been given the same information: Lokoja was in flames, had been virtually destroyed, and there was no point in going there, so he was quite astounded to find all buildings standing and me sitting quietly in my office! Ojukwu had apparently engaged a firm of publicists to feed the press with greatly exaggerated stories about the Civil War and particularly about the bombing. The representative promised the bank would re-open as quickly as possible, and in a day or so having located the Manager it was business as usual. He seemed in no hurry to return to Lagos and was staying in the Rest House.

One morning about lunchtime I heard the sound of a plane and went outside to see the B26 circling over the Township at about 5,000 feet, so low that I could even see if the bomb flaps were opening – fortunately they were not. After another circle round, off he went. Within minutes the *Barclays* man appeared looking quite shaken. He had been taking lunch at the Rest House, heard the plane and dived into the drain trench of the nearby road. He told me that was enough for him! He was leaving at once and bade me farewell.

Lokoja had one more visit from the B26. One evening when it was nearly dark I was passing through the town in my car when I saw the lights of the plane very low overhead. This time I was really frightened – not of the plane but of policemen with rifles firing at random at the plane! One shot through my windscreen or windows and I would have had it! There was another far-fetched explanation for these last two bombless visits: Hassan told me the story. It was rumoured that the expatriate Federal officer in charge of the ferry, still working but closed to all traffic except Army, Police and Government, was Polish. So, too, was the pilot of the B26; this detail had been in the Press for some time. When the Federal officer's steward had asked to be allowed to leave with his family for home elsewhere, his master had said: "Don't you worry, that man in the plane is a friend of mine. We'll be perfectly safe." The outcome was that, particularly at night, many other stewards would go to the officer's compound confident of being safe there! I asked Hassan if he wanted to join them as I knew he had already sent his wife and family home to Bauchi. But he said he would stay with me and, in fact, he stayed until I left in 1978.

Gradually, as it seemed that the bombing had ceased, people returned to Lokoja. My staff came back from the bush but outbursts of trouble did occur, and anyone thought to be Ibo was molested. One could come across decapitated bodies at the side of the road, possibly pushed off trucks and then run over by following traffic. I saw one body of a suspect Ibo left for days. I could not blame my labourers for ignoring it.

I had a Technical Assistant named William who was fat, softly spoken and baby-faced. Any small survey I gave him was meticulously carried out and the results were always reliable. One day, as I was returning through the Township, an open police truck passed me with William and several policemen in the back. He was covered in blood and waved desperately at me. I knew he could only have been caught up in some trouble by accident. Back at the office I rang the Lokoja Head of Police and explained what I had seen and asked if he would check whether William was in a cell. On receiving confirmation I told him that William was not an Ibo, but came from Idah, the result of inter-tribal marriage, and that as he was my Technical Assistant I was responsible for him. I asked him to release William to me, to which he agreed and said I could come to the Station and collect him. The building was about 50 yards from the road where I had to leave my car and walk up the pathway already crowded on both sides with people. I was shown at once into the office of the Head of Police, who told me he was prepared to release William because if he kept him he was likely to be molested.

Now as I write this, I can still feel the awful tension as William, still blood-stained, and I walked down that pathway being grimly stared at by all the people as at any moment William and I could have been attacked and killed. I put him on the floor of the Peugeot and quickly drove to my compound. Hassan took him off to attend to his wounds, then I sent Hassan on his bicycle for the two trustworthy contractors whom I mentioned earlier to come with their transport. It would be too dangerous for me to keep William in my compound as it was bound to become known in the Township and some people would come for him, and I would be regarded as taking sides in the Civil War. The two came within an hour: I explained my position and asked them to take William to some place where he could be kept hidden and looked after until I felt he could safely be transferred elsewhere. They readily agreed, rather taken with the associated air of excitement and secrecy! It was a risk but I had to take it. I told the Head of Police what I had done but without mentioning names. Hassan then told me William's story: apparently some people in the Town had accused him of giving signals to the B26 as to where to drop bombs! He was beaten up and handed over to the police.

Early in September I received, by hand of a driver from Kaduna, this letter of 5th September from Tuku Usman the Chief Civil Engineer at Headquarters Kaduna:

"Sorry for this informal letter, but there was no time for an official one. This is to inform you that Mr Davies, Water Engineer, has been temporarily transferred to Kaduna on 'Special Duty'. Please arrange to send his personal belongings, his car and servants per low-loader and lorry sent.

"The Permanent Secretary on behalf of all of us has asked me to express our deep appreciation in all your help to the Government in Lokoja in spite of the situation."

Mrs Davies had already left Lokoja, as mentioned in my letter to Mr Laird of 13th August. Mr Davies had been long with the Ministry of Works but now had heart trouble. His particular expertise was the use of explosives for driving 'adits' into rock in order to gain water. This would account for 'Special Duty' at this time. I knew, too, that he was restless in Lokoja after his wife had left.

My correspondence with Mr Laird had ceased following his letter of 4th September. However, not long after Mr Davies had left, I was very pleased at the unexpected arrival in Lokoja of Mr and Mrs Wilfred Turner of the British High Commission Kaduna. Although no notice of their coming had reached me, they had been accommodated at the Rest House. I did my best to explain events to them and entertained them to dinner one evening. Here is Mr Turner's letter to me of 4th October:

"My wife and I would like to thank you for all you did to make our visit to Lokoja both enjoyable and useful. We were so sorry that you did not have any notice of our arrival and so we were particularly grateful for the way in which you arranged things for us.

"I have been telling the Deputy High Commissioner about the terrific impression you have made throughout Central West State because of the way you behaved during the recent crises in Lokoja. I found it very gratifying to hear senior officials from the Military Governor downwards speaking so warmly of the contribution of a British person."

It was on 4th October 1967 that Enugu, the Ibo Capital, fell to Federal forces. Ojukwu was defiant and re-grouped with Headquarters at Umuahia. The world media rushed to get to Enugu. Here I should introduce extracts from my letter to my brother of 17th December relevant to my time in Lokoja but written after I had left, about which I need to elaborate further:

"Once it was known that Enugu had fallen these lads came in about three waves mad to get there. He was with the crowd of *BBC, ITV, Daily Express, Daily Telegraph* – I never really did sort out who was who. Then came *Time, Newsweek* and all sorts. Quite a lot got straight back by air to Lagos but this chap with some others came back by road and I gave them drinks so I could hear their stories. It was an expensive expedition for someone. Between them they had written off two cars but no-one was badly hurt. Martin Bell (BBC) stayed on in Enugu and gave some excellent despatches which I heard on the World News. I liked him very much but he didn't come back my way.

"I really meant to write regularly to give you something a bit nearer the truth than all the balderdash in the papers – at least in those I saw. In fact, no journalist, not even a Nigerian one, came near us during the bad period to see how the ordinary people were taking, or not taking, the war. The poor sods were literally frenzied with fear of bombs and the Ibo boys, who for some weeks could have taken the whole area from the Mid-West with nothing but a few policemen with pop guns to try and stop them. I've tried to re-phrase Churchill's famous quote: "Never in the field of human conflict was so much owed by so many to so few," to describe the effect of the lone B26 bomber on the populace. Never were so many so terrified by just one plane. You may at some time have lived surrounded by people stricken with fear – not a pleasant experience.

"The soldiers (Federal) when they did come were *sans* almost everything, including maps, and though the officers were charming chaps and very respectful, the soldiery were very undisciplined. So much so that at times I have wondered whether the people were not more afraid of their own soldiers than the Ibos! Somehow the Federal troops are ahead and if they pull this thing off it will be more by luck than judgement, and probably because the other lads seem just about the same, otherwise they would have followed up their advantage. Probably by the time I come home these events will all be stale, but I must tell you some of the extraordinary things that have happened."

To elaborate first about the media: the 'three waves and all sorts' came with the intention of reaching Enugu by the eastern route using the River Niger crossing at Lokoja, not realising that it might be unavailable. At first the Federal officer in charge refused to open up for them and someone must have come to fetch me. I found a gathering of very frustrated journalists, and after my explanation and pleading I was able to persuade the Federal officer to help. Several crossings were necessary to get them all to the other side, and one of them promised to ring Malcolm at the first opportunity, which he did. Those who came back our way had no difficulty with the officer in charge. A throw-back to that event took place just a few years ago, when my youngest son rang me in the UK and told me to tune into Radio Two, where Martin Bell was talking about his experiences during the Nigerian Civil War. He mentioned my name as the person who helped his team to cross the River Niger *en route* for Enugu. I wrote to him and he replied very warmly remembering the occasion at Lokoja.

After the media came the soldiers, a large contingent under the command of Colonel Murtala Mohammed – of whom more later. The officers, mostly young men in smart new uniforms, clearly had no idea of what might await them. They were *sans* almost everything except for fuel for their vehicles, but there was a problem. In their haste to move off from Lagos they had commandeered several privately owned lorries with drivers and loaded them with drums of diesel and petrol to follow the convoy. Somehow these vehicles had managed to reach Lokoja, but with flat tyres beyond repair and engines at their last gasp, many of these were not in a fit condition to go any further, whilst the drivers were in poor shape and frightened. Workshops could put one or two perhaps in reasonable shape to move on, but the others would have to unload their drums in a MOW Depot and then push off as best they could back to Lagos, to the great relief of their drivers. It was agreed that an Army vehicle would return to Lokoja as necessary to collect drums if fuel was not obtainable as the force moved forward to the East.

That evening I had a nightmare: the drums in the Depot, perhaps up to a hundred, could easily be seen from the air. If the B26 came the pilot could drop a bomb or two or even one of their home-made explosives and bang...! Early the next morning I went to the Depot, had the drums loaded onto lorries and moved several miles out of Lokoja to some deep forest. Here I set up a well hidden Depot for the drums, fencing etc., making arrangements for security guards, relying on the co-operation of the Head of Police. From then onwards I could sleep at night! Gradually the stock was collected by the Army. Whether any of it was 'sold-off' on the way was not my responsibility – and the B26 never came!

One objective of the Federal Army was to push the Ibos out of the West and Mid-West which they had occupied earlier, partly to round-up money from the banks and post offices, and food from the people for themselves. Another was to attempt a crossing of the River Niger from Asaba and capture Onitsha, an important Ibo town on the far bank. There are conflicting references to this event in books about the Nigerian Civil War. I will give some extracts and what was related to me by one of the young officers who arrived back in Lokoja in a pitiful state. This from Forsyth's *The Biafra Story*:

> "On 6th October the Biafrans at Asaba crossed the Niger to Onitsha and blew up the newly completed £6 million bridge behind them to prevent Mohammed crossing."

Not quite accurate – just two spans on the Ibo side were blown up which, of course, effectively barred use by vehicles. A quote from General Obasanjo's *My Command*, gives an experienced professional's view:

> "It is no military secret that an opposed river-crossing operation is difficult even under ideal conditions. But

118

without adequate standard equipment and with poor level of training of soldiers and officers it could become impossible. The 2 Division Commander (Murtala Mohammed) had shown great determination, initiative and resourcefulness by collecting all the ferries in use elsewhere in the country to Asaba. He had also embarked on special training of the brigade ear-marked for the operation in conditions similar to where the actual operation would take place. But the Army Headquarters and Supreme Headquarters had strongly advised against embarking on an opposed river-crossing from Asaba to Onitsha because of inadequacy of equipment and deficiency in the training of troops for such a semi-specialist operation. The superior Headquarters had advised an unopposed crossing at Idah while the Division passed through 1 Division's secure position to capture Onitsha. Colonel Murtala Mohammed, the Division Commander, decided to take a grave and calculated risk which should be called bravado. But if the operation had been successful, as it nearly was, it would have been one of the most praiseworthy operations of the entire Civil War. In the end it failed and the Commander had to take the blame for it.

"On 12th October 1967, the first landing in which the Division Commander himself took part was, by all accounts, as successful as any opposed water-crossing can be. But the subsequent follow-up of men and materials to back up the first party failed to turn up, due to mechanical fault in the second ferry and to rebel opposition. All the same, if the first landing party had been well controlled and disciplined enough to hold the beach-head, which it successfully captured on landing with little or no fighting, instead of running into Onitsha town for whatever booty they could grab, a successful effort could have been made for back-up men and materials to reach them before they were overrun. When things went completely out of control at the other end, individual soldiers and officers ran for their dear lives, some jumping into the river, some running towards the North to Idah and most running southwards into the hands of the rebels. But whichever way they went, only very few of them escaped being captured or killed. It was a great tragedy. I was an eye-witness of part of the tragedy..."

General Obasanjo later in the book:

"After three unsuccessful attempts, the third almost ending in a fiasco, the Division Commander agreed to abandon the idea of an opposed river-crossing and adopted the previous advice of Superior Headquarters. The attempts had been bold and extremely costly. The unsuccessful efforts had taught useful lessons to the Nigerian Army as a whole. The setback had obviously delayed the end of the war by several months. Murtala reorganised and refurbished his division, crossed the Niger at Idah in January 1968 and led with 6 Brigade, then under command of Captain Shehu Yar Adua, through 1 Division areas of operation and captured Onitsha on 23rd March 1968 after a bloody battle, almost six months after the first attempt..."

Forsyth's record is much the same except for: "...the Hausa soldiers set fire to the Onitsha Market, the largest in West Africa and with a stock valued at £3million..."

I happened to have been with the officer in charge of the ferry at Lokoja when Colonel Mohammed's representative came to commandeer the ferry for this first crossing attempt from Asaba on the 12th October. From my experience in the Royal Engineers during the Second World War of the floating Bailey Bridge on pontoons which resembled ferries, I felt I must advise that the ferry, with its slow pace and very limited manoeuvrability, was quite unsuitable for an opposed crossing of the River Niger from Asaba, but he was insistent that it should proceed downriver, manned by the civilian crew, to await the arrival of the assault force of over 500 with whatever equipment they had. This was the young officer's story: the first trip by the ferry had taken the advance beach party across with their guns. The ferry set off again crammed tight with soldiers and some officers, but as it neared the far bank the Ibos who had taken the place of the beach party opened up with guns and rifles. Many died instantly, others including himself jumped into the water and swam back towards Asaba as quickly as possible. Here the local people helped him and by various means he reached Lokoja, his morale broken. I did what I could to cheer him up.

After the debacle the ferry did manage to get back to Lokoja with, I think, one crew member killed and the others wounded, very angry with the soldiers for compelling them to take part.

It must have been in late October or early November 1967 that I received another letter from Tuku Usman, Chief Civil Engineer, instructing me to move to Zaria, North Central State '…with immediate effect,' to take over as Provincial Engineer, no reason or explanation given. I could only presume that he was making arrangements for my replacement at Lokoja. 'Immediate effect' to me meant 'now', so Hassan packed and we left. I sent a note to the Provincial Secretary explaining my action and excusing myself from calling. For all I knew, he may well have been consulted or told of the position. Reaching Kaduna – I had to pass that way – I reported to the Chief Civil Engineer for whom I had always had great regard.

Here I will give the explanation for Tuku Usman's decision to move me so very urgently, as well as describing the background to the general situation at Zaria in which, from now onwards, I was to become so closely involved. Apparently, the relationship between the Army – then the dominant factor in Zaria – and the Ministry of Works had badly broken down and this was of great concern at MOW Headquarters at Kaduna. The two key personalities involved were the Commander of the Military Barracks, Colonel Adekunle, and the Provincial Engineer Ministry of Works. Incidentally, Colonel Adekunle was the brother of Colonel Benjamin Adekunle, a hot-tempered but efficient Commander often in trouble with his superiors but highly effective in the field and known as 'The Black Scorpion'. The Provincial Engineer was a Nigerian recently qualified professionally as a civil engineer following a year or so on attachment to an international firm of Consulting Engineers in the UK, studying to pass the examination required to become a Member of the Institution of Civil Engineers.

The origin of the Barracks or Garrison at Zaria goes back to the West African Frontier Force and elements of the British Army during the early days of the Colonial regime, later occupied by the Nigerian Federal Army following Independence. Its Officers' Mess – all Nigerian – was a sort of 'Holy of Holies' still maintaining the standards and rituals of its British counterpart – dress, silver emblems on the table, toasts etc. etc. Later I was to be invited to become an Honorary Member of the Mess and dined at least once. Over the years the Barracks had grown and developed into a massive complex – probably the oldest and largest in Nigeria – the general maintenance of its buildings, houses, sanitation, water supply and so on being the responsibility of the Ministry of Works Zaria. Without doubt, this was always an exacting business and not without its hazards, and, at this juncture, more so than ever.

Because of the Civil War, the Federal forces needed greatly to increase its numbers. At this time, I was told, it was recruiting mainly in the local market without difficulty amongst the unemployed at the rate of 2,000 a week. Recruits received shelter, uniform, food and some pay, and some rudimentary training before being dispatched to join Divisions engaged in the various areas of activity against the Ibo forces. The losses amongst these recruits must have been considerable. War is War whether International or Civil. Unquestionably, the resources of the Barracks, its services and so on were being severely stressed by this greatly increased pressure which could have aggravated 'outside' relationships, both personal and administrative. Reports had reached MOW Headquarters in Kaduna of MOW lorries on their own business being commandeered by Army personnel for their purposes, and MOW workers sent to do specific repairs or maintenance were being diverted to do other things. This led to complaints from those awaiting attention and, worse still, threats had been made to the person of the Provincial Engineer because of his complete lack of co-operation. Whether this had any ethnic element I cannot say.

The situation had come to a head with the Provincial Engineer refusing all MOW co-operation, so he had to be replaced and Tuku Usman had chosen me! A compliment or not, an expatriate replacement might be effective.

Naturally, I could only promise to tackle the matter to the best of my ability. I would arrange to see the Commander without delay – I presumed that he had been kept informed – and let him know the outcome within days.

North Central State

By the time I had finished with Tuku Usman, the Chief Civil Engineer, and seen to one or two other matters in Kaduna, it was late afternoon before I set out to drive to Zaria, only about 50 miles away on a bitumen surfaced road. I had telephoned to book in at the Rest House for several nights and would go to the Provincial Engineer's office in the morning.

During the evening I gave more thought to what Tuku Usman had told me. Strangely, he had made hardly any reference to the Provincial Engineer, so great was his concern about the situation with the Army. I had to assume that he had personally told the Commander my name and presumably some background. At Lokoja my contact with the Army had been brief, but from now onwards it was bound to be frequent, even daily perhaps, and had to be made effective. I anticipated some open hostility initially, but there was no question of me being 'a soft touch'. I represented the responsibilities of the Ministry of Works, as did also the Commander, to the Army, so co-operation must be on equal terms.

First, however, I should meet the outgoing Provincial Engineer and, hopefully, effect a quick handover. 8.00am seemed to me a reasonable time to report to his office at Headquarters, a single-storey building with car-parking in front. As I walked to the entrance I noticed one room with closed blinds. I gave my name to a uniformed attendant and asked to see the Provincial Engineer. The attendant asked me to wait. When he returned he was accompanied by the Chief Clerk who looked at me with a somewhat puzzled expression. He explained that he did not know if the Provincial Engineer would be coming to the office today. Rather than waiting for him to turn up, I asked the Chief Clerk if he would kindly inform the Provincial Engineer that I had arrived, and was staying at the Rest House where I would expect him to telephone me so that I could go and see him. With that I left, made a quick tour of the Township and returned to the Rest House where I was told there was no message waiting for me, and none came that day.

Next day I went to Headquarters about 9.00am and this time the Provincial Engineer was in his office – the same room I had noticed with closed blinds the previous day. He was taller than most Nigerians with a blotched face and sleepy eyes, and a disinterested but courteous speech and manner. He told me he had left the keys of the house with the watchman and said he would be leaving today for his home town in the North. There were no Handover Notes, he said, but the Chief Clerk would advise me, adding that he was fully aware my first priority was to deal with the Barracks etc. With that we shook hands and he left, which was sad as even in that short time we were together I had felt drawn to him.

I had a long talk with the Chief Clerk asking him to be entirely open with me. He explained that for weeks now they had not known whether the Provincial Engineer would come to the office or not. He was clearly drinking heavily, and sometimes on the Chief Clerk's arrival in the morning, the office blinds were closed, but the door was not locked and he would be lying on the floor, drunk or asleep. Other times, he might come for an hour or so, look at the post, leave a few instructions, and then go without saying anything and not come back for the rest of the day, or he might stay at home for days and not contact the office at all. He ignored messages or calls from the Barracks, and the Superintendents and junior staff dealt with routine matters. The Chief Clerk must have checked up on me somehow, because he said he was sure things would be different now. He sounded sincere, not just trying to 'suck up' to me.

Hassan, of course, was with me and the loads. We went to the house, originally a 'standard' bungalow which, I was told later, successive British Provincial Engineers had discreetly added to. We went round the rooms where every window was screwed up, and extra locks and bolts had been put on outside doors. Lying on the double bed in the main bedroom was a police truncheon. Clearly the outgoing Provincial Engineer was fearful of possible intruders from the Barracks on the order of the Commander. I arranged for all the windows to be opened up.

The Provincial Engineer's bungalow

Now that he had left I thought quite a lot about his case and the factors that may have contributed to his alcoholism. The cumulative effect of a longish period spent in a rather sophisticated professional working atmosphere with the Consulting Engineers and the intensive study necessary for his qualifications in the UK, with its complete change of environment and lifestyle, all may have overtaxed his mental faculties. By contrast, the associated social life of drinks parties, and the general availability of entertainment and so on may have led him to find temporary relief and relaxation in drinking excessive amounts of alcohol. Incidentally, I heard later that another Nigerian engineer on the same course in the UK had almost the same outcome of alcoholism. Whether they continued with this lifestyle I cannot say. Both were Muslims by birth and upbringing.

There was something tragic about these two cases, and I wonder whether they might somehow symbolise or demonstrate the collision of cultures. Our Colonial regime has, with the best of intentions, introduced our alien Western culture, already showing signs of decadence and breaking up, to Africa, supplanting an indigenous culture, with its built-in strengths, which had its origins much further back in history, thereby causing the confusion and instability now so noticeable in the independent and developing countries of this Continent.

Before writing about my first visit to the Barracks to meet the Commander, I quote from a letter to my brother of 17th December 1967, written soon after arriving at Zaria:

> "As you see I've moved. In a way I'm sorry, but the situation in the Lokoja area is much more normal now, and any special use I might have had at the time is over. Zaria is quite different in every way: it is a big place and no-one knows (or very much cares) about the war which is a long way away. There is a lot of noise and traffic, and hundreds of those ghastly education people, professors galore, at the University which thankfully is some way off so one doesn't see them around too much, and as we don't maintain the University buildings I shall not have to go there. The climate is quite different from Lokoja, being very cold in the mornings and evenings at present, and summery in the day. I can even sit in the sun and drink tea which one could never do at Lokoja if one wanted to survive. There is no humidity here and, in fact, it is rather too dry. I feel very strange after the sweaty days and nights.

> "I won't be coming on leave now until June next year. I was asked to take over here for various reasons, so I'll have to stay until then. Another reason I am not sorry to be staying is that, by the time June comes, I should know whether it's worth coming back or not. These changes and the new economic position may bring about too much of a shambles. The effects of this war have yet to be felt fully and then God

knows how it's going to work out once the fighting is over –
if it ever is."

I telephoned the Barracks and asked for an appointment with the
Commander, Colonel Adekunle. This was granted for the following
morning. The Barracks was a large, spread out complex with, typically,
one main road through it from the guard post with frequent branches off
lined with rows of huts and several spacious parade grounds. After a short
wait in an ante-room I was shown into the Commander's office. As I
recall, he was a somewhat haggard, weary-looking man who remained
seated at his large desk and did not offer me a handshake. I stood until he
pointed to a chair facing his desk, still showing no sign of any
introductory welcome. I was not really surprised at this sort of reception:
years of experience had prepared me for what I have come to regard as a
signal of instinctive hostility – perhaps too strong a word – by Nigerians
who had made the top, or near to, replacing the representatives of the old
white-dominated regime.

I came straight to the point: "I have come under instruction from the Chief
Civil Engineer to restore the relationship between the Ministry of Works
and the Army. I fully appreciate the priority position of the Army in the
prosecution of the Civil War, nonetheless, I have to ask you to accept that
I have duties and responsibilities which affect the well-being of the whole
community, including the water supply, the maintenance of roads and
public buildings and, of course, the Barracks. I gather that one point
which has caused real friction has been the seizure by Army personnel of
MOW vehicles and their drivers whilst going about their normal business,
claiming they were needed for emergency use. May we agree, from now
onwards, this practice will cease. All such requirements should be made
to me personally, or in my absence, to a designated staff member." I
explained that I had already set up my usual arrangement of a 'stand-by'
lorry and driver for non-working hours including weekends, together
with my Landrover driver retaining his vehicle with him at all times so
that I could send for him whenever an emergency arose. Experience,
particularly during the prevailing conditions, had shown such
arrangements to be very necessary. I have always regarded myself as a
public servant who should be on duty 24 hours a day.

I went on to say, "From now onwards Works Superintendents directly responsible for repairs and maintenance at the Barracks will be required to submit to me a brief daily list of requests, works in hand etc., as I intend to make frequent visits of inspection." I then mentioned that on my way in to his office I had stopped at a latrine block which had a notice outside – 'out of use'. "It is only too obvious why," I told him, "and I will be making enquiries." I was determined to forestall criticism but, at the same time, I accepted MOW's responsibilities to the full.

As I left, Colonel Adekunle came with me and saw me off with a handshake. After two weeks I felt confident enough to let the Chief Civil Engineer know that the relationship was in working order. I made frequent visits to the Barracks so that even the guards at the entrance began to let me through without stopping, and from time to time I paid a courtesy call on the Commander. There were occasional requests for transport and equally from the Police who certainly required extra vehicles when dealing with social unrest.

There were problems with water supply, specially to the high ground area of Wusasa where there was a large Mission and a Hospital belonging to the Church Missionary Society (CMS). The area was served from a multi-gallon storage tank which was refilled during the small hours of the night when demand elsewhere was low. However, there were times when the tank could get dry before the pumping session began causing a serious situation for the Hospital in particular. This was brought to my notice by the British expatriate Maintenance Officer of the Mission as I made my first visit of many. It was clear that some topping up of supply must take place during the day and I promised I would study the problem.

Yakubu (Jack) Gowon, now Head of State, had provided a modern bungalow for his parents in Wusasa, but they preferred to continue living in their round house so the bungalow was used by his brother, Daniel Gowon (unmarried), who had been a victim of polio. Daniel could move about and had a minor position in the Zaria offices of the *Nigerian Tobacco Company*. When VIPs were visiting, the parents would receive them in the bungalow!

A few days after my first visit to the Mission I received a telephone call introducing Daniel Gowon, who most courteously mentioned that often, just as he wanted to have a bath on returning from work, there was insufficient supply of water at the bungalow. He invited me for tea and I went the next day. Although younger than his brother Jack, he looked older and moved with some difficulty but with determination. He was most friendly and took me to meet his parents in the round house, who glowed with quiet pride about their sons. I explained to Daniel what I hoped to do for the Mission and Hospital which should also improve his supply. Without going into technical details, I was able to put into effect the necessary changes to alleviate the supply problem, except for occasional short interruptions due to burst supply lines or unexpected demand elsewhere for bush fires or the like.

The Maintenance Officer at the Hospital had given me an open invitation to take coffee any morning about 10.30 in the staff room of the Hospital, so one morning, slipping away from the pressures at my office, I drove up the hill to Wusasa. I suppose I was still unwinding from the long period of tension at Lokoja, and from then onwards, whenever I felt the need for mental and spiritual succour to keep going I was drawn to the Hospital for this half-an-hour or so in the company of the staff at coffee time. I was made very welcome by all the staff, comprising the Medical Officer in charge, Dr Tom West, who was obviously adored by his staff, several matrons who were not at all matronly, and a number of nurses; British, Australian and others. They laughed and joked in a kindly way about some of the cases with which they were dealing, and operations which were 'near things', and all the time there was love and dedication to their work – just the tonic I sought. Tom West explained how the Hospital managed to keep going: the Mission was constantly chasing for donations from abroad, because for each Nigerian treated the State government paid them a mere pittance. To put it bluntly, they survived precariously and had been doing so for years, yet Tom was supremely confident that they would be able to continue with God's help.

The Civil War seemed remote and news came only through radio and the papers. Despite the fall of Enugu, Ojukwu was defiant and had regrouped. I return to Meredith:

"After the fall of the capital, Enugu, in October (1967), however, as Biafra came under siege, a different ploy was used. With brilliant success, Ojukwu's Directorate of Propaganda set out to convince the Ibos inside the enclave, and foreign opinion in the world outside, that the Lagos Government was bent on a policy of mass slaughter.

"This theme of genocide became one of the most potent weapons in the war. For the Ibos, gripped by memories of the Northern pogroms of 1966, the fear of genocide was real enough and provided every reason to fight on, whatever the odds against them appeared to be... From early 1968 foreign support for Biafra steadily mounted... foreign visitors too came away from Biafra impressed by the stature of Ojukwu and the strength of Ibo nationalism. But what finally galvanised Western opinion was the spectre of mass starvation among refugees in Biafra as the Federal noose slowly tightened. Biafra for the West became a symbol of suffering and persecution. Its very determination to fight on under such terrible conditions lent credence to the fear of genocide... In the critical months of 1968, as the impact of the Biafran war spread around the world, other help was forthcoming. Four African States... hoping that their actions would improve the chances of a cease-fire, announced diplomatic recognition of Biafra. Though of little practical effort their support, coming at a time when spirits were low, lifted morale and seemed to constitute a breakthrough in the struggle for survival. Even more significant were signs of encouragement from France. Partly in a response to domestic political pressures and public opinion which was running strongly in Biafra's favour, partly because it suited French interests in Africa, de Gaulle at the end of July 1968 expressed his sympathy for the Biafran cause... Whatever the motive was, the foreign aid that Biafra received... all helped to sustain the war effort and reinforced Ojukwu's determination to fight on...."

Day touring sufficed for regular road inspection in the Province and raised the standards of maintenance. At Daura on the road to Katsina further north a bridge had been washed out during the short rainy season. At the present time, traffic was able to proceed on the dry river bed but a Bailey Bridge needed to be provided, and I was able to obtain the necessary components from the stock at Kaduna and build the bridge using local labour.

Building the Bailey Bridge on the road to Katsina
As launching equipment was not available we used steel cribs for support
until the gap had been bridged, when they were removed

In March 1968 I had been in post since October 1966, some eighteen months including the stressful year at Lokoja. At Headquarters Ian Nowell, whom I knew well, had replaced Tuku Usman as Chief Civil Engineer, and on a visit to Kaduna I spoke to him about my next leave. I suggested leaving in July 1968 and returning at the start of 1969, but he informed me that he planned to go on UK leave himself in October or November 1968 for several months during which time he would be arranging for me to act as Chief Civil Engineer during his absence. To meet this arrangement I should curtail my leave, and on his return I would resume at Zaria. I readily agreed since, although I was entitled to six months' leave, it did seem too long and I would be restless to return!

Accordingly, leave starting on 15th July 1968 was approved with the actual date for return to be notified to me in the UK against a posting to act as Chief Civil Engineer. However, late in my leave, I received notice that the arrangement to act as Chief Civil Engineer was cancelled and I should take my full leave entitlement and resume on 2nd January 1969 as Acting Provincial Engineer North Central State at Zaria. The explanation for the cancellation and its consequence came as I resumed duty at Zaria.

Meanwhile, at home I had received the following letter from the Foreign and Commonwealth Office in London SW1, dated 2nd December1968:

> Sir,
> I am directed by Mr Secretary Stewart to inform you that he proposes, on the occasion of the forthcoming New Year Honours List, to submit your name to The Queen for appointment as a Member of the Most Excellent Order of the British Empire (MBE).
>
> I am to request that you will be good enough to inform me immediately whether this honour would be agreeable to you, and at the same time to furnish me with correct particulars as to Christian names, surname and permanent address. I must further ask you to treat this matter as entirely confidential until such time as the Honours List is published.
>
> I am, Sir, Your Obedient Servant
> A.L. Mayall

This letter was quickly followed by another dated 30th December 1968:

> Sir,
>
> I am directed by Mr Secretary Stewart to inform you that The Queen has been graciously pleased, on the occasion of the New Year 1969, to direct that you should be appointed a Member of the Civil Division of the Most Excellent order of the British Empire in recognition of the valuable services which you have rendered.
>
> I am, Sir, Your Obedient Servant,
> W.G.M. Tear

Then in Nigeria I received the following letter from the British High Commission in Lagos, dated 1st January 1969:

> Dear Mr Muggeridge,
>
> Please accept my warmest congratulations on the occasion of the award to you of an MBE in the New Year Honours Lists. It has, I know, given great pleasure to a very wide circle in Nigeria that the value of your services has received this recognition.
>
> I know how highly the Nigerian authorities for their part have appreciated your contribution to the well-being of the country, particularly in these difficult times.
>
> It is through the efforts of people like you, and of many others who are working in Nigeria, that Britain's contribution to this and other developing countries in Africa is most effectively made.
>
> Yours sincerely,
> David Hunt

I had replied "Yes, thank you" to the letter of 2nd December 1968, but 'Entirely Confidential' meant that I could not even tell the family. Then, luckily, the letter of 30th December arrived just as I was leaving for the flight to Kano on 1st January 1969, and shortly afterwards the Honours List was published in the papers. When I showed my name in the MBE

Civil List to my last but one son, Richard, he asked: "What did you get that for Dad?"!

I was very pleased to see the name 'W.A. Wilson' in the same List. 'Bill' Wilson was the Chief Mechanical Engineer at MOW Headquarters Kaduna, and for a time he was Acting Permanent Secretary. As CME he was bound to have had close involvement with the Army etc. concerning transport, fuel and so on. I have included the correspondence simply to place on record, at the time, the comparative rarity of any such awards within the so-called 'technical' Departments, as against the ritual allocation of OBEs, CBEs etc., within the Administration. It's not a question of 'sour grapes' but merely a matter of fact.

Jack receiving his MBE from Sir Leslie Glass,
the British High Commissioner, at Lagos

So began a second spell of duty as Acting Provincial Engineer North Central State at Zaria. My first call, on my way there, was to Headquarters Kaduna. I was curious to find out why the arrangement for me to take over as Acting Chief Civil Engineer had been cancelled almost at the last moment. It was not that I was greatly disappointed at the change, because by instinct I was not a 'Headquarters Man' and had earlier declined an undefined post at Kano when Jonah had wanted to send me there. It was because the arrangement had come from Ian Nowell on a personal basis, that I wanted to know the reason for the cancellation.

First my enquiry was at the 'lower level' of Headquarters which, like London taxi drivers and chauffeurs to top politicians, is always the most reliable source about Cabinet Changes and so on. Thus by the time I was due to pay my respects at the 'high level' I felt well informed. To explain: at Independence in 1960, Nigeria was made up of three Regions – North, West and East with Lagos in the South as 'Capital Territory'. Kaduna was the Capital of the Northern Region and it, too, had 'Capital Territory'. Within the Ministry of Works this area was known as 'Kaduna Division' and its Head known as 'Divisional Engineer' comparable to 'Provincial Engineer' in the Provinces. Over the years, it seemed that, by tradition, whoever occupied this post was regarded as being 'one down' from Chief Civil Engineer, although I cannot say that this automatically held fast whenever the substantive Chief Civil Engineer went on leave or was away on duty for more than a few days. When Ian Nowell told me about the arrangement for me to 'stand in' while he was on leave, I was completely unaware that a New Zealander, Lloyd Hooper, was in post as Divisional Engineer Kaduna. Certainly, his name did not figure amongst Provincial Engineers so far as I knew them. There were, of course, a number of engineers holding senior posts in the establishment of Headquarters who could be selected for 'outside' postings when necessary. It seemed that Ian Nowell had decided to bring me in to act in his absence without reference to the Permanent Secretary, Mallam Armiyau, who, incidentally, was the first Nigerian to qualify professionally and become a Member of the Institution of Civil Engineers UK. Mr E. Jones (Jonah) had decided to retire soon after the coming of the military regime arising from the coup of 15th January 1966. Mr Hooper had complained to Mallam Armiyau, the outcome being that the arrangement involving me had been cancelled.

During my long leave in the UK, July 1968 to January 1969, I had met with considerable interest, if ill-informed, regarding the Nigerian Civil War. But now back in Nigeria, it seemed strange that there was more local interest about the impending marriage of the Head of State than in the Civil War, which seemed forgotten or ignored in the North. There were hints of disagreement within the Biafran Camp – Meredith 1969:

> "... Foreign supporters were also dismayed by Ojukwu's unwillingness to seek terms and international sympathy for Biafra began to wane. After a team of foreign military observers had concluded in 1968 that there was no evidence to support Biafran claims about genocide, the propaganda machine that the Biafrans had used so successfully to arouse concern for their plight lost much of its impact. In military terms, Biafra was faced at best with a grinding war of endurance... although at times the Nigerian military was inert, cumbersome and poorly led, it had every advantage on its side. Against such an Army, Biafra was fighting with makeshift tactics and means. White mercenaries were hired, a miniature air force of light aircraft was raised... and used to bomb Federal positions. But such efforts were of little avail."

Following the wedding of Major General Yakubu Gowon and Victoria, a daughter of a much respected senior civil servant, there would be a Special Thanksgiving Service on Sunday 20th April 1969 at 4.30pm at St Bartholomew's Church, situated in the grounds of the CMS Mission at Wusasa, capacity only 200, to which I was delighted to receive an invitation. I was able to squeeze in standing at the back and also attended the reception afterwards which Daniel Gowon had organised on behalf of his brother. On the next day 21st April 1969, I attended, by invitation, a Reception at State House, Kaduna from 5.00 to 6.30pm by His Excellency, Major General Yakubu Gowon and Mrs Victoria to mark the occasion of their wedding. This, of course, was a great formal occasion in contrast to the happenings at Wusasa.

As the weeks went by the Civil War continued, although it was seldom spoken of during conversation. On 5th October 1969 I wrote to my brother:

> "The war here has become pretty dirty in many ways. I wonder now if the soldiery really want it to be ended. Somehow the economy struggles on and the lads continue to build their houses and live a life of considerable ease and affluence. No-one seems to challenge them. Most people are apathetic, disillusioned and realise that their affairs are rundown but don't really know what to do about it all. I doubt if they see any alternative at present. One of the more intelligent Administrative Officers said to me recently, '...we really don't know what is going to happen to us. Some of us say it would be a good thing if we were colonised again...!'

> "The oil boys, it is said, have had more than enough. The whole business of the war has become very strange, phantom-like, not really happening. The Press make mention of action occasionally but otherwise it seems not there. The oddest thing of all, of course, is that the starving millions seem to have faded away, no longer mentioned except by Auberon Waugh who strains hard to keep mention of them in his articles. No more screams about the thousands dying every day. Of course, they aren't and never were to anything like the extent spoken and written about. How much longer the war will go on is anyone's guess. It may just fold up quickly overnight or go on for years yet. My own feeling now is that disintegration will soon occur elsewhere here, probably in the West where there has been considerable rioting, and then the whole will break up... I've no idea when I'll be coming on leave or of the future here..."

I had become a more frequent visitor to the Mission Hospital at morning coffee time. Nothing seemed to lower their spirits. One day, however, as they saw me off with their usual cheerfulness, Tom West said: "Good bye, I'm afraid you will not see us again, we really cannot go on. Government money has not reached us and our overseas support is not enough on its own to keep us going. We are, of course, praying."

Perhaps a month later, I felt I must check up on the situation there. Coffee time was just as welcoming and cheerful with amusing stories to tell me about the operating room, and everything seemed even better than usual, probably because of the longer gap. Casually, I said to Tom West: "Everything all well now?"

For a moment, he looked doubtful, but then said: "Oh, that! Yes, God heard our prayers and an unexpected and large cheque from Germany arrived." What truly wonderful faith and confidence!

As for my work, there was seldom an evening when I was not to be found at my office dealing with matters for which there was no time during normal working hours. This was known, of course, at the Barracks and at the Police but somehow it became more generally known, including the 'after hours and weekend' with a small reliable unit of mechanics, transport etc. for emergencies. Geographically, too, Zaria was situated on the main road from the far North through Kaduna and on to the South carrying almost unceasingly traffic of all types day and night. One of those seeking help was Mallam Armiyau, then Permanent Secretary, Ministry of Works, returning from a visit to Katsina. His Mercedes had blown one of its water hoses in a very difficult place on the engine. Another, late one evening, was the Nigerian engineer who had walked out, seething with anger at me, when I arrived at Minna Ministry of Works to resume as Provincial Engineer for a second tour and he had to move to Bauchi Province instead of me. By this time, however, he had left MOW for higher things and was very grateful for the attention to his car which had broken down some miles out from Zaria. In general, there were no difficulties with the Barracks regarding maintenance and only occasional calls for help with transport, usually in conjunction with the Police for disturbances.

In a letter I had referred, unfairly perhaps, to "...those ghastly education people, professors galore, at the University..." In fact, Ahmadu Bello University (the only one in the North) was just a few miles out of Zaria and I had discovered that it had a bookshop open to the public. On my first visit, it was a pleasant surprise to find it quite well stocked with both fiction and non-fiction, paperbacks, classics and so on and the staff were well informed. By chance, at some gathering to which attendance was virtually obligatory, I had been introduced to the Head of the Faculty of Engineering at the University who invited me to visit the Faculty. I believe he was British and had come from a similar appointment with a University in an overseas Territory. Some weeks later I telephoned him and made an arrangement to visit. His main concern seemed to be that the Engineering Degree awarded by the University should be recognisably equal to that awarded by Universities in the world, America etc., both for prestige but more importantly, so that its graduates would be on an equal footing with other graduates when applying for employment outside Nigeria as many might choose to do.

Although I could appreciate this particular dilemma, I had to point out that at this phase in Nigeria's progress so soon after Independence, the urgent need was to replace the expatriates in, for example, the Ministry of Works with indigenous qualified executive engineers, civil, mechanical, electrical etc., as soon as possible. To that end, the degree syllabus – certainly for some years ahead – should be framed to include road maintenance, bridging, drainage and water supply, basic services all of which were of the greatest importance to the well-being of the whole community. Possibly, I said, two classes of degrees could be introduced, one appropriate to the current needs of Nigeria, the other for what might be described as 'international' applications. Although I expected to be going on leave in the near future, I offered to take a graduate into my Department as a Trainee Executive Engineer as a test case. He was pleased and said he would make arrangements accordingly.

He also told me that, as part of the programme for the West African Group of Professional Engineers Zaria Branch, he had put together a series of afternoon lectures by representatives of contracting, research, public services and so on, and invited me to give a lecture early in the new year, 1970, on a topic of my own choice. I accepted, the date to be settled after I had determined my leave date which I hoped would be not later than March 1970. Thirty years on it is interesting to re-read my completely non-technical discourse given before an audience of young students, graduates, staff and others from outside on 9th February 1970 at the Department of Civil Engineering at Ahmadu Bello University, Zaria.

Too Much Technology?
By Mr J.R. Muggeridge

Summary

This is a completely non-technical discourse, the question being 'Is there, in fact, too much technology or is it that it's the wrong sort and goes on its way regardless of whether there is demand for more and more, in a seemingly purposeless rush to try to satisfy the virtually insatiable human appetite for material things, so-called material well-being? To where and what is technology leading and from where and what may it be leading man away?

There is a case to answer that technology, as we now see it, is self defeating or, even worse, openly destructive and life destroying. By appearing to solve a problem or to supply the answer to some apparent need, it merely creates another problem, or problems, and takes away, or reduces, the availability of what is already there for man's use or need. What of man's emotional and spiritual life, is it being submerged or drowned by technology which, like the gross national product, must (we are told) each year grow and grow if we are to survive. What of the power and force of nature? For how much longer will nature continue to tolerate man's tampering with its functions? Will nature not at some time decide to kick back – is it not doing so already? Man is handling forces which he thinks he knows about but in fact he knows little or nothing for certain since the basic mystery of life and of death is still beyond him. 1984 is only 14 years away. Will it resemble George Orwell's concept or that of H.G. Wells'?

Opening Remarks

Before actually starting my talk may I just say a word or two of personal explanation. I was delighted, of course, to be asked to give this so-called lecture, and I intentionally chose a non-technical subject as a change from the more erudite papers given by others so much more professionally competent than I could possibly hope to be on my own work as a Provincial Engineer. I was afraid, too, that I might bore rather than stimulate you if I spoke about the largely hack work in which I am so much engaged. I like to think that we are not so deeply immersed in formulae and theories that we cannot come up for a change of air occasionally. Frankly, I dislike 'reading a paper' as the phrase goes and much prefer to speak from brief notes or headings, particularly on such a subject as I have chosen this evening, but naturally I will follow your usual practice and read from a prepared text. I think my lecture is shorter than others but I hope there is enough of it to provoke some worthwhile discussion afterwards and to which, personally, I look forward keenly. Open discussion is usually much more enjoyable and interesting, certainly to the lecturer when he has had his say.

Too Much Technology?

I suppose all of us, at some time, have those quick moments or even periods in life when we feel moved to take stock of our personal affairs, attitudes, thoughts, even aspirations, if any are still left to us, and certainly, I hope, of our shortcomings and inevitable failures. Sixty years of age is, I should say, quite one of those moments – it certainly has been for me. What started it off, I think, must have been filling in some form or other. I forget what it could have been about but there it was, the one certainty on any form, 'Date of Birth', and down it went '15th August 1909'. For some reason, I must have looked at this entry again, not because it was wrong, but because suddenly some fleeting, flashing pictures of what the scene looked like, or must have looked like, those 60 years ago passed in front of me – a sort of 'What the butler saw' series of picture frames! 1909: was I really born into this world at a time when the motor car was still almost a monstrosity striking terror into people's lives, when there was no radio, certainly no television, thankfully no bingo, no birth or fertility pill, few universities with students to demonstrate, and really nothing of what seems now to surround and bewilder us, perhaps to overwhelm us? And was there a word 'technology' then? I doubt it. Thus I was really off on a train of thought – you may know how it is.

My much loved father – when was he born? 1864. And his father, my grand-father whom I never saw, when did he arrive on earth? Perhaps 1825? I do not recall being told. And his father, my great-grandfather? Possibly about the time of Dr Samuel Johnson when, I remember reading, the population of England and Wales was about nine million – today it's about five times that figure. At any rate, by that time about 150 years ago we can be quite sure there was no science fiction, nor, in fact, much science at all as we know it today and certainly not much fiction, if any, of the kitchen-sink or moon-shot varieties now loading the bookshelves.

Thinking afterwards of this mental and, to some degree, emotional going back, I felt more than ever convinced that my father's period – 1864 to 1942 – and which, with my four brothers, I shared with him for my first 30 years or so – was really the period in which the greatest changes took place and in which, for good or ill, man began to take the course on which he now seems so set – to extract or produce more and more material things, perhaps to the point when only the new will appear to satisfy or please, no matter whether it is needed or has a use. There is little doubt that the First World War (1914-1918), of which I have an ineradicable recollection as I have of the Second World War, was the pivotal point of the changes which, once started, have in succeeding years cascaded upon us like an avalanche threatening to engulf us completely. It could be said that the First World War and its immediate aftermath jolted man out of so many fixed ideas and ways of life and that the Second World War, despite the widely different techniques used in its prosecution, was only a further and more dramatic shaking up.

To my mind, the significance of both, but particularly of the first, is that consciously or sub-consciously man's attitude to himself, his future, and his purpose, became not just uncertain and charged with doubt, but took on a sort of desperation: "eat drink and be merry for tomorrow we die" – an indefinite extension of that attitude which during, the war itself, was perhaps understandable and excusable. In other words, what before had seemed solidly based, or firmly set, values had been shown, in the course of a few years charged with drama and indescribable tragedy, not to be so, and had, in fact, been destroyed, discredited by man's own actions. Then with what were these values being, or to be, replaced? None apparently were set up, as there seemed no urge to set up any, and so all became a scramble for what seemed to give at least some transient sense of well-being, and security – the pursuit of happiness or bust! This is actually written into the American constitution!

By now, if not before, you may well be wondering what all this has to do with my question "Too much technology?" The point I hoped to have made is that, once man had fixed his sights on material development and exploitation as being the goals of endeavour, of thought, of life itself, then the scientific and technological era was bound to occur, and bound to go on occurring, and if we are not wary, may well engulf us and all that we have accomplished (whether good or bad), thus bringing to an end this civilisation only to join the earlier civilisations which have crashed for not dissimilar reasons, even if the actual manifestations of their break-up have been different in character or scope. To my mind, the signs are all there and I do not think I need to illuminate them. You cannot fail to see and realise them for yourselves. Let me hasten to say that I know there have been cries, time without number, of "…the end of the world is at hand" and yet the world – apparently at least – is still here. For so long there has seemed to be one great achievement after another each one heralding inexhaustible benefits to mankind on the way to that well-being for all that we crave, with every problem solved or at least accounted for by 'big boss man'. But have we not reached, or are we not about to reach, the moment when suddenly there are signs everywhere of doubt, disintegration and of problems not actually solved but, in fact, become more intractable. Isn't everything rather a whirl, chaotic and perhaps beyond control?

My description may appear too dramatic, all too much like the television news and the words of the journalist just back from the rebel enclave with his photographs of "…the real thing," and, yes, those interviews! It is, of course, not like that now, but is there not a real threat or real danger that it could, and will, become just like that or even worse, if technology and the technologists are not restrained and brought to heel? Is technology "…too important to be left to the technologists" to adapt the phrase once used about broadcasting by the UK Minister of Technology. Is there then too much technology in the sense that we will be surfeited with it and literally made sick by it – even die of it like King John with his lampreys? Or more ominously, is it that, whether too much or not enough, so much is perpetrated without thought as to its effects or aftermath, and some is even actually and openly harmful? There are, I think, definite portends, perhaps unmistakable signs of which we, all of us, whether participants or not in tech activities, must take heed. Pollution of air and water, depletion or squandering of basic resources, spoliation of the countryside, the damage to be wrought by supersonic boom, filth multiplying and so many places daily becoming filthier – and I do not mean just the filth of theatre, cinema, news-papers, television, books and so on. It is almost impossible to open any newspaper or magazine, or listen to radio or watch television without being reminded of, confronted with, the results of technology or, should I say, too much technology – technology gone mad perhaps? For instance, Alistair Cooke the other day commented that the great dread now in the USA is not nuclear war, the outburst of black power, but that, in just a few years if action is not soon taken, the most powerful and prosperous nation in the world will be faced with undrinkable water in an unbreatheable air. If we allow this Earth to become largely uninhabitable because of our wanton activities, then presumably we are to make a mass exodus to the Moon there only to start the same calamitous business all over again. (Ed. The first manned moon landing had taken place six months before in July 1969.)

I would like, however, to delve deeper into the effects of technology, effects below the surface of things, into the very basic structure of man. Effects which I think should be regarded as of even greater significance than those we now know to be arising from pollution, spoliation and the others I have mentioned. Let me quote from a comment in the *New Statesman* recently, referring to 1970 as being 'European Conservation Year': "The real ignorance of modern technology is shown by those who assume that it can safely be left to work out its own solutions, that because no disaster has hit us yet there will never be one – quote: 'people like you wanted to ban the railways'." And so one can find many instances of the concern felt about technology and what it is up to. I should, of course, have mentioned Lake Erin in Canada about which the reports are so appalling that the question mark in my heading seems completely irrelevant.

Now as to the deeper implications of technology and its ever developing and enveloping influence on our lives today. By the tremendous concentration on things technological and all the wonders which supposedly can, and do appear, to come our way, all of us, and I include the technologists themselves, seem to me to be being led into a world of fantasy in which there is to be no limit to things material, all for our comfort, all to render life effortless. Yet the strange thing is that mankind seems more than ever beset with problems: the threat of extinction by nuclear or other horror let loose by some lunatic or luster after power; the poor get poorer, the rich richer; 100,000 persons are killed in a year in accidents on the roads and each year the number increases; violence and lawlessness is erupting in many places, and there is a general breakdown of authority and of moral behaviour. Where then is the peaceful Paradise, the Heaven on Earth which technology and the technologists have been promising us – saying that it is just round the corner? When is the bonanza? Is it perhaps that the advancement into

145

technology which largely, or perhaps only, came about as the result of man's lust for power, for domination over other men, has its origins only in the fear of annihilation, destruction or death and not in the positive believe in life? Is man's fear of himself *vis-à-vis* himself in the guise of someone speaking a different language, having a different colour from himself? Is it that, in the fierce evangelical sense, technology and all that goes with it is evil, the devil ineluctably drawing us into his fold so that at last we will be destroyed once and for all? Certainly, the devil would then have the last laugh because the deed would have been done by man himself. So far, despite every effort known to, or invented by, man for its extinction, life has shown itself to be supreme and indestructible, but we have no means of knowing that it will continue so, so enormous and overpowering are the forces with which man is playing and of which, in his heart, he knows he has little or no real knowledge or understanding or is ever likely to have.

It has always been said that the great advances of science and technology should be dispelling man's ignorance of so many things which before had been beyond him. These advances give him enlightenment and discernment in dark places of the earth and of the mind; the ability to compare and select for himself without having to be told by others better informed than he. They also open up to man the vast spread of communications and means of communicating one with the other, and give to one and all the real facts, the real truth, with no delusions, no exaggerations, and no distortions. But what in fact has happened and can be seen to be happening? Man's credulity is now almost beyond bounds. Within a few days of heavy dosage by radio, television, newspapers, magazines, he will come to believe, and even cry out loud for all to hear, almost anything which those having the power wish him to believe. Whether it is true or false is irrelevant so long as it is believed and accepted at that moment. Later, if it is to be disbelieved for some reason or other, the reverse process is equally easy and is applied without conscience or fear of reprisal. In the end, of course, man comes to believe everything or nothing. So with the growth of technology; we believe that it is right that it must be producing or procuring immeasurable benefits for man, that all of it must be purposeful – how marvellous that dam, how wonderful that nuclear power station, how effortless the daily chores are with all that gadgetry, when it works! Yet almost without warning, all is seen to be a mess, in chaos, something is missing, something has gone astray. Surely, we were told, have had it hammered into us, that technology would go on for ever, each year growing a little more, producing more benefits. But should there not be a little unease, a little nagging doubt that perhaps man is not quite the supreme boss of nature he thinks he is and might he not one day find himself down on the floor with nature kicking back?

And now, where in all this is the very heart of man, his soul, his spirit, his yearning for the thought beyond earthly affairs and possessions which supposedly has made him rise above the mere animal, the mere creatures of the earth? Man surely has not changed even if his environment has been changed for and by him.

At 60 years, possibly without realising it, one is already preparing ever so slightly for the withdrawal from life which becomes a finality with death. Certainly, one begins to notice a feeling of detachment in viewing the torrent of events going on around one, a subconscious acceptance that retirement from the scene will not be too long delayed. Undoubtedly, at 60 there is a great deal more behind one than there possibly can be in front – even the egg-heads, the back-room boys, the heart transplanters, are not yet able to change that – and it is in that spirit of detachment that some of us may hope that man will find it is in himself to be able to control, if not conquer, the technology which seems likely to overwhelm him. 1984 is now only 14 years away. Will it be George Orwell's or H.G. Wells's concept of life which prevails? Better that neither should.

For myself now, I am content to remain the professional hack which, in reality, I have been for some considerable time. My personal technology does not, and will not, go beyond the use of two legs to propel myself through the fields in the gathering end of the day to witness, as I so often try to do, with never failing joy, wonder and thankfulness, the unchallengeable splendour of the setting sun behind Kuffena Rock, remembering G.K. Chesterton's deathless phrase: 'In the fiery alphabet of every sunset is written "to be continued in our next."' (From 'On the Institution of the Family' in *Heretics* published by *Bodley Head* in 1905)

* * * * *

The reaction to the lecture – once it got going – was, I felt, a mixture of puzzlement by the young and challenge by the older. I was able to agree with both.

Soon the selected trainee engineer reported to my office. He was wearing a smart suit, shirt, tie and dress shoes. I had prepared a small room near me for his office with desk, chairs, drawing table and some surveying equipment. As we talked I realised that, as I had suspected, there had been little or no basic training or experience throughout his course. Not for him the heat of the long dusty laterite road, so I made a point of taking him with me – having by then replaced the suit with more suitable bush attire – on visits to the Barracks, the waterworks, out on the roads etc., and then to the site of a short timber bridge in poor condition which I had agreed should be replaced with a Bailey Bridge. I showed him the limits of a site survey he should make (not strictly required but a good exercise for him), and then draw a site plan to a certain scale, which I could see would be a problem for him. He did try very hard but obviously relied heavily on the technical assistants I allotted to him.

Quite soon, it was clear to me that, along with his professional status, he expected an appointment with a well set-up office, secretary, subordinate staff and the appropriate salary. I could only tell him of my start, at the age of 16, as a trainee in the Drawing Office of the Department of the Borough Surveyor of the Local Authority when, going on survey with a senior engineer, I had to carry the level, staff, tripod, some ranging rods, and the 100ft chain – the senior might carry the tape. On Fridays, the Officer i/c Drawing Office would go to the market and buy fish and give it to me to take to his house for his wife, then I had to make tea or coffee for morning break. At least I was given a drawing board with set squares etc. so that I could learn to draw. This was vital as I knew that it I failed to show reasonable aptitude for drawing (with instruments and to scale) I would lose my place. By the time I went on leave I think I had brought him down to earth and could pass him on to my successor with some confidence.

I reported the experience to the Head of Faculty at the University but I doubt if it had any influence. In any case, before I left, I heard that he was moving on to a new University in Papua New Guinea.

The Zaria Local Authority had spoken to me about Town Planning for the Township, which was dominantly northern in character and consisted of jumbled mud round houses with narrow haphazard walk-ways between them and a few roads; the population was probably 50,000. The request led me to give some thought to the preliminaries of a town planning scheme and the factors involved at early appraisal. This brought to mind the occasions when I had clambered up the many steps to the top viewing point of one of the towers of the huge Mosque in Kano Native City and gazed down on the vast spread of, mostly, flat roofs in every direction, where lives the City's population, said to be one million but no-one really knows. Attempts at producing a reliable census have failed due to the constant shifting movement of people into and out of the City for various reasons. Nationwide counts have proved equally unreliable, particularly in the North which is determined to have the highest count, as this is the determining factor for allocation of Federal funds to the Regions. Zaria, by comparison is like a large village. Surely, the first planning criterion to be settled would be, for what standard of re-housing would the Scheme provide? This was crucial so that at least the area and location of land, for what, in effect, would be a new Township, could be allocated. If the Authority were really serious about a Town Plan for Zaria then I would include the subject in my Handing-Over Notes since, with my leave imminent, I would be unable to make a start on the Project. This was how the matter was left with the Authority.

Some of my letter of 18th December 1969 to my brother is worth including in view of what occurred within a few weeks:

> "I expect you are sick of the Nigerian war. I hear that Parliament has had another outburst with Hugh Fraser gushing forth again… as for the ban on arms… the Federal Government is bad and now deep in corruption but it is doing the only thing possible to try to stop the country fragmenting still further. Otherwise the place will be back in the pre-colonial days of tribal fighting and much more bloodshed and privation than ever this war has created. Of course, there is little or no actual fighting going on now anywhere in the areas… people are now quite bewildered as to what can be done or will happen… I'll be going to the Christmas Service at the little Mission Church at the Hospital. The Mission is almost the only place I go to and it's like a tonic. Just half-an-hour amongst the people there with their unshakeable faith and I feel a different person."

Then, only a few days later, to quote from Meredith: "Biafra collapsed suddenly in January 1970." General Olusegun Obasango in his book *My Command:* "At 4.00pm on Monday 12th January 1970 Lieutenant Colonel Philip Effiong announced the surrender of Biafra…"

The surrender formalities took place at Dodan Barracks Lagos on 15th January 1970 with speeches and the signing of documents. It has often been said that the process of surrender at Lagos actually began earlier but was intentionally held back so that the final stage would take place on 15th January 1970, the anniversary of the first military coup (Ibo) at Kaduna in 1966 – Nigerians do have a liking for anniversaries!

From what I was to learn from reliable sources later, the 'surrender' was not the outcome of active military engagement between the opposing forces, nor as sudden as it appeared. First the military aspect: where engagements had been taking place and Ibo forces had been captured by the Federal forces, the officers particularly were seen to be dispirited, all being very hungry despite the talk that much of the food which was being flown in to the Ibo side from outside supporters for the population was being diverted to the Ibo fighting forces. By contrast, Federal officers were able to show strong morale and made sure that the captured Ibo officers received plenty to eat. Then instead of keeping them as prisoners of war, they sent them back to the Ibo lines encouraging them to tell their fellow officers how good it was with the Federal forces. Without doubt, this would have undermined the enthusiasm of the Ibo officers to continue the struggle for Biafra as an Independent State – the game was up.

The other aspect was revealed not long after the peace and seemed to corroborate the rumour that had persisted for some time about the 'oil boys' having had 'more than enough' (see my letter to my brother of 5th October 1969). I have mentioned Felix Nwanko (Ibo), a loyal and efficient Mechanical Superintendent at MOW Minna, who like other Ibos, once the Civil War started, had decided to go to the East with his family for safety. When the war ended he came to see me and told me that, once in the East, he had hidden with his family in the deepest bush for their safety but also to avoid himself being rounded up by the Army to serve in the war, because any man found free was being forced into the fight. There were days when they were so short of food they had to eat rats and scrounge for anything to eat in the bush, but they survived. He had clear evidence of what he described as 'well-dressed men from the oil Companies' going amongst the dispirited Ibo officers and men, giving them money, promising them employment when they were able to start the business of oil again, and encouraging them to give up the fighting. After all, the Companies and particularly *Shell Company* had invested many millions in the East, and for three years it had been dormant and neglected. I give these two instances but others have been able to produce similar examples of the sordid aspect of the Civil War.

One last quote from Meredith:

> "Weary, demoralised and short of food, Biafra's people were desperate for peace. On 10th January, two days before Biafra formally surrendered, Ojukwu fled to exile in the Ivory Coast, still defiant, still warning of the threat of genocide. In a final statement, he explained that he had departed knowing that "...whilst I live Biafra lives." The aftermath of the war, however, was remarkable for its compassion and mercy, and the way in which the memories of Biafra soon faded. In Lagos, Gowon vigorously pursued a policy of clemency, pledging a general amnesty for those who fought against the Federal government and encouraging Ibos in the tasks of reconstruction... Civil servants returned to their posts in the Federal government; and property belonging to Ibos in the North and other Federal areas was restored to them."

My leave was granted as from 31st March 1970 to resume on 29th July 1970 as Acting Divisional Engineer Kaduna being the most senior 'outside' post, one below that of Chief Civil Engineer in the Ministry of Works. By March 1970, I had been serving since April 1958 in Nigeria, about eleven years apart from UK leaves. Aged 49 when I arrived, I was now 60, and the normal age for retirement, depending on the Territory, was 55.

I had, of course, received and kept up to date all the necessary inoculations against smallpox, yellow fever, cholera etc. Also, as advised for Nigeria, I took anti-malarial tablets and favoured Paludrine, because the dose was one tablet a day, and it could hardly be forgotten as the container was part of the breakfast table with the marmalade and so on. However, the additional advice was that if, despite having taken Paludrine, a bout of fever seemed imminent, one should add the stronger antidote of Nivaquin which was taken once a week, so I kept a supply available. Incidentally, these pills were not an issue, one had to purchase them at drug stores.

Up to then, I had been fortunate, especially at my age, to have suffered nothing worse than an occasional bout of 'the runs', which was almost inevitable in the tropics. It was during my second tour at Zaria that, for the first time, I really felt I was running a fever. I certainly had a ghastly sore throat so I took one tablet of Nivaquin. After a day or so the sore throat was so bad that I decided to consult Dr Tom West at the Mission Hospital rather than the State Hospital. He had no doubt about my throat – quite the worst he had ever seen – and at once sent me to the Hospital Pharmacy with a note to get some pills. I suppose I was so concerned about the throat that I did not tell him about taking the anti-malaria pills. That night, lying in bed tossing and turning, with my eyes closed trying to sleep, I had the most terrible hallucinations. I was lying in broken glass with large serpents crawling all over me, and sleep or rest were quite impossible.

In the morning, I went straight to see Tom West and told him what I had experienced. Only then did I casually mention the Paludrine and the addition of the Nivaquin I had been taking. Apparently, it was the Nivaquin which had 'warred' with the pill he had given me to overcome the sore throat. He gave me another dose and told me not to take any more anti-malaria pills for a day or so. By this time the throat had cleared and normality was restored, except for one extraordinary and inexplicable change – I had no desire at all to smoke, it had gone completely! I had been smoking about two packets of 20 *Bicycle,* the cheap and rough local cigarettes, every day. To this day, the desire has never returned and, if I have to, I can be with others who are smoking without being tempted at all. I now look out for non-smoking areas only because I realise how unpleasant the habit is. I sometimes wonder if my ghastly sore throat experience could be marketed to help others who find so much difficulty over trying to kick the habit!

Again, and I am sure unrelated, it was at Zaria that I found I could do without alcohol, especially whisky, but, in fact, all alcohol drinks. I never checked, but I believe that all such drinks were forbidden by law in Nigeria, particularly in the Muslim dominated North, and that the multi-shops etc. were breaking the law by selling them openly on their shelves. Certainly, the reputable brands of imported whisky could be purchased at low prices compared with the UK, as could many wines. The Civil War curtailed supplies of imported spirits etc. and it was difficult to get hold of, but I knew I could obtain it through the Officers' Mess at the Barracks. I had been informed of this during one of my rare visits to the Officers' Mess, but thought it unwise to take advantage of the privilege. The nearest international boundary was that with Niger, and I was introduced to a trader who went regularly over the border for his own 'business' and was quite prepared to bring in whisky for me at £15 a bottle – quite exorbitant, of course. I used the trader for a short time but it was too costly to continue, and I settled for a glass or two of wine in the evenings, which was still available locally. Then, like the smoking, I found I wanted neither and, on the few occasions when I had to go to drinks parties, I found no difficulty in asking for orange or apple juice!

There were two climate changes for me to adjust to in Zaria: firstly there was a long dry season and a short wet season. During the former the heat was greater but drier, which I found easier to cope with when outside working. For a day's exposure to the sun, bridge building, road maintenance and so on, I wore a floppy hat to protect the back of my neck. I always carried a large thermos of water with me but experience had shown that it was best to put off taking a drink of water for as long as possible – even all day – because once having started one had to continue. So I resisted until I reached home where Hassan would immediately produce a large pot of tea with extra hot water and I would drink mug after mug until I felt ready for a bath to remove all the day's dust and sweat. I never asked whether this was the right approach to avoiding dehydration but not once did I experience it.

Secondly there was the Harmattan wind, the 'mistral' of the Tropics, a very cold and dusty wind of the evenings in the dry season. The drop in temperature was quite dramatic and equally in the morning as the sun rose so did the heat; I then understood why the living room of my house had a fireplace, iron grate, mantelpiece and all – no doubt one of the 'improvements' added by an expatriate predecessor. Hassan would judge conditions so that some nights, when I returned from my late working at the office, there was a log fire burning in the grate and the room was cosily warm! Then I would sit by the fire enjoying the large bowl of mixed fruits – jungle pudding as I called it – which Hassan had left for me in the refrigerator.

Zaria remains special in my memories, both for the Mission Hospital and for the walks I was able to enjoy each evening as the sun began to set, casting a warm glow over the surrounding hills.

Kaduna Division

I returned from leave on 29th July 1970 with mixed feelings, knowing that I would be taking over as Divisional Engineer Kaduna. I was not keen to be so close to MOW Headquarters, which I regarded as a place to be avoided. Zaria, 50 miles away, was also comparatively close by, but at least my visits there would be at my choosing.

I would be taking over from Mr Lloyd Hooper who had stood in earlier as Chief Civil Engineer while Mr Ian Nowell had proceeded on leave. So far as I was concerned, this posting was just normal procedure, the start of a tour of duty at a new Station for the appropriate period – I had no reason to think otherwise.

I had some general idea of the duties and responsibilities of the Divisional Engineer, picked up during visits from Zaria. An important one was Kaduna Waterworks, naturally much larger than those in the Provinces yet water treatment by use of chemicals was not greatly different anywhere. The Senior Water Engineer at Headquarters, Mr A. Cheema, had recently been promoted following the retirement of Mr Bill Calder, Chief Water Engineer of long standing. There had been some minor differences with Mr Cheema over allocations of annual running and maintenance costs for Provincial schemes, particularly for the new ones settling down as local demand inevitably increased. These I had to refer to Mr Calder for review. Now that Mr Cheema was in charge I had to be watchful.

My contacts with Lloyd and Mrs Hooper had been largely at social occasions where attendance was almost compulsory. Lloyd was tall, well over 6ft, and his large body seemed to sag loosely on its frame. His face was pale and he spoke so softly that he was known as the 'Whispering Giant'. By contrast, Mrs Hooper was short and stockily built with a sallow complexion. She spoke in a strident voice, clearly determined to have her way. There were three children – all boys, I think – at boarding schools in England where she would spend regular periods during tours.

My office was on the upper floor of a square building at the Divisional Headquarters. On the first day of taking over I arrived at my office at about 8.00am. To my surprise, seated round three sides of the large square room were robed Nigerians who rose as I entered. From my side of the desk I asked why they were present. One explained that they came every day to wait for Mr Hooper to give out contracts. They had assumed that I would continue this practice while he was away. Tersely, I asked them to leave – I would deal with contracts in my own way – and the morning assembly was not repeated. Within a few days, I was writing to my brother a letter dated 2nd August 1970 from which I give the following extracts:

> "Here I can only see the shambles I have come to expect wherever I find myself taking over, so I will be busy. In any case, it is better to be fully occupied, as this will give me an excuse to keep out of the vapid social life which prevails in Kaduna, being a large Headquarters and commercial centre. I gather corruption at all levels is now blatant and rife, and little or nothing is done to check it or even locate it.

> "The oil business further south is on the boom and more and more concessions are being granted particularly for off-shore exploitation. If you do make Lagos you can fly on afterwards direct to Kaduna and stay for a time with me, and I can then take you on to Kano for your return."

Apparently, there had been some suggestion within the *BBC* that the TV programme *The Question Why*, which Malcolm led, might embark upon overseas visits, and Lagos had been considered but nothing came of it. Also, that he might go to Yaounde (Cameroon) to interview a Roman Catholic Bishop in charge of a Leprosarium near there, who was in some conflict with the Pope – that is how I understood the situation but, again, nothing came of that either.

I had yet to introduce myself to the Administrator of Kaduna, Mallam Magaji Mohammed in control of the Native Authority with responsibility for Kaduna Township, its roads, services and so on. There seemed to be a rather loose understanding, particularly regarding amenity matters within the Township generally. Already during my first quick tour of the Township, including the Central Market, I had come across great heaps of refuse completely blocking some Township roads. Clearly, because of the lack of any system of collection and disposal, over the years these foul-smelling dumps of assorted refuse had become well established. Open-sided drains were also blocked with rubbish, no doubt causing flooding during heavy rains. After talks with the Administrator I offered to take early action to clear these great heaps and prevent their continuation by providing suitable containers for refuse disposal. There was always a plentiful supply of empty oil and bitumen drums in depots etc. and these could be placed on the roadside in the business and residential areas and in the surrounds of the Central Market.

Sidi Ali, a loyal and trusted Foreman, came to join me at Kaduna bringing his large family with him. He soon settled down in Kaduna and together we tackled the problem of the refuse heaps, operating on mutual trust. The refuse had to be loaded either manually or with small mechanical shovels into tipper lorries and taken for disposal at 'borrow pits' sited along the roads leading out of Kaduna. 'Borrow pits' are where laterite has been dug out for the purposes of maintaining dirt roads and the verges of black-topped surfaces. These pits are quite a feature along northern roads and can be seen in the bush a short distance from the roads. Not all laterite, however, is suitable and, after it has been spread, clay or earth is sometimes used to bind the rock granules together when watered and rolled.

I mentioned to Sidi Ali about the contractors who had waited on me on my first day in the office, but told him he was to make his own enquiries regarding contractors as well. The contract was to be at an inclusive price for loading the tipper and dumping in the selected pits. At the heap being cleared there should be a 'checker' (on MOW pay roll) who must ensure that each tipper was full before being allowed to drive off to the pits, the number of trips being recorded. At the pits there must also be a checker taking the name of the contractor and the number of trips etc., so records at each place should tally. Within a few weeks all the heaps and the side drains in the Township had been cleared, and the replacement drums were being emptied regularly by MOW tippers. Later, the scheme for drums in the business and residential areas was set up, including disposal at the pits, and the large heaps did not reappear.

The local press had spotted the activity and gave it some prominence. No doubt it was this which led to the Secretary to the Military Government, Alhaji Garba Ja Abdul Kadir, summoning me to his office to be told that the Military Governor, Colonel Abba Kyari, wished to see me. I had met Colonel Kyari formally on a few occasions during my time at Zaria but we had only exchanged a few words. Now he expressed his appreciation of the clearance of the refuse heaps and asked me if I had any plans to develop the service on a firm basis, including the financial aspect. I had to explain that I had no specific allocation of funding at present. He said, "How much do you require?" Off the cuff, I suggested one million Nairas; he made a note and I left. Within a few days I received an allocation of the one million! Now I was fully committed and a regular refuse collection and disposal service was established using contractors, and each day I made a point of visiting a different area to check up on them.

My understanding with Sidi Ali was simple: I did not interfere with his selection of contractors but all rates must be agreed with me. He was fully aware of the standard below which both he and the contractor would be in trouble with me - the contract would be terminated without paying the contractor who would certainly be struck off the list. I accepted, of course, that Sidi's large family would be looked after: chickens, other food stuffs and perhaps some clothing would be passed to them, but no money. Though unorthodox and risky, this meant I was able to free myself from any attempt at bribery, (which, in any case, would have been rejected) and yet retain control over the contractors engaged and the work done.

Kaduna Central Market was a vital element in the social and economic life of Kaduna and the focal point for a large surrounding area. However, the access roads were hopelessly congested with 'overflow' traders from the

Market and it was impossible to carry out any effective maintenance. I made regular visits to the area which, like all markets had its fascination despite the appalling conditions: it was a maze of narrow muddy walk-ways between the rickety stalls with no drainage or amenities such as vehicle parks or water supply etc. etc. However, many thousands of people used it every day and it was still the best place to buy cheap imported cotton shirts and shorts, so long as one could stand the smell and the mud! At this stage I had no inkling of what lay ahead for me in regard to the Kaduna Central Market.

What did concern me was the Waterworks which, like those in the Provinces, needed chemicals for water treatment. These, I expected would be supplied on indent from the bulk store purchased by Headquarters as in the Provinces. But according to a written directive from the Chief Water Engineer, Mr Cheema, the Kaduna Waterworks should purchase its requirements direct from the local supplier. Payment was to be made from the annual funds allocated for running costs, general maintenance, wages and so on, yet I could see no specific sub-heading for chemicals. According to my calculations the sum required would seriously affect the amount allocated for wages, fuel and other equally vital running costs. The situation had to be faced at once.

I wrote to the Chief Water Engineer explaining that it was my duty and responsibility to ensure that the water supply served to the large population in and around Kaduna was of the required quality at all times, and that, should it appear that this was likely to be adversely affected because of his recent directive regarding chemicals for treatment, I would not hesitate to overspend and inform him accordingly. I believe in my letter I used the words: "One cannot half-run a Waterworks." There was no reply to my letter.

Then, just before Christmas 1970, I became embroiled in a real clash over water supply. A problem was brought to my notice by the Officer in charge of maintenance at Kaduna Airport. He explained that he himself lived in a house within the boundary of the Airport, but his staff, technicians, porters etc., with their families were housed in a large block of flats on the road leading to the Airport, rented out by the Federal Government in Lagos from the owners, the State Government.

Apparently, the Federal Aviation Department at Lagos were years behind with payment of the annual rent for the building and the State Government had decided to take some punitive action by turning off the water supply to the building. The Officer believed the action had been instigated by the Chief Water Engineer on his own initiative, or perhaps under direction by the MOW Permanent Secretary, Mallam Armiyau. There was now great concern amongst his maintenance staff, their wives and children at the lack of water, particularly as Christmas was only a day or so away. The occupants felt they were being victimised for something which was not their responsibility, as they did not pay the rent. Naturally, I saw the unfairness of the action and said that I would deal with it at once. The termination of the supply had been taken without reference to me as the Divisional Engineer, the Officer in charge of Waterworks.

First I went to the building to find one of the turnkey staff of the Water Department on guard at the valve chamber to prevent interference with the valve. I told him to tell his Foreman to come to my office before the day was over. When the Foreman came he was told to be at the building at 7.00am the next day with the key to the valve to carry out my instruction, as Divisional Engineer, to turn on the supply. Meanwhile, I wrote a letter to the Permanent Secretary MOW. I explained the action I was taking in the interests of the occupants of the building, and that, as this meant I was countermanding an instruction which I assumed had been given by him, I was now submitting my resignation from MOW with immediate effect.

I met the Foreman at 7.00am the following morning and saw to the resumption of supply to the great joy of the assembled wives and children. The Foreman was to place a guard at the valve chamber and to inform me at once if there was any difficulty.

Later that day, I was summoned to the Commissioner of Works Alhaji Nuhu Bamalli at Headquarters. I had met him a number of times and liked his direct manner. He was alone in his office and he came to the point at once. He said he understood from the Permanent Secretary that I had submitted my resignation from the Ministry with immediate effect and he wished to hear from me how this had arisen. I explained the circumstances and that, as I regarded the action taken as wholly unfair to the occupants of the building, I had exercised my position as the

Divisional Engineer to order the restoration of the supply, thus countermanding the directive to turn off the supply which appeared to have originated with the Permanent Secretary. Accordingly, I had no alternative but to tender my resignation from the Ministry. Without hesitation he said he supported my action. I was equally direct and said that, of course, I would now withdraw my resignation – it was all over in about 15 minutes. I went to the building to check that the water was still running, sent the guard off and told the tenants that all was now well – Happy Christmas! I was pleased at the outcome but realised that it would be added to the creeping character assassination.

The next matter that concerned me was the traffic in Kaduna, increasing by at least 10% annually causing congestion of roads in the core of the business and commercial area of the Capital. This comprised banks, Commissions, the library and Post Office, and some early residential parts, within a layout of narrow black-topped roads with inadequate drainage. However, some foresight had been taken in planning to set back the buildings, leaving deep verges on both sides of the roads on which two rows of trees had been planted which were now fully established and providing much-needed shade. Nonetheless, the front row on each side was restricting the passage of two-way traffic. Inspection showed that the removal of the front row of trees on each side would enable the road to be widened, while still leaving the second row of trees to continue to provide shade and amenity. These roads were in the care of Division but out of courtesy the Administrator needed to be informed. It was not long before 'Candido' was on the attack in the *New Nigerian* of 31st March 1971:

> "Please, Administrator, please…
> "I have tried to contain my anguish about the fate of trees in the Kaduna Capital Territory. Some axe-wielding butcher has done a great deal of felling of our precious trees. I am sure no-one meant harm but in many cases that was the result achieved all the same. Lucky fellow, the mania for ecology that has gripped some parts of the world has not yet reached this country! Mind you, I am not saying anything about the deforestation of Kaduna because I think the Administrator means to explain the situation to concerned citizens eventually... Please, Administrator, please."

I, of course, was the 'axe-wielding butcher'.

The so-called butchery also came to the notice of the well-known Architect and Town Planner, Max Lock who in 1965 had been commissioned by the Federal Government to town plan Kaduna and some other Provincial Capitals, and had continued to be involved with the work thereafter. He complained bitterly about the removal of the trees, saying that it violated his Town Plan for Kaduna which had laid down that some roads should be closed to traffic. I believe I met him briefly on the evening he visited Kaduna to give a piano recital before an invited audience at a hotel. If so, I am sure I would have explained that, since his plan in 1965, traffic in Kaduna had substantially increased and action had to be taken to relieve congestion in 1970/71. (Max Lock died in 1988, aged 78, the *Daily Telegraph* obituary ended with the words: "His day was incomplete without a spell at the piano.")

I can only say that the press and the public generally favoured the action taken to remove the trees. But it was now March 1971 and I would be 62 in August. I began to think of leave, and this time I was seriously considering not returning. I was uneasy at Division and was aware that character assassination was being nurtured against me using the incidents of the alleged 'overspending' and the water supply to the Federal staff building. Lloyd Hooper had returned from leave, no doubt confidently expecting to resume at Division – his 'rightful preserve' – which I continued to occupy. Maybe there was some attempt to unseat me by bringing the 'overspending issue' to the ear of the Acting Permanent Secretary, who happened to be Mr W.A.W. Wilson (substantive Chief Mechanical Engineer). When he looked into this matter he found no over-spending had actually taken place. I was grateful for his understanding and support for the action which I was prepared to take to ensure there would be no interruption in water supply to the public.

As the year progressed, the time came when I decided to apply for leave in July 1971 (having by then completed a tour of twelve months), indicating that I would not be returning. This must have come to the notice of the Secretary to the Military Government, Alhaji Garba Ja Abdul Kadir because he asked to see me. He rather pooh-poohed my mention of character assassination and expressed the concern of the Military

Governor and himself at my decision not to return. He said they had already earmarked me for the post of Chief Engineer to the Kaduna Capital Development Board (KCDB) to be set up as from 1st January 1972, with the specific objective of speeding up the carrying out of development projects urgently needed in Kaduna and a surrounding area to be designated in the edict establishing the Board. I was taken completely by surprise and asked for 24 hours to consider the proposal, to which the Secretary agreed, and before I left him he outlined the Board's specific functions and considerable powers.

By the morning I had decided to accept, for several reasons: I would be leaving the Ministry of Works to be employed by the Board, so operational constraints would be lessened since the Board would be provided with its own funds by Government and, most vitally, would have powers to borrow money from banks etc., (under Government guarantee) to finance development projects which it would decide upon and implement. For me this appointment presented an exciting challenge both personally and professionally. Also I felt that the offer was an acknowledgement – though never sought or expected – of my years of Public Service since 1958, and in this new role I would have a grand opportunity to continue and, perhaps, enhance this service.

I returned from leave on 5th November 1971 refreshed and keen to face a new beginning with the Board as its Chief Engineer, the first task being to set up its Engineering and Works Division.

Kaduna Capital Development Board

Returning to Kaduna on 5th November 1971 I found that, during my leave period, a Secretary to head Kaduna Capital Development Board had been appointed. Office accommodation, including a Board Room, had also been rented above the Mercedes premises in the centre of the commercial area, and a Board Chairman had been appointed. The Secretary was Mr Freddie Sheridan, previously in Administration in Uganda at the time of Idi Amin, and the Chairman, Alhaji A.B. Dikko, was a respected local dignitary. The Members of the Board, about 12-15 strong, would be drawn from local interests, including the Administrator of Kaduna and the Chief Civil Engineer of the Ministry of Works. An Assistant Secretary and several staff had been brought in from Government Departments. The Secretary had secured some finance from the Ministry of Finance and opened a bank account for the Board.

An office had been reserved for me but, as yet, no technical staff. The edict formally establishing the Board with effect from 1st January 1972 had yet to be promulgated by the State Government. I discussed with Mr Sheridan the setting up of the Board's Engineering Division under me as Chief Engineer, and its duties and responsibilities. These would include the maintenance and improvement of roads within the Capital Territory and, of course, the implementation of development projects directed by the State Government and others initiated by the Board itself. I was aware that a new Central Market for Kaduna would be first priority and had decided to devote time to investigating the site and the role of the Market in the life of the community. I discovered it was much more than a 'shop', as it served an area much larger than Kaduna Township. A great deal of trading of various kinds took place there.

For road maintenance a works Depot with plant, lorries, mechanics etc., would be required. This would have to be sited in the industrial area known as Kaduna South; Kaduna North was predominantly a residential area containing the Capital School, Colleges and general amenities, while in the heart of the Capital were the Parliament building, the House of Chiefs, Ministers Houses, High Commissions, top class hotels, Clubs, the Race Course, all of which had once been 'Colonial' and now were 'Government'.

Driving around the industrial area in search of a Road Maintenance Depot, I came across an ideal site. The international Firm of *Greenhams Plant Hire* were closing down their branch in Kaduna through lack of worthwhile business. With the developing economy, Ministry of Works and prospering indigenous contractors were in a better position to purchase road-graders, rollers, bulldozers etc. outright, or on short-term hire purchase, from stocks being imported by the manufacturers of such plant in Europe or the USA. The Depot consisted of a brick-built administrative block, a well-equipped mechanical workshop, a spacious parking area, security fencing and gates, lighting, power and water supply. All this belonged to the Firm and was up for sale, the site being held on a Certificate of Occupancy which could be transferred to the Board without difficulty.

I was in discussion with *Greenhams* about those of the office and mechanical staff who wished to transfer to the Board – not all were Northerners but that could be overcome in the circumstances – when, in mid-December 1971 (I had only been effectively with the Board for about six weeks) I was told by Freddie Sheridan that the Secretary to the State Military Government, Alhaji Garba Ja Abdul Kadir, wanted to see me. As he gave me the message I thought there was an amused gleam in his eyes. What had occasioned this I was about to learn. As an aside, I would record that Sheridan and I were getting along very well, and he had given me a free hand.

This would be my second 'summons' to Alhaji Garba Ja, who spoke perfect English and was absolutely charming. Being over 6ft and of sparse build he was, I am sure, of Fulani origin. Welcoming me back from leave and to the post with KCDB I heard why he had called for me.

Jack's house in North Kaduna

Jack in his office at KCDB with clerical staff

During the official visit of the Head of State, General Yakubu Gowon, to North Central State from 6th-14th December which had just concluded, he had revealed to the State Military Governor and the Secretary that his Imperial Majesty Haile Selassie, Emperor of Ethiopia was shortly to make a State Visit to Nigeria, part of which would take place in Kaduna on 20th and 21st January 1972. The highlight was to be a Durbar at the Race Course. Already four of the Northern States – North Western, North Central, Kano, and North Eastern – had been informed that each was to provide 500 horses with riders, grooms etc. This made a total of 2,000 for the Durbar which would be programmed for two hours during the morning of Thursday 20th January 1972. The other two Northern States, Kwara and Benue Plateau, would be giving a display of traditional dancing during the afternoon at Ahmadu Bellow Stadium.

My instructions were to prepare a Camp for the horse contingents totalling 2,000, with accommodation for riders, grooms, other support personnel and the necessary amenities. The contingents would be expected to arrive in Kaduna not later than 15th January to allow for settling down and rehearsals on the Race Course. He had already spoken to Mr Sheridan about the assignment as I would need to be fully engaged on it for the next month – would I not indeed!

Durbars, displays of horsemanship which had originated in India, were a feature of North Nigeria. I had been present at one or two small ones during my tours in the Provinces but to have to prepare for one involving 2,000 horses was really beyond my comprehension – and worse was to come. I had to ask Alhaji Garba Ja to give me 48 hours to make enquiries, inspect possible sites, attempt to assess expenditure and put together at least a tentative plan of action to submit to him. Of course, it was quite impossible for me to refuse the instruction but it certainly took me into wholly unfamiliar activity and responsibility – a challenge too far perhaps?

The time available was only four weeks as it was now 16th December 1971. The Camp must be finished and ready for the incoming contingents by not later than 12th January 1972 in case any contingent arrived early. Clearly, time off over Christmas and the New Year were out as far as I was concerned, and others whom I must induce to help. All I knew about horses was that they were beautiful animals which took part in hunts and ran races at Race Courses and now Durbars. How much space would 2,000 horses and their contingents require while preparing for the Durbar? Somehow I recalled the Chief Veterinary Officer at Minna at the Federal Elections at Minna in 1964, and found out that, by sheer luck, he was now at his Department's Headquarters at Kaduna! When I told him about my involvement with the Durbar he was most helpful and kindness itself.

He explained how horses tethered in the open for long periods without proper exercise could become restless and bad tempered and might bite at each other if too close together. Therefore the radius of the tether must keep them away from other horses. He sketched out how rows of tether posts about 20 feet apart should be staggered to achieve this. It was obvious that a very large open area would be needed for 2,000 horses and this was the next search for me. The Race Course itself had to be ruled out as this must be available for the horses to muster for the presentation for the Durbar. Any open space in the industrial area of Kaduna South would be too far from the Race Course and, in any case, the restricted access and traffic conditions would impede the movement of the horses to and from the Race Course for rehearsals and on the Day. Kaduna North, which was developing fast as a residential area with Colleges and the Capital School etc. was certainly more hopeful. Just beyond the newest development I found there was plenty of open, more or less level land stretching into the distance, which could be cleared of scrub. Nearby was a large four-storey building under construction. The roof was on but the openings for windows and doors had yet to be provided with frames etc. I found a watchman on the site who was able to tell me that it was a new College building but work had been halted for the time being. I decided to try to take it over just as it was for the period of the Durbar, and the windows and doors would have to be 'closed' with matting as the nights were cold in December.

By now the 48 hours had expired and I must see Alhaji Garba Ja. I had noted other items – access roads within the Camp, lighting, water supply, rows of rumfas for the grooms near the tethered horse lines etc. etc. – and I decided to mention my 'guesstimate' figure of N200,000. Now the Government was committed – and so was I – to putting on the Durbar, and I must be in a position to meet any contingencies which were sure to arise. I outlined to Alhaji Garba Ja what I had been doing and thinking since I saw him, adding that, of course, I accepted his directive but I had to express one condition. This was that I should not be beholden to any Committee which he might be setting up for the Durbar and if I was to succeed in the time already desperately short I must be trusted and given an absolutely free hand. He told me he had asked one Member of the Executive Council with a small group to be responsible for administrative matters, protocol, programmes, seating at the Race Course and so on, but the Camp, the participants etc., were for me. He suggested I make a courtesy call on the Member and his group in case any common matter arose. I mentioned the building under construction which I intended to take over for the duration which might give rise to some compensation to the contractor for any damage done, and possibly halt the work for a few weeks, also that I would be using as much as was necessary of the vacant land beyond the building, which I assumed was 'free' and unallocated, for the tethering of the horses and the shelters for the grooms etc., and all would be cleared up afterwards. Finally, I explained that, while I could give no exact figures of likely expenditure, I had in mind N200,000 but I could not be tied to that amount. In the main, I would be engaging contractors telling them that they would be paid after the Durbar. I would submit full details to him so that he could make arrangements for payment as the Board was not viable as yet. I left having secured his full agreement to my proposals.

I knew I had no time to waste. But then came the shock from Kano. I had not known this at the time, but a great rivalry existed between the Emir of Kano and the Shehu of Bornu (North East State) regarding horse displays at national Durbars staged for visiting Royalty, Heads of State and the like. Kano regarded itself as the 'premier' provider of horses for such 'top' occasions, and Bornu, headed by the Shehu, would challenge this claim. Now, apparently, Kano had calmly announced that it would be bringing 1,000, not 500, horses which had immediately led Bornu to raise its contingent to 1,000, and soon the other two States followed – a total of 4,000 horses! For me the outcome was that more or less everything I had been planning had to be doubled: the land for tethering, the shelter for grooms, supply of fodder etc. etc. There was some solace in that I had mentioned the figure of N200,000 but now it could well be exceeded.

I was thankful that the mustering of the horses and the Durbar itself, with all its ceremonial, was not my responsibility – this was for other hands. I did wonder how 4,000 horses dressed 'overall' with their riders could muster on the Race Course and still leave the considerable open area required for the Durbar Ceremony proper. I had to ensure that the 4,000 horses would leave the Camp in good order in the early hours of Thursday 20th January to muster at the Race Course not later than 9.00am to start the Durbar by 10.50am. Fortunately, the road route of about two miles from the Camp was mostly through the residential area of Kaduna North which would be closed to traffic as necessary with the co-operation of the police. In any case, the route would be tested for the two rehearsals which would take place, the first with no regalia, the second with riders and horses dressed overall. The rehearsals would take place during daylight hours but on the day itself the Camp would have to be alerted from 5.00am onwards for everyone to be ready, fully decorated, for the move off; a point I had to bear in mind when setting up the full-scale lighting system for the whole Camp.

By now I think I have described enough to indicate the many aspects which evolved as the Camp progressed. By 12th January when the first contingent reached the Camp (having arrived in a number of goods trains), the Camp was ready with access roads, water supply, all-over lighting, rumfas for the grooms, the building converted into a 'dormitory' for riders and followers, some of whom might, however, put up with relatives or friends around Kaduna. As the Camp developed, I had realised the need for other facilities, such as food stores, canteens, Police Posts and parking areas as thousands would be there for a week or more. Watering for the horses was greatly eased when I was told of a 'lake', probably an old gravel or laterite pit, only a short distance from the horse lines. Taking them there would also provide exercise helping to reduce restlessness.

By 15th January the other three contingents had arrived, some by transporters and some trekking by road having left a week or so earlier. I was given wonderful co-operation by MOW and others: for example, I just took the electricians round the whole Camp pointing out where I wanted lighting particularly for the horse lines to help the grooms in caring for the animals at all times. Someone said that about a million light bulbs and miles of cable were used. Certainly, seen from Kaduna about three miles away, the Camp looked like a Gin Palace at night and before the Durbar it became the nightly outing for many car-loads of people to drive round and see the sights. Impromptu native dancing and music and parties were held, giving the whole affair an air of fiesta. Although the lighting was connected to the mains supply, I made sure of generators in case of breakdown and some electricians were on standby during the night. The police might have had to deal with one or two tribal incidents but they were not serious.

I was at the Camp every day and later up to 9.00 or 10.00pm as things quietened down. Parties of expatriates with their wives and children also joined in the evening outings, and the press came to see and write it up for the newspapers. Then on the day of the Durbar I was there by 4.00am to make sure that the contingents of horses and riders, all dressed overall, left in good order for the Race Course.

The previous evening Alhaji Garba Ja had turned up, so far as I knew for the first time, and from his reaction I could see he had not realised what was involved in creating the Camp – neither had I until I started on it! He was really impressed and intrigued, and asked if I would be attending the Reception at State House in the evening of Durbar Day. I said I had not received an invitation, and one reached me in time.

After the stressful days of preparation, I was determined to take my seat in the Grandstand, so after all the contingents had left I made my way to the Race Course. According to the programme the Emperor was to arrive at 10.15am. At 10.20am the Military Governor of North Central State, Colonel Abba Kyari, would make a speech, at 10.25am the Durbar would start, finishing at 12.40pm for the Emperor's speech, which allowed just over two hours for the Durbar. Finally, at 12.50pm the Emperor accompanied by the Head of State, General Yakubu Gowon, would leave for a private lunch at Government Lodge.

During touring over the years, I had on several occasions happened to be staying in a bush Rest House near a town – Kontagora for example – when a local Durbar was due to take place on a convenient open space to mark some traditional day or occasion, and I would be invited to be present. Thus I was aware of the ritual to be followed: Town dignitaries, guests etc. would be seated at one end of the ground while the horsemen – perhaps 50 to 100 dressed in their regalia and holding their long spears – would muster at the other end. As for time, the programme could be short or long: a long one might comprise speeches (which I would not really understand) followed by displays of prowess by individual riders, including some of a comic nature, culminating in the grand 'charge'. I shall never forget the first time I witnessed this: I was seated in the front row alongside the local Chief or Headman with other guests. The horsemen with their spears were arranged in a single line at the other end. At the given signal they set off at once, spurring on their horses to full speed (maybe 30mph) shouting and waving their spears, towards the other end perhaps 100 yards or so away where we were sitting. On they came, still at full charge and greatly excited, to within five yards or so of the front row, when they reined in their horses which reared up on their hind legs and came to a full stop. On the first occasion, I instinctively half rose from my chair in fright. The next time, although I kept my seat, I was still mentally prepared to flee!

Now, on the Race Course it would not be so dramatic as we would be in the Grandstand well protected if anything should go wrong. First, there was a procession of the four contingents past the Grandstand. Then in turn, selected horsemen from the Kano contingent gave a display of their particular prowess culminating in the traditional charge by 40-50 horsemen representative of the contingent. Allowing for the time taken for the procession, no contingent could be allowed more than 25-30 minutes for its presentation. After Kano came the presentation by North Central State followed by that of North Western each keeping closely to the time allowed, and to finish, that from North East State. When their individual riders began their ritual others joined them and developed variations which showed no sign of coming to an end. By now, the Durbar should have ended and the Emperor should have made his speech,

173

but the display continued and the charge had still to take place. I could see consternation on the faces of those sitting near the Emperor. At last the charge took place and the Emperor gave his speech, but the end was a good hour late! Apparently, the Shehu of Bornu had instructed his contingent to ignore the organisers and give his State's full Durbar ritual – strong man indeed!

Dog-tired as I was, I was determined to go to the Reception at State House timed from 7.00-8.30pm. The Emperor, seated on a sort of throne, had the Head of State on one side and the State Military Governor on the other. Other VIPs were standing around or mixing and talking. It was a packed assembly, with everyone in magnificent multi-coloured robes, the all-pervading odour of unwashed sweat blending with overpowering eastern perfumes to produce 'bouquet d'Afrique' (an expatriate phrase!). The whole spectacle, enough to make one blink, was what the Western press would describe as "…a glittering occasion".

I felt a little conspicuous in my black suit and tie and very hot, although I had managed a bath. I got as close as I could to the Emperor who at 81 was small and frail. Born in 1891 he was crowned in 1930 and, after the Italian conquest of Abyssinia from 1935-1936, he had settled in England. After the liberation by British forces he was restored to his throne in 1941 and he played a crucial part in the early 1960s in founding the Organisation of African Unity (OAU). However, opposition to his reign had existed since 1960.

(Soon after this State Visit to Nigeria, in 1973 there was a terrible famine in Ethiopia which led to economic chaos, industrial strikes and mutiny amongst the Armed Forces, and eventually to his overthrow in 1974 in favour of the Crown Prince, but the monarchy was abolished. He died in 1975 in unexplained circumstances. (Adapted from *Chambers Biographical Dictionary*))

At the Reception several people spoke appreciatively about the Camp, having visited it in the evening when it was all lit up. I did not stay very long before returning to the Camp which was really '*en fête*' with riotous parties, music, dancing and obviously much drinking! There were one or two affrays but the police kept control.

The next day, it would have been midday before I was able to get to the Camp.. Astonishingly, it was almost empty! I was told the exodus had begun at first light. Contractors were already there to remove the rumfas and other temporary structures, the matting at the building etc., and I had told them they could take away all materials used in lieu of being paid for clearing up to which they had agreed. Payments for work done had been agreed at the time of allocation of contracts, and on the understanding that they would not be paid until after the Durbar. The building had received minor damage, due to a few fires which had been lit inside, and we agreed a small amount of compensation with the building contractor. I was agreeably surprised when he then admitted that work on the building had been halted because of the failure of the supplier of the door and window frames etc., to deliver them to the site in the agreed time, so the carpenters and labourers had been stood off. Consequently he would not be claiming any compensation for interruption to the building works. The tether posts were being removed by the contractors who had supplied and put them up and the area was otherwise unaffected as the scrub would soon grow again when the rains came and prevent erosion. No-one had appeared to challenge the use made of the land, and anyway, the horses had manured it well!

I prepared my details for payments to contractors etc., most of whom I had known at Division and could be trusted. They had performed well under pressure and, I think, they thoroughly enjoyed the involvement with the Durbar where I had spotted some of them amongst the spectators. Incredibly the total cost came to a few thousand under my guesstimate of N200,000. I sent the bills to Alhaji Garba Ja for settlement, and as no-one complained to me of non-payment, I presumed all were satisfied.

The Sheridans had seen the Durbar and driven round the Camp and were very appreciative. To finish with the Durbar affair, here is an extract from a letter dated 20th December 1971 which somehow I found time to write to my brother:

"...it is likely that I will have to be flat out organising a Camp for 4,000 horses and 20,000 people for a Durbar in honour of the Emperor of Ethiopia who is due on a visit to Nigeria and may well come North for a day or so. I'll have just about

175

three weeks from scratch if it comes off. Quite absurdly little time but somehow I suppose I'll get it done. It is fantastic what one can get done in this Country once the pressure is on. Of course, one just has to lash out on expense – 'regardless' is the word – the Nigerians love that sort of thing because it means they get paid almost what they ask without any of the customary bargaining. I imagine you may have seen these Durbars in India or elsewhere. Small ones occur, of course, at the various Moslem Festivals, but for special occasions, such as this would be, they really are pretty impressive. This one could hardly be as tremendous as that for the Queen when she came here in 1956. I did not see this, of course, but I am told that it was the Durbar that beat all Durbars. All was Colonial then and I think the cost was about £2 million. Horses, Chiefs, Emirs came from far and wide with all their regalia. I've mentioned the figure of N200,000 for the one proposed. Food and fodder for the suggested number of people and horses for about ten days will cost a good amount! The Emperor seems indestructible and must be well over 70 – I can only hope he says that the trip here will be too much for him so that the idea is off..."

Now to KCDB. The edict had been promulgated from 1st January 1972 and I think a preliminary meeting of the Board had taken place. A monthly meeting of the Board was due at which Members would determine the list of projects in order of priority. First, I was sure, would be the new Kaduna Central Market, then road improvements within the Capital Territory, a comprehensive system of refuse collection and disposal, a Bus Service to cover outlying areas, improved street lighting etc. The Secretary had secured operational funds from the Government and an accountant and sundry staff had been engaged. Because of the delay I was fearful that I might have lost the *Greenhams* site, although I had seen the local Manager earlier to ask him to hold the place for the Board, explaining that I was being directed to other work and would be unable to deal with the negotiations over their Depot for some weeks. But all was well; the Manager was authorised to negotiate on the basis of

N10,000 for the premises and one or two items of plant to be agreed. Frankly, I regarded the amount as nominal for what was available, but obviously it suited the Company's plan for closure. The Secretary agreed and the Chairman gave approval pending formal authority by the Board. The Foreman and the mechanics were pleased to be employed by the Board once *Greenhams* had left – the first example of the freedom the Board enjoyed! Now, too, I could wean Sidi Ali from Division so that he could take charge of the Depot for the time being.

Under the general control of the British Council, Voluntary Service Overseas (VSO) had been initiated by the British Foreign and Commonwealth Office for sixth formers, after leaving school but before moving on to University or into trainee employment, to assist developing countries. However, their usefulness proved too limited due to their lack of worthwhile experience, so now VSO encouraged new graduates to apply for one year's service overseas before starting their chosen career.

The scheme was proving attractive to young men and women due to its mixture of opportunities for adventure and usefulness to ex-Colonial territories and the like, which were striving to improve literacy, technical know-how and so on. North Central State had agreed to take a number of these graduates and three – representing Engineering, Town Planning and Agriculture – would be based in Kaduna. Nominally they would be under the care of the British Council which would arrange their housing, perhaps a motorcycle, and payment of a modest monthly allowance with which to maintain themselves, but the Department to which they were allocated would have overall responsibility for them.

The Board accepted the Engineer and the Town Planner, and the Ministry of Agriculture accepted the Agricultural graduate. The three would share a Government house and its running costs in Kaduna. VSO had strict rules that volunteers should not involve themselves in national or local politics, though naturally they were free to take part in the general social life of the city, playing tennis, rugby, and going to the Club etc. The American equivalent of VSO was the Peace Corps, some of whom had apparently become involved in politics thinking that was part of their role, and had to be sent home.

The contrast between Peter Guthrie, the Engineering graduate, and Julian, the Town Planner, could hardly have been greater, although both were tall and long-haired. Peter was always smiling, open-minded and enthusiastic, while Julian was taciturn if not gloomy, always questioning and in conversation 'leftish'. I wondered how they would manage living in the same house! The Agricultural Graduate I only met casually, but he seemed normal, if not rather dull against the other two. I was anxious to make use of Peter as quickly as I could so I took him to the Depot, now fully with the Board, and introduced him to Sidi Ali and the Mechanical Foreman. Sidi Ali already knew what I had in mind, and returning to the office I told Peter that from the next day onwards he should go to the Depot and take charge, and I did not wish to see or hear from him for a week unless he was in dire difficulties.

Peter Guthrie (third from left) with KCDB staff and another VSO

After the week I went to the Depot and was pleased to see that he and Sidi Ali were getting along very well. We discussed a general programme of road maintenance for the Township and the business areas which would show that KCDB was already in action and Peter would develop it under guidance from Sidi Ali. The Foreman of the Mechanics was well able to deal with vehicle and plant maintenance and, in conjunction with the small office staff and the Board EQ accountant, Peter would soon learn the routine of ordering fuel and oil, paying wages and keeping a check on expenditure etc. I would check on things from time to time but for me the plan for the new Kaduna Central Market was absolute priority, and I was aiming to present a preliminary design to the next meeting of the Board. This was another case for my habit of evening and weekend working, first on site and then at the drawing board.

From my local enquiries I gathered that various attempts had been made over many years to bring about a new Central Market, and although the Ministry of Works had looked into the matter nothing had come of it. The Market probably dated back to 1912 on the present site which was squalid in the extreme, greatly overcrowded and lacking in any amenities. Additionally, stalls of very poor standard have been allowed to encroach on the roads in the immediate area, creating difficulties for traffic. It was clear to me that it would be quite impossible to produce a new Market on the site while the traders remained, so everything would have to be moved to a temporary site. As usual, I had no problem in recruiting junior technical staff from Division and MOW HQ to help me on site with measurements and levels, which I could then check against what plans existed so that I could produce a site plan sufficiently reliable for the preparation of a preliminary layout for the new Market.

The Administrator's Market office told me that rent was collected from about 2,000 traders at present, excluding those illegally located on the roads. Thus a new Market allowing proper spacing etc., should aim to provide at least 3,000 permanently constructed lock-up stalls each 10ft by 10ft with proper amenities. Consequently, I concluded that the 20 acres of the existing site would be quite inadequate. The shape of the site was roughly rectangular with a depth of roughly three times its width, the land sloping slightly. On one long boundary there was a high fence in poor condition through which could be seen an area of land much overgrown and seemingly vacant. Rough measurements showed this area to be about 10 acres which would make a significant addition to the Market area. The Administrator's office was reluctant to provide any information about this land so I had to see the Administrator himself for clarification. He, too, was obscure about the land but when I suggested that it should be absorbed into the new Market scheme I was preparing, he raised no objection. I took a chance and made a site plan of 130 acres on which to prepare the preliminary scheme. I spent two whole days in the existing Market talking to a great variety of traders, including their leaders in the specialist sections such as butchers, fishmongers etc. It emerged that, for the majority of traders selling 'dry' goods, a covered lock-up stall of 10ft by 10ft, with a front which could be opened up for business, would be appropriate. 'Wet' traders such as butchers, fishmongers, vegetable and fruit traders and so on, whose produce was brought in and sold on a daily basis would need covered counters on which to display their produce, the leftovers being removed when the Market closed for the day.

Then I considered the question of amenities, which were wholly lacking. A lorry/van parking area for 100 vehicles with adequate access to the area of the Market was essential, since no vehicles would be allowed into the Market proper except those which would be essential to the management of the Market for clearing refuse, general maintenance, fire fighting etc. As part of the parking space there should be some lock-up storage for the use of traders but under the control of the Market management. Another parking area would be designated for the use of general public in cars and on motorcycles ,as well as taxis, when visiting the Market.

Other requirements would be: a base for the management, a Police Post, a maintenance yard to include accommodation for a 24-hour fire-fighting unit with Landrover properly fitted with hoses etc., some tippers, septic tank emptier for clearing the toilets, water distribution system served from a 100,000 gallon storage tank (probably sited in a corner of the lorry park), general security lighting for the management unit, Police Post and maintenance yard, but not for the stalls or the 'wet' blocks since this would be impracticable. Virtually, the whole 30 acres would be surfaced with concrete which would prevent traders extending their stalls with

KADUNA CAPITAL DEVELOPMENT BOARD

rickety makeshift additions so noticeable at present. For the lorry and car parks the concrete would have to be substantial, but elsewhere it would be of lightly reinforced concrete on which the block stalls could be directly built. A system of open drain channels protected by iron fencing would be provided to take the heavy run-off from the 30 acres during storms. The final discharge outlet for the run-off could involve a considerable extension away from the surrounding built-up areas to a stream or even the river, and this would call for detailed examination.

I was satisfied that on the extended site plan I could lay out my preliminary design for the new Market showing a total of 5,000 stalls in blocks of varying lengths, the 'open' blocks and the amenities and put it to the Board at its next meeting. As for cost, I could only suggest a 'Guesstimate' of N3-4 million, but I did not expect any difficulty over cost at this stage since I knew that the State Government was strongly behind the Board's plans, and particularly for a new Market which would be very popular with the public.

Now to the drawing board for some long nights and a weekend, and I was ready with the layout plan and a few line drawings showing the type of stall and ancillary buildings. I showed the drawings to the Chairman and the Secretary and received their support. The Board met and after some routine business I showed my plan to the members, and I could see a look of disbelief in their faces. Before their eyes were plans for a new Central Market for Kaduna, which they had been waiting for many years. One or two expressed their great surprise and in response I just said they had given me an instruction and I had tried to carry it out, at least on paper to begin with. A general discussion took place, during which some helpful suggestions were voiced, but the plan was given general approval. However, I needed much more than this if the momentum was to be maintained, since a layout plan and a few line drawings were only a beginning and many detailed working drawings would have to be drawn up in preparation for seeking tenders for the construction of the whole project. I had no technical supporting staff and, moreover, I could not possibly give myself full-time to what would be months of preparation. This, I suggested, was the crucial moment to seek authority to engage a

Firm of Consulting Engineers to take the project through all the necessary stages to physical completion in good time.

I was aware that Brian Rogers, a Senior Engineer in the Water Division of MOW Headquarters had left some time previously and had recently been in Kaduna representing the well-known Firm of Consulting Engineers *Ward Ashcroft and Parkman* based in Liverpool UK. I knew him well and he had been to see me at Division. In 1972 there was still little or no call for competition between Consultants over engagements, since fees and charges were covered by standard Agreements established by the Association of Consulting Engineers in UK to which most Firms subscribed. Explaining the situation to the Board, I asked for and obtained its approval to engage *Ward Ashcroft and Parkman* to ensure that the New Market Project would go forward expeditiously and tenders sought for its implementation. The Government would be kept informed through the Minutes of the Board meetings.

From then onwards progress with the project went well to the stage when Bills of Quantities etc. for tender had to be prepared by the Consultants. The most important element of the work would fall into the category of Civil Engineering i.e. 30 acres of concrete, drainage, water supply, security lighting, and incidental improvements to roads leading to the Market. The construction of the stalls and ancillary buildings would, in the main, be simple block-work structures, repetitive but still substantial. The former would be organised and carried out by a major contractor, with adequate plant and finance, producing a high standard result to a strict timetable. The latter could perhaps be within the physical capacity of several of the local indigenous contractors but would also require significant finance and the time factor would be crucial. Unfortunately, it was known that indigenous contractors did take on contracts beyond their capacity to bring to completion, leading to difficulties and delays. I had been thinking about these two aspects for some time and how best to deal with them to ensure that the outcome would be a well-built Market in reasonable time, the time factor being particularly sensitive as the traders would have to be moved to a temporary site and undue delay could adversely affect their business. Also, because of the finance involved, whatever contracts the Board approved must be put to Government for sanction.

After discussion with the Consultants, who had produced the necessary working drawings based on my design, I decided to seek the Board's agreement to go to tender for all the Civil Engineering works already outlined, to be followed after their completion with a tender for the building works, the stalls, ancillary buildings etc. This process was agreed by the Board and, after I had appeared before the Executive Council, accepted by the Government.

Jack is seen showing Governor Abba Kyari (centre) the plan of the Kaduna Central Market. On the left is the Administrator M. Magaji Mohammed, and on the right of the Governor are Alhaji A.B. Dikko, Chairman of KCDB, and Alhaji Armiyau, Commissioner for finance.

From *New Nigerian* 3rd July 1973

An advertisement for tenders resulted in submissions from several established contractors including *Taylor Woodrow Ltd., Costain Ltd.* and one local indigenous contractor. Not unexpectedly, the local tender was considerably lower than any of the others. When examined by the Consultants, it was clear from his pricing of the major items of the Bills of Quantities that he had not appreciated the magnitude of, for example, the laying of 30 acres of concrete which would call for adequate plant and the continuous supply of stone aggregate, cement etc., if this alone was to be completed with expedition.

The lowest of the other tenders was that of *Costain Ltd.* at, as I recall, slightly under two N2 million. The Board accepted the recommendation of the *Costain Ltd.* tender which was put to the Executive Council and agreed. Next, a day for the traders to move from the present site was agreed with the Administrator who issued the necessary instruction. I visited the site on the afternoon of the day only to find that no movement had taken place, and decided that the police would have to be called the following day. However, the next morning I went again and to my utter astonishment the whole site was clear! A concerted move to the temporary site must have taken place during the night or in the early hours; yet another example of the unpredictability of Nigerians! *Costain Ltd.* moved on to the site and made an impressive start with clearance, levelling, setting out and general progress. Boundaries to the site were properly established so that the 8ft-high boundary wall could be implemented, including two arched entrances with ornamental gates traditional to African/Nigerian culture.

I was in constant touch with the Consultants' staff on the site settling any points which arose as the work progressed. I was very anxious for Board Members to see the scale of the work bearing in mind the second phase, namely the building of the 3,000 stalls and the ancillary works yet to come. Bills of Quantities, specifications etc. were being prepared by the Consultants for this work, so crucial to the successful conclusion of the whole Project. Although it had been advisable – in fact, strategic – for the Civil Engineering works to be carried out first and by a competent contractor I had hoped that the Board, having seen physically the outcome, could be persuaded to accept my, and the Consultants', recommendation to negotiate a contract for the building work with the contractor already on site, namely *Costain Ltd.* There was obvious merit in this arrangement since there would be continuity of work and much quicker progress towards completion. I would have to emphasise that despite the simpler character of the work I was doubtful if a local indigenous contractor had the capacity to fulfil the building contract of N1 million in the prescribed time.

Put to the Board and supported by the Chairman and the Secretary, it was agreed to negotiate with *Costain Ltd.* against the Bills of Quantities prepared by the Consultants. The resulting tender – from memory slightly under N1 million, was accepted by the Board and – let me put it delicately – seen through the Executive Council successfully after I had put the reasons for approval. From then onwards construction in all aspects went at full pace. There were some problems but they were easily settled.

The traditional arched entrance to Kaduna Market with 'Northern Knot' and 'King of the River' designs

So the first major project of KCDB, initiated on paper in March/April 1972 was officially opened by the Military Governor of North Central State, Brigadier Abba Kyari, during February 1975.

The Opening Ceremony in February 1975

Jack and members of the board meet the Governor,
Brigadier Abba Kyari

Jack showing the Brigadier and his entourage around the Market

The return of the traders, at considerably increased rents, was in the hands of the Administrator who would have to take charge from then onwards.

View of the market stalls before the traders took possession!

View of the market showing the lock-ups and drainage system

One final comment on this Project: I asked the Board to provide an amount in its annual estimates for the maintenance of the Market. "But," said the Members, "It's new." I told them that already on the first day of opening misuse of one of the toilet blocks had occurred and its drains were blocked. There would be need for daily maintenance. I had experienced the same answer in the Provinces regarding new Colleges and Hospitals: "But they're new."

With the Market Project completed and opened, I asked for and was granted, a few weeks' UK leave from 6th April to 12th May 1975 – my first break in 3½ years!

On my return, I was told that visitors to the Market were impressed and complimentary. One must have been Lt. Col. Umaru Mohammed, a senior officer based in Kaduna, whom I had met socially once or twice. His house was in the residential area of Kaduna North, not far from where two houses had been secured for the Board, one being occupied by me. On one occasion he had mentioned that the water supply to his house, one of extended housing in one of the new roads in Kaduna North, was unreliable. I had looked into this and deduced that the supply pipe in the road, originally laid for the first few houses, had been repeatedly extended as new houses were built, but by some oversight the extension for his house had been a smaller diameter pipe. Through previous connections, I was able to arrange for the situation to be rectified for which he was grateful. He showed interest in KCDB and its functions which, it will be seen, had an outcome for me.

VSO Peter Guthrie had proved a great help in pushing on with road maintenance and improvements etc., and his year going all too quickly. Sidi Ali and all the staff at the Depot pleaded hard with me to persuade him to stay. I even heard that some were in tears! But, of course, this was impossible, as he must start his career. (Our relationship which began in Nigeria has continued to this day, and he is now a Director with one of the leading Consulting Engineers in the UK. He told me once that he has never forgotten what the chance I gave him at KCDB did for his future success.)

At the Depot Peter Guthrie was followed by a Nigerian graduate, Buhari Dikke, who was well connected, drove a Ford Capri and, I believe, had a lively social life in and around Kaduna. We too were to meet again at Federal Capital Development Authority (FCDA).

Julian, the Town Planner, devoted his year to the preparation of a Town Plan which, when completed, enabled the Board to operate effectively in the future. Under the Edict, the Board was also the Town Planning Authority for its prescribed area, deriving its powers and authority from the Town and Country Planning Law which had been in existence in Nigeria since 1946 and was still extant.

A Transport Officer for the Kaduna Bus Service, Mr L.S. Webb, had been recruited for the Board and various services had been started under his direction. Amongst other projects sanctioned and implemented by the Board were eight buildings at the Kabala Housing Estate comprising four four-room units and four two-room units, with a further twelve four-room units to follow. Additionally, the comprehensive system for refuse collection and disposal in the Township and the residential areas was brought into operation, succeeding the earlier effort by Division. Earlier in July 1973, in conjunction with the Board, high-grade lighting had been provided for Ali Akilu Road, the dual carriageway developed by the Federal Government, which leads from Kaduna to the Airport. The lighting was switched on at a Ceremony when the Military Governor's little daughter pressed the button to light up.

Although I had only been away for a few weeks on leave, I sensed some of that earlier feeling of 'something has to give'. According to *Soldiers and Oil: The Political Transformation of Nigeria* edited by Keith Panter-Brick, Gowon's continued inaction, despite his firmly declared intention to appoint a new set of Federal Commissioners and to reassign the State Governors, prompted the inescapable conclusion that, short of a change of leadership at the highest level, the country would simply continue to drift in a sea of corruption. What happened is complex and not really relevant to this Memoir, but the military coup of 29th July 1975 ousted Gowon in favour of Murtala Mohammed who, in turn, was assassinated in Lagos on 11th February 1976 when the Chief of Staff, Olusegur Obasanjo took over as Head of State.

The first coup resulted in the replacement of the twelve State Governors and most of the Federal and State Commissioners. As for the Board, already Freddie Sheridan had served his contract and been replaced by Alhaji Sani Sambo, a round-faced man who was always cheerful with whom I got on well. But then came the blow, at least for me. The Chairman, Alhaji A.B. Dikko, with whom I had had throughout an excellent relationship, was replaced by the Permanent Secretary of the Ministry of Finance with whom I had failed to come to any rapport while in that capacity. I knew he had not agreed with the N1 million I had been given while at Division – although I received it so quickly! Perhaps he had raised queries, too, about the near N200,000 I had spent on the Camp for the Durbar, and then there had been the funds for the two phases of the new Central Market. It was difficult to find an explanation for his antagonism towards me which, even on his first day at the Board as Chairman, underlay our discussion. He was mistaken if he thought I was receiving any favours from contractors, Consultants, *Costain Ltd.* et al. Maybe I was too sensitive but I decided I would not stay with KCDB under his chairmanship. Also since returning from leave there had been rumblings that the Board was encroaching on the responsibilities which, by tradition, belonged to the Administrator and this had been hinted at during Board meetings. Maybe the time had come for a qualified Nigerian to become Chief Engineer to the Board. Anyway, the following paragraph appeared in the *New Nigerian* of 14th October 1975:

KCDB Chief Engineer Quits.

"The Chief Engineer of the Kaduna Capital Development Board, Mr J.R. Muggeridge, has withdrawn his services from the board with effect from 11th October this year.

"This was contained in a statement issued by the board in Kaduna at the weekend. The statement explained that a civil engineer of the board, Malam Buhari Dikko, has been appointed to act as the Chief Engineer. The contract appointment of the Transport Officer of the Kaduna Bus Service of the KCDB, Mr L.S. Webb will also expire at the end of this month. According to the statement the board has decided to appoint Malam B.B. Mohammed as the Chief Transport Officer when the present one quits."

191

But yet again, my decision to retire was changed for me! Following the changes of Military Governors, Colonel Umaru Mohammed was now Military Governor of North Western State, Sokoto, and must have seen the above paragraph in the paper because a third party approached me on his behalf. One of his immediate actions would be to set up a Development Authority for Sokoto on the lines of KCDB and he asked me not to leave the country but await an offer by letter to move to Sokoto. The contact pressed me hard to wait, promising no delay, and I agreed although I was, in fact, already packed to travel in a day or so. Fortunately, Brian Rogers of the Consultants kindly allowed me to stay in a small chalet the Firm had for visitors etc. In the event, I arrived in Sokoto on 21st November 1975.

I would like to record paragraph four of the letter from the Secretary to the Military Government of North Western State to the Permanent Secretary, Public Service Commission Sokoto, regarding my appointment which reads:

> "4. One point of interest is that Mr Muggeridge is 66 years old but he has confirmed – and those who know him agree – that he '…can still do a good long day's hard work, possibly more so than those younger.' In view of this we believe that his special experience and the value of his services in establishing the SUDA should make the question of age a secondary consideration."

On to another challenge. I could face it with some confidence having had the experience at KCDB, but, oh, that 66 years of age!

North Western State and
Sokoto Urban Development Authority

My service with the (then) North Western State, Sokoto, was formalised through paragraph two of the letter of 8th November 1975 to me from Alhaji Muhammadu A. Carpenter, Secretary to the Military Governor of Sokoto State, Colonel Umaru Alhaji Mohammed, which explained:

> "In view of the Government's intention to establish the Sokoto Urban Development Authority, His Excellency considered that the services of Mr Muggeridge will be most useful in setting up the Authority. I have, however, discussed the possibility of employing Mr Muggeridge with the Permanent Secretary Ministry of Works who agreed that Mr Muggeridge can be employed to fill the vacant post of Chief Civil Engineer, with a view to posting him to the Development Authority when it is constituted."

Fortunately, I already knew Alhaji Shehu Mohammed Kangiwa, Permanent Secretary Ministry of Works, from the time when he was Secretary to the Kaduna Polytechnic. Later, in 1980, he was to become Governor of Sokoto State but, tragically, his end came soon after in November 1981 when he was killed playing polo at Kaduna Race Course. There is no doubt that he had yet to make his full contribution to the well-being and progress of Nigeria.

The formalities of my appointment were soon completed and I assumed the role of Chief Civil Engineer, Ministry of Works, Sokoto on 21st November 1975, in the full knowledge that I would move to the Sokoto Urban Development Authority (SUDA) following its creation. I was given no indication as to when this would legally take place. Naturally, during this waiting period, I had to engage full-time in my responsibilities as Chief Civil Engineer Ministry of Works.

However, there was no doubt in my mind that the Military Governor, having brought me to Sokoto specifically for the proposed Development Authority, and in particular for the new Central Market, would expect me at least to give some early consideration to those matters as circumstances allowed. In fact, when I began as Chief Engineer with the KCDB in 1971, much of the conception and design work for the new Central Market for Kaduna had been done in my own time – in evenings and at weekends – so there was no difficulty in adopting this habit at Sokoto.

From initial enquiries, I became aware that earlier studies to replace the existing Market, and its often water-logged lorry park, had been carried out by the Ministry of Works and a site in the Township was already dedicated by the Sultan of Sokoto. I visited the site, almost in the centre of the Township, and using a local map worked out that its area was in excess of 50 acres. It was entirely open, with a slight fall in one direction, and the surface was a dry, loose sand. On all its boundaries, there were a variety of buildings accessed by service roads. Later on, once the Edict setting up SUDA had been promulgated, one of these buildings solved my problem of finding a Headquarters for the Authority, a prime essential if it was to show it meant business.

I was determined to use this waiting period to advantage to put on paper an outline design for the new Market and its supporting services which I could submit to the Authority at its first meeting, whenever that became possible. For this purpose, I first prepared an enlarged scale plan of the Market Site from the local map which would be sufficient for me to prepare a preliminary layout for the site. This time I had the benefit of the valuable experience gained at Kaduna, where shortcomings, mistakes and, most importantly, omissions had inevitably come to light once the Market became fully operational.

For Sokoto, on a site this time in excess of 50 acres, compared to the 30 acres at Kaduna, it should be possible to provide upwards of 5,000 Kaduna-type stalls together with lorry and car parks and a range of ancillary buildings and facilities. With time seemingly in hand, however, it seemed wise to undertake site checking of my enlarged plan, so that at least the depth, length and falls on the site should be determined with some degree of accuracy.

As Chief Civil Engineer, I had ready access to surveying and levelling equipment, a drawing board etc. I asked several of the junior technical staff in the Department whether they were prepared to work with me on site for one or two weekends to take measurements and levels. They agreed; grateful, I felt sure, for the extra money which I paid out myself. The outcome was a plan on which I was able to develop my initial concept to a final design to provide the facilities mentioned above for eventual presentation to the Authority for approval.

The day came, 1st July 1976, when Edict No.10 was promulgated setting up Sokoto Urban Development Authority (SUDA). The Edict was similar to that which had established Kaduna Capital Development Board (KCDB) in 1971. The Authority would select members representing local interests, the Native Authority, relevant Ministries and a Chairman, all to be appointed by the State Military Governor. Its financial resources would be provided by the Government but, most importantly, it would be able to borrow from banks for its capital projects under Government guarantee. In addition, the Authority would be the Town Planning Authority under the existing Town and Country Planning Law for its prescribed area.

I was now called to a meeting at the office of the Military Governor at Government House to be told that, as from 12th July 1976, I should assume the post of General Manager and Chief Executive of SUDA and proceed as quickly as possible to set up the Authority. In fact, as at Kaduna, the Edict provided for its Head to be 'Secretary' so an amendment to the Edict had to be quickly tabled and approved. This amendment of title was important to me to ensure that the holder controlled the administrative structure, being responsible for implementing policies as determined by the Authority.

One fear I did have – which, thankfully proved groundless – was that suddenly, without warning, a collection of administrative, financial and other staff would be sent to me by well meaning Government Departments before I had even been able to locate and secure suitable premises for the Authority. My aim had always been to set up the Authority from scratch, creating an administration gradually, properly framed to fit the emerging requirements.

Now I could return to the location of the new Market and the range of buildings on its boundaries. My eye settled on one unoccupied bungalow-type building fronting a well-made-up road, behind which there were other buildings resembling workshops, and an open area on which were parked a number of vehicles and items of mechanical plant. I was reminded of what I had come across in the industrial area of Kaduna South when looking for suitable premises for the Works Division of KCDB in 1971.

Local enquiries led me to the administrative office in Sokoto of one of the major British Engineering Contractors in Nigeria, *Taylor Woodrow & Co.* What I had found was a self-contained Works Unit which was now surplus to their requirements. The Firm held the plot under a Certificate of Occupancy which was soon due for surrender or renewal. The existing buildings were their property. Allowed the keys for inspection, I soon realised my good fortune; here was the almost perfect headquarters for SUDA! On entering the hall of the bungalow to the right was a large living room, ideal for meetings of the Authority, with toilet facilities leading off; to the left were various rooms which had been adapted as offices for administrative staff etc., and again toilet facilities. On land at the rear was a row of open-fronted workshops, store sheds etc., and a good-sized parking area for vehicles and plant. Services of water, electricity and telephone were still connected. In all, it could hardly have been more suitable for my immediate purposes.

There was no difficulty agreeing terms with *Taylor Woodrow* for takeover. Clearly the Firm was pleased to be able to dispose of their assets for a public purpose. Moreover, they had an empty quarter for rent in the Government Residential Area which solved my personal accommodation problem since, from my arrival in Sokoto in November 1975, I had stayed in the *Sokoto Hotel* due to a serious shortage of Government housing. As an extra gesture, the Firm provided me with a typist's desk and two chairs. I employed the Firm's night-watchman as the first 'staff' and SUDA was on its way!

The waiting period was over and the challenge for me was to bring SUDA alive. My immediate responsibility was to create the administrative structure to enable the Authority to function effectively: the Board room had to be appropriately furnished for members to meet; offices had to be set up for clerks and typists etc.; funds had to be obtained from the Ministry of Finance and a bank account opened in the name of the Authority, and other essential arrangements completed.

At a private meeting with the Military Governor I learnt that the appointment of members of the Authority was well in hand and negotiations were proceeding for the appointment of the Chairman, Alhaji Shehu Shagari, Turakin of Sokoto, a most distinguished resident. I knew of him in name only as a greatly respected national figure who, after the military coup of 29th July 1975, had returned to Sokoto to spend more time on his farm at Shagari.

The Military Governor had earlier remarked how keen he was that SUDA should establish a Bus Service in Sokoto and its environs. (He was aware that KCDB had set up a successful Bus Service in Kaduna). So keen was he that, in advance of the first meeting of SUDA, the nucleus of a service was started prematurely under Government initiative with a few buses. An inauguration ceremony was held in the Township attended by local dignitaries. On arrival, I was directed to a seat in the front row of guests. Then someone was ceremoniously conducted to an adjacent seat and for a few minutes we exchanged glances until I thought I ought to introduce myself. Smiling, he said in a quiet voice, "So you are Mr Muggeridge." He was, of course, Alhaji Shehu Shagari. We were talking when Alhaji Muhammadu Carpenter, the Secretary to the Military Government came across and said, "I can see you have introduced yourselves," and apologised for not having arranged for a formal introduction at an earlier date!

After the ceremony, I explained to Alhaji Shehu Shagari that when his office was ready in a few days' time I would let him know so that I could formally welcome him as Chairman to SUDA. He was about to leave in his car when he asked me if I knew where his house was in Sokoto, inviting me to go with him and see its location, adding that his driver would bring me back to collect my car, an example of the many thoughtful gestures which eased our relationship during the next two years. We parted outside his modest house right in the centre of the Township. Understandably, our approach to each other at this first meeting had been rather guarded. With all sincerity, I can say this soon disappeared.

The large living room was now furnished as the Board Room with a long table and chairs. Taking a chance that the Chairman would use one end of the Board Room as his 'office' I had installed a large desk and chairs, telephone, bell to my office and so on. When he came a few days later I showed him round the bungalow, the workshops and the parking area at the rear. He was pleased that the set-up had proved suitable for SUDA and said he was fully satisfied with his 'office'. I asked him whether I should appoint a secretary for him, but he said that would not be necessary as he could share my secretary for his correspondence. Already, I was beginning to understand his inborn modesty. He explained that his current part-time engagements as Chairman or Director of some public and private Companies would occasion his absence from time to time and he would keep me informed.

On 28th October 1976 the Military Governor came to SUDA Headquarters formally to inaugurate the Authority. During the weeks beforehand, the Authority had its first meeting under the chairmanship of Alhaji Shehu Shagari with an agenda of proposed projects: the new Market which was already under design; the takeover of the Sokoto Bus Service; the development of an organised system of refuse collection and disposal similar to that successfully initiated by KCDB at Kaduna and well received by the community there; and other general procedural matters such as monthly meetings.

It was probably at this first meeting that I explained how, once my final design for the new Market had been approved (hopefully at the following meeting), the engagement of Consulting Engineers was essential to prepare a mass of detailed working drawings from my layout and design, specifications, and contract documents etc. This would enable tenders to be invited for construction. I probably also mentioned that based, pro rata, on costs of the new Market at Kaduna, I thought a figure of N20 million must be considered. I gave the name of international Consulting Engineers *Scott Wilson Kirkpatrick & Partners* who had a long-standing reputation with the Federal Government and other State Governments. The Firm would set up a team of qualified engineers in Sokoto to see the project through to completion by a date to be specified in the contract documents. Throughout, there would be constant reference to me, particularly if any changes of significance were found to be necessary.

Before the next meeting I was pleased to welcome Mallam Isa Dabai, a Senior Administrative Officer who had formerly acted as Private Secretary to the Military Governor, Colonel Usman Faruk, as Secretary to the Authority. His appointment would allow me to devote more time to the development of the approved projects.

On 28th October 1976, the Military Governor came to SUDA Headquarters formally to inaugurate the Authority. The following speech was given by the Chairman, Alhaji Shehu Shagari welcoming the Military Governor.

"My Lords, Honourable Commissioners, Ladies and Gentlemen,

"May I first, on behalf of myself and all Members of the Sokoto Urban Development Authority, bid you and our other guests a warm welcome and thank you for sparing time to honour us with your presence on this occasion to mark the inauguration of our Authority.

"We who have been chosen to serve are very conscious, Your Excellency, of your own personal involvement in the creation of this Authority, and we know, too, of the close and active interest you have taken in its initiation, an interest which, undoubtedly, will be sustained into the years ahead. In the setting up and conduct of any new Body or Organisation, there is always the element of challenge. We accept the challenge and are determined to work hard and with a spirit of dedication for the success of the Authority, knowing that by our efforts we will be making our contribution to the Development of our Capital, Sokoto, and to the increasing well-being of the whole community of the State.

"The Instrument or Edict which we have been given, and through which we will function, is both comprehensive and powerful. Should we fail – and fail we must not – it would not be the lack of authority or of the means to take decisive action but because of ourselves. Nonetheless, the Sokoto Urban Development Authority is a new body, its purpose, duties, responsibilities and status are not yet generally or widely known or, perhaps, understood and, when known, may not always be immediately and readily acceptable to some who may view us with a degree of apprehension. This reaction is, perhaps, only to be expected when nationwide new Authorities for so many varying purposes, to meet the demands of our rapidly expanding and developing economy and educational and social systems, are springing up almost daily. However, we of this Authority intend, in no uncertain manner, to register the Sokoto Urban Development Authority firmly in the hearts and minds of the people of Sokoto through the works and projects which we will plan and execute with every expeditiousness.

"With Your Excellency's kind support and encouragement we are determined to prove ourselves, and the new Authority, as worthy instruments of progress and development, ready and willing to contribute our own quota towards the fulfilment of the aspirations of the people of Sokoto Urban area in particular and of the Sokoto State in general. Of course, we will need money and we look with every confidence to Government to aid us in that all important regard. Already considerable progress has been made in our first and supremely vital project of the New Sokoto Central Market which will rise upon the large area behind us as we sit here. Today, in fact, at the end of these proceedings, straightaway we will be engaged in the consideration of the layout and design of the new Market which covers an area of 50 acres, with lorry and car parks, water supply, security lighting, toilets and many other modern amenities and provides for 5,000 stalls embraced within a road network to the most modern standards to cater for the heavy concentration of traffic which the coming of the new Market will generate. Your Excellency, with the support of your Government, the Authority will be planning its programme to have the new Market finished and ready for use by the end of March 1979.

"Our Authority was given legal substance by Edict as a Development Authority from 1st July this year. Simultaneously, Government resolved that we should be made the Town Planning Authority for our prescribed area. In that capacity, which is separate and distinct from that under the Edict, the Authority will operate through the Town and Country Planning Law which has been in existence since 1946. We are aware that it will take time before we can establish ourselves as the Planning Authority and could be frustrated or even defeated if we do not apply our duties, powers and responsibilities as the Planning Authority with vigour and determination. Again, Your Excellency, we trust the Government will give us its full support to implement the very law which, by its own action, we have been directed to administer.

"Since our birth on 1st July, there has also come into being the transformation of Local Government throughout the Country. Even now, although we are both very new, it can be seen that, in some important aspects, our two Organisations will be complementary or parallel and Government may find it desirable and necessary to decide on some degree of division of duties and responsibilities as between the two.

"Your Excellency, let me conclude by emphasising that in our future work and efforts we look forward with keenness and confidence to the help, co-operation, stimulation and understanding of all the elements within the community of

Sokoto aimed at the common goal of a Capital City for Sokoto State of which every citizen can be proud.

"It is now my sincere pleasure to call upon Your Excellency formally to inaugurate the Sokoto Urban Development Authority."

His Excellency The Military Governor, Colonel Umaru Alhaji Mohammed, responded with the following speech:

"Your Highness The Sultan, Your Lordships, Honourable Commissioners, Mr Chairman, Members of the Sokoto Urban Development Authority, Distinguished Guests, Ladies and Gentlemen,

"Since my arrival here a year ago it has always been my dream to see the metropolitan city of Sokoto develop into a modern capital worthy of the State. Frequent Market fires and near-complete lack of Fire Service, drainage problems in the rainy season, very poor condition of streets in the town and lack of proper planning in some parts of Sokoto are physical reminders to all of us that something serious must be done about the development of this city. It is therefore with the joy and happiness of seeing one's dream come true that I perform the inauguration of the Sokoto Urban Development Authority this morning.

"As you have mentioned, Mr Chairman, the development of the Sokoto City into the capital town we all envisage is not going to be an easy task. I am glad, however, to see the determined manner in which you have already started to tackle the preliminary organisational problems of the Authority. I have no doubt that you and the members of your Authority have the experience, patriotic dedication and the ability to measure up to this gigantic challenge. On its part the Sokoto State Government will be keenly watching your progress and will always make itself available for any support the Authority may need. The resolution of the Board to hold monthly meetings is an eloquent testimony of the seriousness with which you intend to conduct the affairs of the Authority. It is most encouraging to note that, so soon after the inception of the Authority, you are already in a position to consider and finalise the general layout and the designs of the new Sokoto Central Market and with this enthusiasm I hope you will be able to beat the target date for the completion of the Market by 1979.

"Another facility which will be of great importance to the life and well-being of the community is the provision of easy and cheap means of transport within the city and its environs. The Bus Service you have already started, though on a small scale, has already made very valuable impact on the life of the city-dwellers, and I hope that you will soon expand it in order to cope adequately with the public demand for this service. At this juncture, I wish to inform you that, in order to ease the problem of the transportation of children to and from their schools, the Government intends to approach your Authority for the establishment of an auxiliary Bus Service solely devoted to ply routes specially selected for carrying children to and from schools. We believe that this service will be a great relief to parents who now have to devote a lot of their time to provide this facility to their children themselves.

"Mr Chairman, in your speech you made mention of your Authority having the second capacity of being a Town Planning Authority. You also touched on the question of the relationship of the Authority in these capacities with the Local Government of the area. I would like to take this opportunity to explain that the Sokoto Urban Development Authority was established in view of the fact that the development of the State Capital is of State-wide interest and importance, to the extent that it cannot correctly be treated as local affairs. The need for the existence of such City Planning and Development Authorities is fully provided for in the Federal Guidelines on Local Government Reforms. It must be realised, however, that a very intimate relation must exist between your Authority and the Local Government. It is with this in view, that adequate provision has been made for the representation of the Local Government of the area on the Board of your Authority. In its capacity as a Town Planning Authority it is supreme, in its area of activity, in that all land development plans – whether for commercial or residential purposes, public or private, including the Government itself – must be first brought to the attention of the Planning Authority for consideration and approval before they are put to execution.

"Your Highness, distinguished guests, ladies and gentlemen, before I bring my address to a final close, I would like to appeal to all Sokoto people who may be affected in one way or another by the Sokoto Urban Development projects to give the Authority their maximum co-operation and goodwill, with the full understanding that the Authority exists only for their own service and interest.

"With these remarks I have the great pleasure and delight in officially inaugurating the Sokoto Urban Development Authority this 28th day of October 1976. May Allah bless the Authority, and give His guidance and wisdom to all those associated with the execution of its development plans, so that the Authority will grow to be one of the most useful organisations in the service of our people. Amen."

It was interesting to me to hear the warning in each speech against suspicion, possibly resentment, that the Authority might take over, even usurp, powers and functions long entrenched in Native Authorities and Local Government generally. The emphasis was for the whole community of Sokoto to welcome the Authority and show co-operation with it. I had experienced such growing tension in Kaduna as KCDB proceeded with its activities and particularly that of Town Planning.

The vital meeting of the Authority took place, as the Chairman had said, immediately following the Ceremony on 28th October 1976. I had already established with him that I would always discuss each agenda item with him before meetings. In this way I could be confident that agendas included only items which he would support and could ensure that they were approved. I soon came to rely on his way of achieving approval; he would allow members some time for free discussion and then choose just the right moment to say, "Well, thank you, that's agreed," and proceed at once to the next item. This technique never failed – no vote ever took place!

My final plans, and the engagement of the Consulting Engineers, *Scott Wilson Kirkpatrick (Nigeria) and Partners*, to carry forward the complete project were approved at this meeting. There was also the crucial question of funding which would be by loans. The Chairman, and, indeed, the Members, were emphatic that no contract for construction could be entered into until the required loans had been secured. (In the event, the necessary loans were secured from the State Government and three commercial banks, as follows: State Government N10 million; First Bank, originally Standard Bank, N8 million; United Bank of Africa N4 million; Bank of the North N2 million.)

From then onwards at its meetings the Authority was kept informed of progress with the project, culminating in tenders for construction being invited in August 1977. A number were received and, after close scrutiny, that of the German Firm, *Messrs. Kueppers (Nigeria) Ltd.*, in the total of N22.3 million was recommended for acceptance. In the Appendices can be found the speech made by the Chairman of SUDA, Alhaji Shehu Shagari, in October 1977 on the occasion of the signing of the formal contract Agreement, and the response by Mr Siegfried Winkel.

The Contractors started on site in December 1977. An impressive process of mass fabrication of different elements of the construction was set up. The Consulting Engineers responsible for supervision established their office on site. I would, of course, make frequent visits to observe progress and settle any problems which might arise. Other objectives of SUDA had not been overlooked. The Works Yard had been set up with mechanical staff for the maintenance of the expanded Bus Service for which more buses were purchased: also acquired were a number of covered tipper lorries for the daily, including weekend, collection of refuse from the drums placed at frequent intervals in the streets of the Township and in the service roads of the residential areas. This service actually arose from the early call to the Authority from the Executive Council of the State Government, at 24-hours' notice, that there must be a 'Clean Up Sokoto' Campaign, which was continued on the permanent basis described. The public responded well and the 'clean' condition at Sokoto received favourable comment in the local and national press.

Senior Mechanical staff at SUDA

The sandy site of the new Market

The blocks of stalls were so laid out that, from the air, their roofs, painted brilliant red, represented the famous symbol known as the 'Northern Knot' which had also featured at Kaduna

The market at a later stage after the roads had been surfaced

That I could feel pleased and confident with the progress and success of the Authority up to this point – the beginning of the year 1978 – must be attributed to the personal relationship which had grown during the past months between the Chairman, Alhaji Shehu Shagari, and myself. His understanding and encouragement were always available but I was well aware that he would not countenance failure – he told me so once: "You know, Mr Muggeridge, I do not take on an assignment without seeing that it succeeds." There were times when we talked of wider affairs including the national scene which was moving towards a return to political – and thus civilian – rule in 1979. It was during these talks that I began to sense his personal anxieties and concern as to the political pressures to which he might be subjected during this year.

Other personal factors, too, had now to be taken into account. As 1978 began I had had no UK leave since May 1975 when I had returned from a few weeks' leave to my position as Chief Engineer to KCDB. Then in October 1975 came my resignation from KCDB and the move to Sokoto in November to be ready to set up the Sokoto Urban Development Authority (SUDA). Those years in Sokota had been exacting, rewarding and inspiring, but there were now signs of growing tension regarding the attitude to me at SUDA of some of the elements within the local Community. It was similar to what I have mentioned earlier regarding KCDB at Kaduna. These are best explained by quoting from my Handing-Over Notes, dated 20th September 1978, following my letter to the Secretary to the Military Government of Sokoto of 19th August 1978. This sought permission to proceed on UK leave on or about 20th September 1978, also indicating that it was most unlikely that I would be returning for further service with SUDA.

Handing Over Notes

1. Origins of SUDA

Fortunately, the Secretary, Mallam Isa A. Dabai, has been with the Authority since October 1976 so he has a wide knowledge of the origins of SUDA, its duties, functions and responsibilities as laid down in Edict No.10 of July 1976 (which inaugurated SUDA) and as these have been varied and enlarged by direction of Government. He will also be able to produce on file various papers, memoranda etc., which have been prepared from time to time when SUDA was called upon to put forward a brief about itself, for example, a visit by the Head of State, or, more recently, the change in the set up of Government. Edict No.10, however, should still be regarded as the legal basis on which SUDA is founded and on which it exercises its powers.

2. SUDA as Planning Authority

To be clear on SUDA as a Planning Authority (separate from its status as a Development Authority by virtue of Edict No.10) it is advisable to study the various Memoranda which have been submitted to the Authority at its meetings during the last twelve months. The necessary files and papers can be produced. It will be seen that it was not until April 1978 than any significant action could be taken even to accept and deal with routine aspects such as the submissions from developers wishing to embark upon construction on their plots. At least it will be seen that the Authority is now properly and legally the Planning Authority, but it is still only at the beginning of the lengthy legal process leading to the approval of a fully authenticated Planning Scheme which lies at the heart of any effective control and achievement of development, the protection of the environment, and the overall well-being of the whole community. It is vitally urgent to secure the permanent services of an experienced Planning Officer to carry through the whole process, otherwise it will soon be too late to prevent the sporadic and haphazard outcrops of building of all types now taking place from spreading, to the extent that control is lost and the appearance of the Capital permanently marred. The Town Planning Officer must have the supporting technical staff since there is a great deal of field and drawing office work to be done.

3. Public Services

The rapid growth of the Capital, its commerce, business, population and general activity, have created stresses and strains on the public services so that the urge for overall development has been matched, or even overtaken, by the need to provide such services as public transport, refuse collection and disposal – a vital environmental element – proper roads and drainage, street lighting and so on. SUDA, not only because of the provisions of its Edict but because of Government direction, has, so soon after its inception, had to embark upon the setting up of certain public services which has, apart from other aspects such as shortage of suitable staff, caused it to be distracted or diverted from its primary function of development. Thus its preoccupation at present is the day to day, seven days a week, operation and control of these public services, so that, in the public eye, they should be as effective and efficient as it is possible to make them within its limitations of manpower and, of course, finance.

It may be said with some pride that SUDA does meet with a fair measure of general acclaim for what it has done, and is doing, in the way of environmental control and improvement but, in truth, this is not its proper, or even intended, role. Moreover, with the coming of the Local Government Edict and the reiteration by the Federal Government that Local Governments are so important and must be made more effective, some clash of interest, inevitably, must arise because SUDA, and not the Local Government, is providing public services, which, rightly or wrongly, over the years, have been regarded as the prerogative of the latter.

There is then some dilemma for SUDA. If it guards its reputation as, of course, it should do, it must strive to perform these public services well and even improve upon them, yet, by so doing, it may find itself neglecting, or giving only secondary consideration to, its prime role of development.

Yet the latter, if effectively pursued – and, for this, of course, liberal finance must be available or made available – would certainly earn SUDA much more general appreciation and praise. Of course, development can and does take place alongside or parallel with the carrying out of public services, but to do so SUDA will require to expand very considerably and must carefully select its staff to fulfil the two distinct roles. For this, much more finance in aid will be essential and it is difficult in present circumstances to see Government providing more finance to SUDA. There are also the political/social attitudes towards SUDA, both favourable and the reverse, which should influence the position.

For what it is worth, the opinion is offered that the moment is quite near when there will be definite moves to change or modify the role of SUDA within the overall pattern of Government, and this may be for the better or for the worse, whichever way SUDA is looked at by those closely involved in its existence and well-being. On a personal note, this opinion is not related to the going of the present General Manager, although he has been conscious of impending changes for some time."

* * * * *

In item 1 'Origins of SUDA', there is reference to "…a visit by the Head of State". In September 1977, during a State Visit to Sokoto State by the then Head of the Federal Military Government in Lagos, General Olusegun Obasanjo, he visited SUDA accompanied by the State Governor, Colonel Umaru Alhaji Mohammed. I had known the General as the Chief Engineer of the Corps of Engineers in the Federal Forces (similar to the British Corps of Royal Engineers). As I was introduced to the General he said, "Oh, Yes, you're the man who works in his office on Christmas Day." Colonel Mohammed would, every now and again, drop in to SUDA on an evening or during a weekend knowing I would be there. Sometimes he brought with him another State Governor visiting privately. He must have told the General how, on Christmas Day 1976, he had found me working in the office at SUDA!

Apparently, Governor Umaru Mohammed told the Chairman, Alhaji Shehu Shagari, that General Obasanjo was so impressed with the cleanliness of Sokoto town that he asked whether Alhaji Shehu Shagari could be persuaded to offer his services to the Lagos State Government so as to help clean the city of Lagos! Alhaji Shehu Shagari told the Governor: "It was not me who made Sokoto clean but Mr Muggeridge, therefore the invitation should be passed to him." When he told me this story later, the Chairman added, "The irony of this was that, up to that time, General Obasanjo did not envisage that I was to go to Lagos to succeed him rather than to help clean Lagos!"

Early in 1978, looming ahead and gathering momentum, was a proposal to return to civilian rule in 1979 promised by the Federal Military Government led by General Obasanjo, who was generally regarded as someone who would keep his word. To that end, party politics, officially banned nationwide since the first of the military coups on 15th January 1966, were made legal in September 1978. There would be a new Constitution based on a presidential system with national elections for President and members of a National Assembly in Lagos.

A consideration for me arose from the decision by the Federal Military Government, as one of the preparations for the return to civilian rule, to replace the State Military Governors by 'Military Administrators'. Colonel Muhammadu Gado Nasko replaced Colonel Umaru Alhaji Mohammed at Sokoto, probably during July 1978. It was inevitable, with Alhaji Shehu Shagari and Colonel Umaru Alhaji Mohammed going or gone, that my position would be exposed and I would not remain to see the new Market through to completion but it was going ahead very well. Most likely problems had already been settled with the Consultants in whom I had full confidence.

Clearly, it would be better for the future of SUDA, as my Handing-Over Notes had envisaged, to be worked out by an indigenous General Manager and Chief Executive under a new Chairman and, no doubt, new Members, of the Authority. Besides, I was 69 and badly needed leave!

First, I had to tell the Chairman of my intention to go on leave and not return. It may seem ironical, but the opportunity came on 1st August 1978 through an exchange of private letters concerning, I feel certain, the first and only misunderstanding during the two years of our relationship. The cause for the disagreement is irrelevant now. The Chairman expressed 'sincere regret' and I was 'more than grieved' – end of matter.

Actually, by this time, I think both the Military Governor and the Chairman would not have been surprised at my decision, bearing in mind the changes. I proceeded on leave on 20th September 1978. Having tendered my resignation, I cherished the following farewell letter received from the Chairman:

15th September 1978

My Dear Muggeridge,

I am writing to you on behalf of the Sokoto Urban Development Authority, at which I am the Chairman, and also on behalf of myself to thank you most sincerely and to express our deep appreciation for the invaluable service you have rendered to the Authority within a short time of its establishment.

I need not tell you how disturbed I personally felt when you told me about your desire to retire. This is obvious because of the cordiality and mutual understanding that has existed between us, and the excellent working relationship that has made my work as Chairman of the Authority so easy and enjoyable. I have always been so confident that the Authority will always succeed in its numerous undertakings under your able management. I have felt proud myself to have been associated with a person of such high sense of responsibility and unquestionable integrity. Yours has been a dedicated life to the service of our country and of the Sokoto Urban Development Authority in particular. The testimony of your hard work and dedication to duty is manifested in the well-established services now being run by the Authority,

NORTH WESTERN STATE AND SOKOTO URBAN DEVELOPMENT AUTHORITY

and the permanent landmark in the form of the New Sokoto Central Market which you initially designed and personally supervised its construction. How sad that you will now not be available to see to its final stage! I have no doubt that you will continue to be remembered affectionately by the people of Sokoto whose lives you have made so significant contribution to improve.   This is indeed a remarkable achievement on your part.

It is in realisation of your selfless service and dedication to duty that the Sokoto Urban Development Authority, at its Meeting held on Thursday 14th September 1978, unanimously passed a resolution of thanks and appreciation for all your efforts in establishing and managing the Authority from its very inception to the pride of place which it now enjoys in Sokoto and beyond. We will always remember and cherish the enviable position into which you have placed the Sokoto Urban Development Authority. We wish also to place on record our appreciation of the patience and encouragement of your family, particularly your dear wife who has endured your long absence from home, so that you may put your best into the job that you loved so much.

Finally, may I therefore take this opportunity once more to thank you most sincerely, on behalf of the Authority and myself, for all you have done for us and also to wish you long life and a very happy retirement from Nigeria's public service.

With kindest regards and best wishes
Yours sincerely
Alhaji Shehu Shagari

Turakin Sokoto
Chairman Sokoto Urban Development Authority

Jack with the Mechanical Staff at his send-off from SUDA

All the staff and Board Members of SUDA at a farewell party for Jack

Alhaji Shehu Shagari is seated on Jack's right

England Interlude

Although Alhaji Shehu Shagari had announced publicly that he could best serve his country as a Senator, many others regarded him as the obvious choice for President. For this, not only was he well experienced in government, but universally he had a high reputation as a man of integrity and honesty and was a strong advocate of unity amongst all the diverse peoples of the country. Our personal relationship was such that prior to my leaving Nigeria we had talked openly both about his position *vis-à-vis* his chairmanship of SUDA and my own position, should he cease to be Chairman. I had became aware of the pressures being widely applied to him, including local demands including those from The Sultan, all of which he resolutely resisted.

He even revealed to me on one occasion that he was "…frightened of power" – he was quite determined only to be a Senator. Another time, he told me that his supporters were threatening to turn his own people in the village of Shagari and the district against him! Over the years, he had seen how the pursuit of power, and the ruthless tenacity to hold on to it, had destroyed other leaders. In the end, he was driven to give way, explaining, "This was the most trying period I have ever gone through in my life."

He was the most reluctant President who was elected on 11th August 1979, eleven months after my return to England.

A few days later, on 15th August 1979, General Obasanjo again visited Sokoto to lay the Foundation Stone of the Administrative Building of the new Sokoto Central Market, by then well under construction.

Early in March 1980, I was delighted to receive the following letter of 28th February 1980 signed by Abubakar Ibrahim Illo, Secretary for General Manager Sokoto Urban Development Authority:

New Sokoto Central Market Official Opening Ceremony

"Sokoto Urban Development Authority has all along been associated with your name (Mr Muggeridge), being its first General Manager and one who has been responsible for designing most of the present projects being executed by the Authority. One of these projects designed by you is the present New Sokoto Central Market which, unfortunately, you could not stay to see the actual construction of. The construction work is now at the final stages and, all things being equal, the entire project will be completed by March 1980. It has already been officially confirmed that the New Market will be officially opened by His Excellency the President of the Federal Republic of Nigeria, Alhaji Shehu Shagari on 15th March 1980.

It is in the light of the above that I am pleased to convey to you the Authority's invitation to the opening ceremony. The Management of the Organisation will bear all expenses arising from the trip. On behalf of the Organisation I wish you a safe journey to Nigeria."

I certainly never expected to see the new Market completed let alone to be present at its Official Opening Ceremony and by Alhaji Shehu Shagari as President!

Gerry Summerhayes, whose father had been in the Administrative Service in Nigeria for many years, was in Sokoto at the time, holding the rank of a Permanent Secretary in the Cabinet Office at Sokoto for Political Education and Training, and he gave me hospitality.

Before the Ceremony I watched the excited and colourful crowd comprising motor-cyclists, cyclists and drummers etc., a typical Nigerian display, following the President's entourage on its way into Sokoto and the new Market. At the new Market an even greater crowd was waiting.

Alhaji Shehu Shagari speaking at the Opening Ceremony

The President and VIPs inspecting the Market
from the bridge between the two administrative buildings

All I could do was to push my way through towards the VIP Party. I managed to catch up with it as it went into the open base of the Tower, one of the striking features of the Market. This Tower had a highly practical purpose for the Market Fire Brigade to watch for outbreaks of fire anywhere within the complex. The Party were standing looking up to the top of the Tower, and as I moved forward, the President, obviously much surprised, saw me and called out, "So you're here," and immediately embraced me. Presumably, he had not been told that I had been invited by SUDA. It was a really great moment for me. I could not stay with the President's Party – in any case, he was surrounded by people and security guards.

Later, I called at his house and left a note with his Secretary telling him I would be at Summerhayes' telephone number and could I be called to come and see him at a convenient time. Somehow no message reached me so I did not go. Months later, on 5th December 1980, replying in his typical manner to one of my letters, he wrote:

> "I was delighted to see you at the Ceremony of opening the Sokoto Market last time but was rather disappointed that you were not able to call on me afterwards. I had wanted to invite you from there to visit me in Lagos so that we could have a few minutes together to discuss the past, present and future which will no doubt interest you."

Further on he wrote:

> "I have not forgotten that, during your send-off at SUDA, you offered me your services in the State House if I became President. I in turn offered you a job on my farm – remember? Now, you have a choice of either working in the New State House at Abuja (when completed end of 1981) or at Jan Zomo Farm Shagari which I am now developing in preparation for my retirement in 1982."

He was correct. As I bade farewell to him and SUDA, I had said, somewhat light-heartedly I think but nonetheless meant, "When you're living at Lagos as President just remember I'll be happy to come and look after the drains at State House!"

The New Market in use

Early in 1981, the press here announced that the Nigerian President would be coming to the United Kingdom on a State Visit. I wrote to him on 4th March 1981 saying what a great joy it would be for me if I could see him even for a few minutes. I received a message to see him at the residence of the Nigerian High Commissioner in Kensington Gardens London. He was just the same person I had come to love and admire at SUDA. I told him, "Abuja please – I will await your call," and wrote on 2nd April 1981:

> "I hardly need to say how good it was to see you during your recent visit to the UK. To me, you were just the same person I came to love and admire so much when we were together at SUDA. Power is not now going to change or corrupt you so you have the strength to guide Nigeria through the stresses and strains of the years ahead, certainly for the two periods during which you can and will be President.

"I am, of course, delighted at the opportunity to serve you and I choose Abuja, if only because it means I can be with you the sooner! I shall just await your call to work when you want me – very much something to look forward to from now onwards!"

During those three and a half years in England, I was able to maintain interest in African affairs through a weekly journal *West Africa*. In the issue of 9th June 1980, I was shocked to read that Brigadier Umaru Alhaji Mohammed was one of 17 people who died when a Nigerian Air Force aircraft crashed into the Atlantic Ocean near Escravos in Bendel State. The plane was carrying an official delegation to the Sao Tome and Principe Islands off the West African Coast. I wrote through the Ministry of Defence in Lagos to express my condolences to his family.

Federal Capital Development Authority

The President's call started with this telex which reached me on 16th January 1982:

> "My letter of 7th December 1981 refers. Federal Capital Development Authority requests you report in Lagos urgently for immediate employment. Looking forward to seeing you. Private Secretary."

I answered by telex: "No letter received." In reply, I received a telex on 26th January 1982 asking me to contact DHC Usman at the Nigerian High Commission London who would arrange visa, air passage etc. Next, I received a letter of appointment dated 9th February 1982 from the Permanent Secretary, Federal Capital Development Authority. As I recall, I would be a 'Consultant' to the Authority.

I left London by air on 11th March 1982 reaching Lagos Airport in the evening where I was received with every courtesy and privilege by two staff of State Protocol and accommodated in the Federal Government Special Guest House. The following morning I went to FCDA Lagos office and also to State House, Ribadu Road where I was asked to see The President the following evening, Saturday 13th March. He greeted me warmly and I remained with him for about two hours.

I was already aware, of course, that work was in progress at the site of the new Capital and I was anxious to hear from the President about progress and, in particular, what he was expecting of me.

On two previous occasions I had been made aware of the proposal for a New Federal Capital for Nigeria. The first was in the early '70s – probably when I was Provincial Engineer Zaria – when the then Federal Military Government had publicised its proposed consideration for a new Federal Capital to replace Lagos. I had heard that a Commission

223

had been established to prepare a report with recommendations for what, undoubtedly, would be an enormous Project. The chairman of the Commission was Justice Akinola Aguda.

I had only been in Lagos twice when going on UK leave or returning to a posting in Northern Nigeria, but even these brief experiences were more than enough to ensure that nothing could ever induce me to accept employment in Lagos. A journalist's description of Lagos:

> "Lagos is overcrowded, congested, and built on islands between creeks and lagoons, which gives it little room to expand. It is also deeply in the Southern area of Nigeria where the Yoruba – one of the country's three dominant tribes – live."

I will be quoting again from this journalist.

States, Local Governments, Public Bodies and other interest groups, had been invited to submit recommended locations for the new Capital, bearing in mind climate, existing or potential sources of amenities, water, electricity, roads etc., and, of course, land which could be taken over with the least disturbance to existing occupancy and use. I believe some general idea was given as to the area of land required for what would become the Capital Territory and also the ultimate population envisaged. No doubt the clear objective was to choose a site which could be regarded as ethnically neutral, bearing in mind the bitter experiences of the Civil War from 1967-1970.

I had put forward the suggestion for an area which I knew well, having twice been Provincial Engineer Niger Province for a period of three years. This included the Township of Abuja, about 60 miles from the Provincial Capital Minna, which I had visited at least once a month, normally staying two or three nights in the Government Rest House. Situated on a high hill overlooking the whole Township, this was a typical round bush hut with thick, mud walls, a grass roof and a deep verandah, which made it delightfully cool, though there was a risk of encountering a snake which had once decided to sleep in the rafters directly above the bed! Lying under the rather weak 'protection' of the mosquito net, I could eye its presence until I fell asleep, and it was gone in the morning.

There was a Gateway into Abuja Township where the Emir of Abuja, Suleman Barau, posted his 'spy'. I soon learnt that if I failed to call on him within a short time of arriving, a messenger would appear at the Rest House to tell me that the Emir was expecting me! I looked forward to these visits when we would go to his garden, which was laid out just like an English Garden and talk together. He was a grey-haired, quietly spoken man with good English. He was a devout Muslim and greatly respected by his people for his constant attention to their well-being.

The area of 500 square miles eventually chosen for the new Capital Territory was not greatly different from that which I had suggested. The physical characteristics were similar: hills, plateaux, valleys, forests, availability of water from streams running through deep ravines (with potential for dams and electricity generation), the relatively equable middle-belt climate of six months dry and six months wet, and low humidity. Links to main roads would have to be developed, and there might be a problem over the siting of an international airport. Much of the area was virtually uninhabited or, to use a western description, 'green field' land. A planner given an assignment for a new Capital City would have regarded this terrain as near perfect, offering a wonderful opportunity for imaginative arrangements of administrative, business and commercial centres, light industry, leisure pursuits, etc., in the plateaux and valleys, with housing well spaced out on the rising and higher ground. Roads within the Capital itself and in the residential areas could be carefully planned to retain most of a splendid variety of trees and fauna. I could envisage the absolute delight of the visitor to the City and its environs appreciating the care taken to blend functional needs with the breathtaking natural beauty.

The selected area did not actually incorporate Abuja itself which had been founded by Abu Ja, the great grandfather of Suleman Barau. So that the new Capital could take the name 'Abuja', Government and the Emir agreed to rename the Township and the Emirate 'Suleja', thereby honouring the founder Abu Ja and his great grandson, Suleman Barau. A significant part of the Federal Territory, especially the site of the new city was in the domain of the Emir of Abuja. Sadly, the Emir died before the new Capital was completed. All maps of Nigeria would define the Federal Capital Territory with Abuja as the name of its Capital.

In the press, Abuja was described as...

> "...close to the geographical heart of Nigeria... ethnically neutral, that it can become a symbol of national unity... does have the potential for tourism with its dry, neat rolling savannahs scattered with high hills and cut deeply by streams...etc."

For myself, having witnessed the bitterness, destruction and human misery of the Civil War in the country I had come to love second only to my own, just the announcement of the new Capital, with all the immensity and excitement which that created, was inspiring, particularly as it was to be centred in one of the most beautiful environs anywhere. This, then, was my first contact with the proposal for a new Federal Capital.

My second came early in 1979 when – as I then thought – I had finally 'retired' from service in Nigeria and, indeed, from any professional activity. I was living in a small village in Buckinghamshire a few miles from the New Town of Milton Keynes, which I knew from the local Press was still being implemented by a Development Corporation. My interest was aroused by an article which mentioned the Corporation's connection with Nigeria through its Chief Architect, who had recently had the opportunity to visit the new Federal Capital at Abuja in Nigeria, then in its early stages of implementation. The primary need was housing for the multi-disciplinary staff – administrative, clerical, technical, general workers etc. – required for the Federal Capital Development Authority with overall control for the Federal Government. As a follow-up, a senior representative of the Authority visited Milton Keynes and was much impressed with the layouts of housing, including three and four-storey blocks of flats, and decided to engage the Chief Architect and his staff to prepare a scheme for a section of the area of the Capital City being allocated to staff housing.

It seemed only natural that I should make contact with the Corporation. The Chief Architect welcomed my interest and invited me to his office to talk with him and his staff working on the scheme. So it was there that I first saw the Master Plan for the new Capital, Abuja. Their involvement was in an area of what had been designated as 'The Accelerated District' i.e. for those essential government works I have listed above.

Given a chance next to study the more detailed plans being prepared and to discuss them with the staff, I was taken-aback to learn that none of them had even been to Nigeria, let alone visited the site of the Capital City! Having never been to the African Continent, they were unaware of African culture, the low standard of living and housing for the vast majority of the population, their local customs and family traditions and so on.

Consequently, on the site plans they had been given they were producing layouts of blocks of flats on the lines of those at Milton Keynes – more or less typical of Local Authority Housing Estates in the UK. These blocks of one or two-bedroomed flats, three or four storeys high, were set back only a few feet from the roads they were fronting, with little distance between blocks and no surrounding garden or open space for air. This was completely alien to the traditional Nigerian way of life, with lots of children and, being Muslims, possibly more than one wife in one dwelling.

The Chief Architect gathered the staff together and allowed me to describe how I saw their proposals ought to be reconsidered. It had been mooted that I might possibly be offered engagement with the Corporation as their representative at Abuja, but after one or two further sessions it was obvious I had made myself unpopular and silence followed!

So these early misgivings, arising from this rather cursory study of the Master Plan for the new Capital (which I had noted had been prepared by an American Firm named International Planning Associates) were in my mind as I now talked with the President in Lagos some three years later. I knew, of course, from our time together at SUDA that the unity of his country was his abiding concern. Without the setting aside of ethnic differences, prejudices, and so on, the development of Nigeria in the best interests of all, sharing its many basic resources, would be held back by periodic outbursts of unrest, rioting and killing, such as had beset other ex-colonial territories. I mentioned earlier that whilst at SUDA he was satisfied to use my secretary – at least, I presumed, for his 'open' correspondence – so I could hardly fail to see such letters, and I was struck then by his amicable contacts with politicians and other prominent Nigerians of all shades of opinion nationwide, who clearly held him in great esteem.

That he could use the Presidency to advance unity may have influenced him finally to give way to enormous pressure to accept nomination. The creation of the new Federal Capital would be a powerful demonstration to the public of his goal of unification.

As he began to explain the role he had for me, I realised that, paramount in his mind was the movement, if only partial, of the seat of Government away from Lagos to Abuja. He had already determined that the National Day of Celebrations on 1st October 1982 must take place at Abuja and the previous Military Government had already decided to bring back partial movement to Abuja to 1983 in place of 1986.

Soon after reaching Abuja and joining the Federal Capital Development Authority (FCDA) I heard how this change of date had created consternation in all the operational Departments now confronted with having to revise their work programmes drastically. It was clearly imperative that, before the end of the first four years of the Civilian Regime in October 1983, the new Capital must be seen, on the ground, to have reached a stage of implementation from which there could be no turning back or abandonment of the Project. This meant that prime Government Ministries and, indeed, Government itself, should, as soon as possible from October 1982, function, if only part-time, from Abuja.

It was known from the beginning, that powerful forces in the South and in Lagos had strongly opposed the concept of the new Capital at Abuja. Later, in July 1982, another journalist, after visiting Abuja in the making, wrote:

> "...you might imagine that the top brass in Lagos, a noisome hellish spot, could hardly wait to get to the sylvan delights of Abuja. But civil servants view the move with alarm, since many of them have what might gently be termed commercial interests tied up in Lagos. Shagari is pitted against both

inertia and hostility. Yet beneath his self-effacing ways, he is tough and adroit enough to be the favourite for next year's election to win another term to push Abuja forward."

So to my special role on behalf of the President at Abuja. One of the prestigious buildings under construction was the Presidential Complex. I was only to see this once I reached Abuja, but from the President's description of it – one block for the President's suite, offices, family quarters, staff and others, and other similar blocks for visiting Heads of State, security provision etc., the whole enclosed by a high ornamental wall, all accounting for hundred of millions of Naira – in no way could it be available even for him for 1st October 1982. Moreover, its very grandiose style was utterly out of place for Alhaji Shehu Shagari to use. So he had asked for a President's Lodge to be built with four or five bedrooms, reception rooms, a study and family quarters, all in typical Nigerian style, which could later become a Rest House for the President's private and personal guests or relatives when the Presidential Complex was completed. Plans had been drawn and construction had been entrusted to an Italian contractor.

However, the determination that the President and elements of Government would operate, if only for part of the time, from Abuja after 1st October 1982, meant that the Lodge must now incorporate a suite of offices, a Conference Room for meetings with Ministers, and other supporting facilities. Fortunately perhaps, work on the site using the original plans had been rather slow, and when I arrived was more or less at a standstill awaiting details of the new changes and additions. In fact, after about six months of construction, only the foundation work had been carried out so the matter was now urgent.

The President explained all this to me before I left Lagos, which had accounted for the urgent telex in January. Had I not promised him to come if called? It was now March and he was handing the task over to me. The Presidential Lodge, as now updated, must be ready for his use by the end of September 1982 for the 1st October Celebrations at Abuja!

This was an awesome assignment with such an absolute deadline. However, even before I had started on it, or seen the state of the project in the new City, I determined to succeed come what may, such was my

229

regard for Alhaji Shehu Shagari. I was soon to realise I had made a rash undertaking!

Arriving in Suleja on 15th March 1982, I reported to the Permanent Secretary of FCDA, Alhaji Aliyu Mohammed, exchanging the ritual greetings. As we talked, it become clear that I had been engaged by the Authority as a 'Consultant'. No reference was made to the special assignment which, as I understood, accounted for my coming. He was anxious for me to familiarise myself quickly with the City Project as it was progressing, and to that end I should devote the next two or three days to a tour of inspection in the company of Mr F.C. Obinani (status not given) and then report back to him. I readily agreed and thanked him for his welcome.

As we toured I found Mr Obinani – so far as I could gather, an 'adviser' – very open in his comments , and quite prepared to stop for inspection as we entered the 'Accelerated Area' where construction of blocks of flats, houses etc., was the main activity. The misgivings I had expressed in Milton Keynes about the design were confirmed, but worse still was the poor quality of the work which should have been condemned.

On the third day, before parting from Mr Obinani, he introduced me to the Directors of the various technical Divisions of FCDA, where I was warmly received and found several Nigerian professionals I had known earlier, including Mr Buhari Dikko as Chief Engineer under the Director of Engineering. I had engaged Mr Dikko as a newly qualified Executive Engineer when I was Chief Engineer with Kaduna Capital Development Authority (KCDB). Now I had to prepare myself for reporting back to the Permanent Secretary, realising that my misgivings were increasing and that I could not withhold strong comment.

On 18th March I met with the Permanent Secretary, and opened up to him about my concerns, whilst admitting that my adverse comments resulted from a fairly cursory inspection of works in hand. He appreciated my concerns and asked me to prepare a full report in which he encouraged me to be entirely frank. I was grateful for this assurance since, by now, I was wondering whether I could hold back my strong feelings from the President.

By 21st March, working on it by day and late into the nights, I had submitted my written report to the Permanent Secretary with an attachment. (See Appendices) Once I had prepared this I realised that I could not avoid being fully embroiled in the whole City Project from then onwards. As will be seen, the Permanent Secretary took action which made that inevitable.

My next task was to enquire within FCDA regarding the Presidential Lodge. In my mind – and particularly after my tour of inspection and generally doubtful feelings about FCDA – I had determined that I could only be confident of success with this crucial assignment if I took direct control and responsibility for its conduct. As it happened, this became essential.

To my surprise, I found that the Presidential Lodge Project was with the Engineering, rather than the Architectural, Division. Moreover, the officer in charge of it was Mr Buhari Dikko, whose initial welcome turned somewhat sour when I explained the position to him, and that from then onwards the Project would become my personal responsibility. I had yet to visit this Project, which I gathered was being controlled on site by a small team of junior officers with an Italian Contractor.

The outcome of my report to the Permanent Secretary was, I suppose, inevitable. I had observed that the professional Directors seemed to need a team leader and suggested the use of the designation 'Chief Project Director' as being more suitable than 'General Manager', which is commonly used at Development Authorities. I was not putting myself forward for that position. I had only just arrived at FCDA and – as I had understood – for a special assignment more or less on a personal basis for the President.

My Report, however, by its very criticism of the Capital City Project and of FCDA itself, drew me inevitably into the overall situation at FCDA. The Permanent Secretary directed that I become Chief Project Engineer with particular responsibility for the key Divisions of Engineering and Development, and the Project Controller Central Area. I had to assume that my personal responsibility for the Presidential Lodge was incidental to the appointment, and so it remained.

From then onwards I was expected to attend certain meetings which brought me into close contact with Ministers and particularly with the Senior Minister, Chairman of the Board. Certainly, he was aware of, and much concerned about, the Presidential Lodge, no doubt being questioned about its progress by the President in connection with 1st October 1982. Thereafter I emphasised to the Senior Minister my promise to the President and that, having now taken personal responsibility for it, I relied on his understanding and acceptance that I must have complete freedom to act, if success was to be achieved in the time available. He would, of course, be kept fully informed. My 'complete freedom' was understood.

Thus, within a few weeks, I found myself deeply involved professionally as Chief Project Engineer to FCDA in the City Project, about which my misgivings were increasing daily, together with the over-riding personal commitment to the President which had really been the purpose for my presence in Abuja.

Early in April, an opportunity arose for me to write, on a personal basis, to the President. He had announced an 'ethical revolution' to counter the 'canker worm of corruption' in Nigeria. My letter to him of 12th April 1982 (see Appendices) expressed my support for his action and fervently wished him success. However, I could not avoid also writing about FCDA:

> "...I cannot help but let you know how very disappointed I am and there is no absence of the worm here."

I had just heard of his coming to Abuja early in June, so I wrote how anxious I was to see him privately during his visit. Moreover, his coming increased pressure to concentrate progress regarding the enlarged Presidential Lodge.

However, I now had to discuss with Directors their work and responsibilities in more detail, as referred to in my Report. I had already sensed that from an early stage in FCDA – or, perhaps, from Government itself – there had been what can only be described as a rush to engage Consultants for many of the proposals of the Master Plan for the City, and, particularly, for the variety of buildings which were considered priority for the movement of Government from Lagos to Abuja by 1986.

No co-ordinated strategy for this seemed to be in place. Then had come the Government decision to move part of the Government to Abuja by 1983, before the next Federal elections, and I had expressed the consternation I found amongst some of the Directors when confronted with this change of date. I suggested there was urgent need for a new strategic plan which must also take into consideration signs of a deteriorating financial situation within the Authority. The question of over-consultancy now, more than ever, had to be addressed.

During May I saw the Permanent Secretary and he directed me to prepare a Report on Consultancy as soon as possible. To that end, I asked all relevant Directors to let me have copies of Consultancy Agreements, Letters of Intent to Consultants etc., with necessary supplementary details without delay. One hundred or more reached my office, leaving little spare space! Most days I had to be in the City on inspection and at the Presidential Lodge, so long evenings and weekends were directed to studying the Agreements etc., and preparing a detailed and comprehensive Schedule to go with the Report.

As I wrote the Report my fears about FCDA greatly increased, so much so that I could not wait for the June visit of the President, and put together my letter of 22nd May to him which speaks for itself: "...this FCDA is rotten right through." (See Appendices) I commented about the figures in the Consultancy Report:

> "I find that as at 31st December 1981 there were over 256 Consultancy Agreements extant distributed amongst 160 Firms with a total fee commitment of N265 million, N102 million having been paid out against these up to 31st December 1981...."

From memory, I think the final figures in the Report were appreciably higher but, in any case, the fee commitment alone was not far short of the total Government allocation of funds to FCDA for the whole year of 1982! Major finance for the City Project was expected to be provided by a further outside loan of N600 million. This, however, was already known to be doubtful because of the Federal Government's existing heavy borrowing.

Now, in 1998, reading again my letter of 22nd May 1982, perhaps there is a touch of hysteria in it, but its content certainly alerted the President – if such was needed – to see for himself when he came in June, rather than follow the prearranged itinerary of inspection. Its effect is clearly reflected in the record of the meeting the President held with Ministers and officials on 6th June 1982 (see Appendices).

As I had hoped, the President saw me privately after his tour of the City and the subsequent meeting. He was fully appreciative of my letter of 22nd May 1982, and I was able to elaborate about Consultancies. Obviously, the figures I had given in my letter influenced what took place at the meeting as shown in the Record:

> "Item (XVI)Consultancy. The President observed that the Ministry for FCT had engaged far too many Consultants at great cost to the extent that the bulk of the money being spent on Abuja is going to Consultants."

Before returning to Lagos the President inspected the work at the Presidential Lodge with me. As we parted, even though I know he trusted me, he said: "Do you really think it will be ready?" I promised it would be and really meant it.

In my letter to the President of 22nd May (see Appendices) I recommended that…

> "…all building works should be halted and proper inspections and assessments made regarding standard and even design, to check the state of the work and to decide whether they should be continued and, if so, on what basis. To be effective, a ruthless objective exercise must be well prepared and carried out independently of FCDA by reputable experienced professionals who, I am sure, would do this as a gesture to the Project without charge. I am sure this could be arranged. They would expect, however, to be given the fullest support and to know that their recommendations would be carried out."

Jack showing the President the model of the Abuja project
New Nigerian 8th June 1982

Increasingly involved as I was in FCDA and the whole Project, the June visit of the President, his meeting with Ministers and its Record, my private talk and so on, brought me ever closer.

"Item (XIV) of the Record – The National Assembly. The President's criticism of the design of the building. As a result, the Ad Hoc Committee to review the building was set up. I became a member as did the representative of *Kenzo Tange*, the Japanese Architects. The outcome was a re-design of the central feature of the building which had been thought quite out of keeping with Nigerian culture."

235

In fact, with all speed I prepared and submitted to the Permanent Secretary an Assessment headed 'The New Capital City of Abuja' dated 13th June 1982 (see Appendices). In this will be seen my views on aspects of the Master Plan, some of which had been discussed at the meeting on 6th June and figure in the Record. The situation regarding the whole Project had become so crucial that I determined to include an Immediate Strategy. By now I was copying my reports to the President, being convinced that he would be expecting them.

My Review of Consultancy was not considered by the FCDA Board until its meeting on 27th July, at which I was present, though copies of the Review, under strict confidential cover, had been with Board members for some time. It was obvious that members were taken aback at the excess of Consultancies revealed by the Report, and in essence, they accepted the suggested procedures for implementation. At the end of the meeting, members were told by the Chairman (Senior Minister) to hand back their copies to me as they left, so concerned was he that its contents might be made public!

The opportunity to act on the Report was at the next meeting of the Co-ordination Meeting of FCDA Consultants which eventually took place on the 17th and 18th August. All Consultants were warned that from then onwards the continuance of their Consultancy was regarded as being in doubt. A Form 'A' would be distributed at the meeting in which to give full current details of their Consultancies. These would be closely examined and assessed against the future strategy and decisions relating to the City Project to be taken by the FCDA Board. Consultancies would be tested and placed against five Groups, and then the Firms would be informed of the decisions regarding future prospects. In effect, those to be placed in Groups 4 and 5, for example, covering projects years ahead, must be regarded as at least halted or deferred indefinitely. After the Minister had outlined the position at the meeting, I explained the dire necessity for the proposed action. Mixing with the representatives afterwards I found the general reaction one of understanding and willingness to co-operate. Many, I thought, were not really surprised at the turn of events.

As the Permanent Secretary had not attended the Board meeting nor the FCDA Consultants' meeting on 17th and 18th August, I prepared a Report to him dated 2nd September (see Appendices), a copy of which was also sent to the President.

In early September, within a few weeks of the deadline for completion of the Presidential Lodge, I had to review my feelings and position regarding FCDA. It is fair to say that since arriving at FCDA in March 1982, I had quickly become engrossed with FCDA affairs and, after my engagement was formalised as Chief Project Engineer, I was under constant pressure within the Authority, on top of my commitment to the President regarding the Presidential Lodge.

During the succeeding months, I witnessed the general overall situation at FCDA deteriorate to the extent that, by the time of the August meeting with Consultants, I was consciously considering whether there really was a useful and productive role for me within the Authority. My Reports had become more insistent and outspoken about incompetence, corruption, the dire need for a re-appraisal of the City Project and, above all, the serious financial situation. Several major contractors with outstanding claims for very large sums came to tell me that cheques they had been given were rejected by banks, and that when they complained to the Director of Finance he simply admitted that cheques had been issued knowing they could not be honoured, but he wanted the contractors out of his office! Come what may, I was determined to see the completion of the Presidential Lodge – I had made a promise and I would keep it.

Despite being involved in other matters, I spent whole days at the Lodge. Its site was probably the most beautiful and spectacular in the City with magnificent views. I had discovered that the building was really a copy of the VIP Guest House in Niger State, in which Alhaji Shehu Shagari, as Federal President, had stayed and with which he was much taken. He knew that the prestigious Presidential Complex at Abuja could not possibly be ready by October, and in any case it was not at all to his taste. So he had asked for a Presidential Lodge to the design of the Guest House at Niger State with its arches and deep verandahs which fully expressed Nigerian culture and way of life.

Now, by careful planning, we were able to add to that design the additional buildings, such as: offices, committee/conference room, family quarters, enlarged personal staff facilities and even a small mosque. Nearby several houses for the entourage of officials serving the President were already under construction, and elsewhere on the site were houses for the police, and Security etc. In an isolated spot, a generator (with standby) would be housed to supply electricity to a local overhead distribution system. Water and drainage systems were also in hand, and all these facilities were at various stages of progress by contractors. I insisted that all work must be completed, tested and fully operational by not later than mid-September 1982.

However, certain vital provisions had not been planned: the steeply sloping area in front of the house had to be levelled to provide a surfaced car park for at least 50 vehicles, and a short spur access road off the nearby artery of the City must be constructed to finish at an arched entrance with guard rooms. Time was already too short, so I had to call in one or two of the major road contractors for these outside works. They co-operated to the full and accepted my assurance about payment, although the cost could have been 'lost' in one of their major road contracts already awaiting heavy back payments!

One day in late July while at the Lodge, I was met by an elderly, articulate Italian who had learnt of the Presidential Lodge under construction at Abuja and come to offer his help. His name eludes me now, but he presented me with a priced schedule of furniture, furnishings, electrical items and fittings relating to the Lodge, based on the Niger State Guest House design, for which he had apparently been responsible. He owned and ran an emporium in Lagos and another in Kaduna, and claimed to have well-established connections with Government Departments, supplying them with all grades of furniture, fittings and so on. He was a saviour to me! Obsessed with the building and ancillary works I had quite overlooked the vital requirements without which the Lodge, offices and many facilities would be useless!

I was able to check the gentleman's credentials with our Italian Building Contractor and other sources, but time was against us finding other suppliers, so I gave him a copy of the plan of the much enlarged Lodge and asked for a fully comprehensive and detailed, priced schedule with delivery and fitting out guaranteed for not later than mid-September. He delivered it within a few days. The total cost must have been around N50,000. When deliveries began – and to time – to my great relief on most of the consignments I saw the name *Heal's of London* – I had been fearful as to quality. Clearly, he was an Agent for *Heal's,* taking his 'cut'. In the original schedule he had shown me, one corner of the spacious lounge was to be fitted out with a bar counter and high stools, which might have been all right for the Niger State but not for Alhaji Shehu Shagari – so out it went!

For internal decoration I had opted for white throughout – predictably, there was no time for devising a colour scheme. However, the walls of the large lounge, the conference room etc., demanded some relief and when I mentioned this to my Italian supplier, he suggested large framed murals depicting Nigerian culture and great national events, such as Durbars etc., customarily organised in honour of visiting VIPs and the like. Recalling the Durbar which I had arranged for the visit to Kaduna of His Imperial Majesty Haile Selassie 1, Emperor of Ethiopia in1972, I concurred. The Italian's contacts were quite remarkable: within 48 hours a young Ibo artist arrived on site with paintings and sketches of his work. I was delighted. He explained that for large murals he worked with aerosol sprays, which were available in many colours, using oil paints with a paint brush for touching up faces and adding details.

I gave him three weeks in which to produce six framed murals, each about 12ft by 10ft. I think the total cost was of the order of N5,000 which he was paid through the Italian furniture supplier. The murals were ready on time – he told me he had worked to exhaustion – and once in place relieved the bareness of the walls admirably. (Sadly, in November 1999, I heard that most of the murals had been consequently removed on the orders of General Babangida.)

(My letter to the President of 25th July 1982 is in the Appendices.)

The Security System for the Lodge, devised by representatives of the Security Firm who must have inspected the building when I was not present, was quite preposterous. Certainly, it was a 'death blow' and very nearly made me pack my bag overnight and leave. I saw the Senior Minister with the proposal and he agreed to go to Lagos about it at once. I believe a much modified System was eventually installed.

September arrived and the President was due in just three weeks' time! I had kept the Senior Minister informed of the actions I had taken and the progress made. His anxiety that the Lodge should be ready for the President was even greater than mine and sustained me in exercising the freedom to act under tacit ministerial approval.

By now I was experiencing two contrasting feelings – apart from sheer weariness. One was of confidence that, despite all the problems, the Presidential Lodge would be ready on time – I had never allowed myself to think otherwise. The other was that, as days passed, I had to face my doubts about a continuing role for me at FCDA. In fact, with the Lodge assignment completed, the moment for decision had arrived. I recognised that I was stressed and overtired, and after all, I was 73! I made up my mind to speak frankly to the President during his coming stay in Abuja for the Independence Day Celebrations on 1st October 1982.

As the day approached members of his office and domestic staff arrived and installed themselves in their respective quarters to be ready to serve the President. During the small hours of the day on the evening of which the President would arrive at Abuja Airport and be driven straight to the Lodge, I was personally giving the newly laid fitted carpets a final run-over with a vacuum cleaner to remove the fluff. I was keyed-up, anticipating the moment when I would show the President that his doubts in June were unfounded, and this mundane task helped contain my excitement.

As he alighted from his car I greeted him with, "Welcome, Mr President, to the Presidential Lodge," and led him through the spacious entrance hall into the large lounge. As he settled into one of the deep settees I said, "You know, Sir, it really has been hard going," or words to that effect, and his characteristic response was, "Well, here I am in this beautiful lounge and you tell me there's a bedroom and bath upstairs, what more can I want?"

A large framed mural depicting a Durbar in the Conference Room

Ministers and officials began to arrive to see the President so I was able to leave for the Rest House. My faithful driver with the Range Rover was waiting to take me there – his overtime for weeks had been enormous. I could not have driven myself.

Each day, I went to the Lodge early to check that the water and electricity services were working properly and to make sure that the kitchen staff were satisfied, while the President was fully occupied with meetings and interviews. On 1st October I witnessed the Independence Day Ceremony at the Parade Ground and the President's address.

I was able to arrange to see the President on his last evening. My mind was now made up to ask for leave now that the assignment for which he had called me had been fulfilled. As for my return, from the various reports and personal letters I had been sending, he must already have been aware of my growing concern as to whether there could be a useful role for me within FCDA, unless it was drastically reconstructed to overcome widespread incompetence and corruption. Moreover, the outlook for its financial resources with which to progress the Project effectively seemed increasingly bleak. I believed, too, that, by now, the N600 million overseas loan had failed and an idea was forming in my mind. This time, should the President ask me to go to Lagos to see his family I would go for reasons which will soon become clear.

As we talked that evening, it was obvious that he was as troubled as I was – probably more so. After all, he bore the heavy burden and responsibility for what he had rightly conceived as being his greatest contribution to his beloved country – bringing together as one nation the ethnic and religious divisions so detrimental to its future well-being. A new Capital away from Lagos was just one element towards that end. Nigeria, the Giant of Africa, was engaged in fighting itself.

We talked on, perhaps the longest talk we had ever had. When I asked for permission to proceed on leave, I explained that I would have to consider the circumstances in which it might be possible to return. The remarks I had made in my letter to the President of 22nd May about an independent inspection of the work in progress seemed ever more relevant, and this might be the opportunity to take it further.

Realistically, the City Project ought to be halted or severely restricted due to the lack of funds. So I put to the President a proposal for what I would describe as 'UK Technical Aid'. This would take the form of bringing together a number of experienced professional engineers, who had worked for varying periods in public service in Nigeria, as a team to re-appraise the whole City Project and make recommendations. They would come with a sense of dedication to a country and people whom they had come to regard with affection. Their salaries and allowances would be met through UK Technical Aid. Nigeria would be responsible for their transport, quarters, lighting, offices, support staff and so on. I would join them, perhaps as Manager and to liaise with FCDA, and I told him I could think of several people who would be only too pleased and honoured to be invited to come. To put this idea to the UK High Commission in Lagos would be my reason for accepting the President's invitation to go to Lagos to see his family.

The President agreed to my going on leave and, as I had anticipated, he again asked me to join the plane taking him back to Lagos, and there see his family, an honour in itself. This would be only the fourth time I had been to Lagos during my many years in Nigeria, and then only because of going on or returning from leave, otherwise I used the International Airport at Kano in the North.

In 1982, it was well known that it took several hours to make the 12-mile journey to or from the Airport at Lagos because of the fearsome traffic congestion. This time, however, there was no such difficulty since the road had been closed to all traffic for the President's car with police outriders. I was put in an official car following the President and within half-an-hour I was dropped off at the Special Federal Guest House in Lagos. I would be returning to Abuja in a Nigerian Air Force transport plane so it was important to make contact with the UK High Commission quickly. Attempts by telephone failed but I left a message. The next day, I was taken to Dodan Barracks – the President had followed the Military Heads of State in using Dodan Barracks as his base rather than the State House, for obvious reasons – to see the President, who took me to the family quarters where I was introduced to his two wives and his many children, altogether a great privilege. In the evening, I had supper with him and one of his Ministers. We embraced as I left.

In the car returning to the Guest House, I felt a terrible sadness that we might never meet again. Happily, this was not so, but there were turbulent years ahead for Nigeria before this was to happen. I left early the next day to fly back to Abuja sitting on the hard floor of the Air Force transporter surrounded by various packages etc. – a distinct contrast to the President's flight!

It later transpired that there had been a muddle over telephone numbers, which had led to my failure to contact the UK High Commission. Now I had to prepare for leave. Most important was to arrange for the decisions regarding Consultancy to be carried forward. To that end, I placed the details in the hands of the Director of Architecture (see Appendices). I can only conjecture as to their implementation.

I saw the Senior Minister and the Permanent Secretary and formally asked for leave, although I think by now both had realised that it was most unlikely that I would be returning. I was, however, able to see the Deputy High Commissioner in Kaduna on my way to Kano for the journey home on 21st October 1982 for leave, and explained my proposal for possible UK Technical Aid for Abuja, which the President had agreed I should mention.

So ended my years of service in Nigeria which had begun with my arrival at Kano Airport on 18th April 1958 and finished with my departure from that Airport on 21st October 1982 with a break from 22nd September 1978 to 11th March 1982.

Many expatriates who have served in Nigeria would, I think, agree that credulity has no limit as to what happens, or is alleged to have happened, at any one time. One learns to make a judgement in each instance as it arises, or is threatening to arise, in order to decide how to react.

My departure from Kano airport on 21st October 1982 was a perfect example of credulity stretched to its limit. Before catching the *Nigerian Airways* flight to London Heathrow scheduled for 4.30pm, I had lunched with a colleague of long standing based in Kano who dropped me off at

244

the Airport at about 3.30pm. When I presented my documents at the *Nigerian Airways* desk, the Nigerian Duty Officer indicated that there would be no flight that evening, as the aircraft had not yet left London. (In 1982, although *Nigerian Airways* had a number of aircraft for internal flights, it was generally thought that there was only one aircraft for international flights.) When I asked for an explanation, he said that London had informed him that a rat had got into one of the aircraft's engines and had yet to be captured and removed!

Anywhere else one would have treated such an explanation with derision and scorn as an obvious lie, but not in Nigeria if one sought co-operation regarding any alternative which might be available. I happened to know that an hour later there was a *British Caledonian* flight to Gatwick Airport in the UK. (As Nigerian Government officers we were required to use *Nigerian Airways* services.) I asked if perhaps the officer could arrange for me to be put on the *British Caledonian* flight as I was going on leave, and my family were expecting me. He said he would make enquiries, and then told me that he had been able to arrange a seat for me. My hand was not empty as I reached for my documents and to shake his hand expressing my grateful thanks. Even so, one had to be just a little doubtful whether such 'help' was actually genuine. Fortunately, that evening it was and I went through *British Caledonian* check without demur. (Before we took off I had found the true explanation: the Head of State – then General Gowon – had commandeered the one aircraft for a State Visit to Canada!) Once settled in my seat, I asked if a message could be sent through London to my home, to divert my youngest son to meet me at Gatwick and not at Heathrow.

To round off the story of this journey, on giving his usual welcome on board the flight, the Flight Captain gave his name as "...Muggeridge" – I did not catch his first name properly – and his accent had a touch of Australian or New Zealand about it which made me curious. After checking the surname with a stewardess I gave her my card and asked her to take it forward to the Captain, and she returned to invite me to meet him. He was a burly pleasant-looking middle-aged man and he explained that, though normally on the North American route, he had been called at very short notice to take over this aircraft from Gatwick to Nigeria and back because of staff illness. As we talked we worked out that we were probably second cousins! I knew that one of my father's brothers had emigrated to New Zealand as a young man and he would be the link.

Captain Muggeridge lived in Guildford, Surrey, and when at home all telephone calls had to be answered, no matter the time of day, in case – as of now – he was required to fill in for an emergency. As I was about to return to my seat, he said how much he admired my brother Malcolm when he appeared on TV and radio, but added that, since he was listed in the telephone directory as 'M. Muggeridge' there had been several occasions when he had answered the telephone in the small hours, to find that the caller wanted to talk to him about Jesus!

Arriving at Gatwick I was overjoyed to find Terry, my youngest son, waiting for me with his near-vintage Triumph Vitesse Convertible. When I insisted that we stop at a pub to have a drink I got my first shock. I had been away from the UK for only three years but drinks had gone up by almost a quarter!

Back in my daughter's home in Maidenhead, I received a letter dated 26th October 1982 from Mr Brian Austin, the Deputy High Commissioner in Kaduna:

> Dear Mr Muggeridge,
> I hope that you had a good journey back from Kano and are now enjoying some well-earned leave in the UK. As agreed I reported our discussion to the High Commissioner, Lagos, but I was not able to contact you before your departure.
>
> The High Commissioner did see the President personally during a visit by Mr Heath to Lagos on 20th October. In the course of the interview the High Commissioner gave the President an opportunity to raise with him the matter which we discussed, but the President did not do so.
>
> The High Commissioner shares some of the doubts which I mentioned to you about a solely British involvement in any review. We should, however, be willing to consider carefully the proposal should we receive any Nigerian approach.
>
> If you hear any more of the idea please let me know.

Of course, I should have realised that the time was far from propitious to raise my proposal. I am afraid, too, that even if the team had materialised, it would have encountered countless frustrations.

Consequently on 11th November I wrote to the Permanent Secretary, Alhaji Aliyu Mohammed, informing him I would not be returning from leave (see Appendices).

Postscript

After a long period of military rule, His Excellency Alhaji Shehu Shagari was democratically elected the First Executive President of Nigeria in 1979 and then consequently re-elected for a second term in September 1983. As President, he was the Commander-in-Chief of the Armed Forces of Nigeria. A decent, honest and peace-loving man, he gave democracy pride of place, abhorring any form of corruption, violence or excesses. Rocketing oil prices in the latter part of the 1970's had provided the Nigerian government with a period of relative prosperity and during his tenure, agriculture, housing for all, external relations and general standard of living improved considerably. However, a world recession was to lead to the ending of the oil boom and by 1982, mounting corruption and other crime problems changed the economic atmosphere and helped plunge Nigeria into a cycle of massive debt with large scale unemployment.

On 31st December 1983, his democratically elected government was overthrown in a military *coup d'état*, and he was subsequently imprisoned for two and a half years, no charge ever having been proven against him. General Buhari's arrival in power was initially welcomed by many as an answer to the widespread chaos in the country, but it also heralded the collapse of the democratic experiment. However, in 1985 Buhari was ousted in a further coup led by General Babangida, and he in turn by General Sani Abacha in 1993. Nigeria embarked on one of the most brutal and ruthless periods of military dictatorship since its Independence.

With a fluctuating oil market, prices largely affected by the politics of the Middle East, Nigeria fell into a progressively deeper trading debt and annual inflation reached three figures. Politics was seen by many as the only way to wealth. A get-rich-quick mentality seemed to seize many gaining a significant public office, and millions of Naira were spirited out of the public purse into private ones abroad. The cost of fraud and corruption to the Nigerian citizen rose ever higher as inefficiency was encouraged and rewarded, and excessive margins were built into public projects and contracts to meet personal interests. Even low-paid public servants joined in, often inventing needless new bureaucracy with the sole intention of providing opportunity to extract a payment or gratuity. Corruption also caused tensions within the armed forces already divided along religious and ethnic lines. Soldiers in the elite National Guard were seen to enjoy vastly better pay and facilities than those in rank and file forces.

General Abacha died in 1998 of a heart attack and was succeeded by General Abubakar, who promised to restore democracy in stages. On 29th May 1999, Olusegun Obasanjo, a former political prisoner under Abacha was sworn in as Nigeria's first democratically elected president since the toppling of Shehu Shagari in 1983, some sixteen years earlier. In fact as military ruler from 1976 to 1979, he had previously handed power over to Shehu Shagari. Obasanjo has managed to consolidate Nigeria's position as West Africa's political heavyweight and a key player in the Commonwealth, but even with restored democracy the country continues to be beset by violence, especially in Lagos, the Central Plateau and the southern oilfields.

Ethnic, religious, political and economic problems beset the government and progress to reform will be slow. Fraud, corruption and an endemic absence of trust – the Nigeria Disease – hinders achievement of a climate conducive for doing business, and foreign companies and Nigerians alike have learnt to be cautious before investing. With higher OPEC prices, oil exports are once again leading the way in restimulating the economy, the country's daily oil production increasing to 2.5 million barrels of crude. Nigeria, despite its seemingly intractable problems, is potentially rich.

And for the time being at least, after many dark years of iron-fisted rule, Nigeria once again enjoys a period of democracy and relatively stable government – Olusegun Obasanjo gained an overwhelming victory in presidential elections held in April 2003.

David Williams
March 2005

250

Appendices

Speech by the Chairman of SUDA, Alhaji Shehu Shagari, in October 1977 on the occasion of the signing of the formal Contract Agreement for the new Sokoto Central Market and new Central Lorry Park

It is now almost exactly a year since His Excellency the Military Governor of Sokoto State came here on 28th October 1976 and formally inaugurated the Sokoto Urban Development Authority created by Edict No.10 from 1st July of that year. That was, of course, a momentous occasion. In his speech, His Excellency was kind enough to refer to the enthusiasm with which the Authority, so soon after its inception, had forged ahead with the New Market Project and hoped that we would beat the target date for completion. Well, we may be just a little behind our schedule, but with the signing of this Contract Agreement today the way forward should be clear to the finale by June 1979. Then the Opening Ceremony will indeed be a moment for real celebration for the State, for Sokoto City and, naturally, for SUDA and for all those who will have contributed to the splendid achievement.

The signing of a Contract is, of course, a decisive stage in the process of creating the reality of construction from the planning, design and documentation which have to come first. A Project of the magnitude of the new Market and the supporting works has called for much thought and consideration, and it should be made known that the Authority has devoted a great deal of time and has sought suggestions and advice from a number of quarters aimed at ensuring that the final result will be not only the best possible but will meet with general satisfaction since, above all else, a Market is for the well-being of the whole Community.

Let me now take this opportunity to make public the many interesting and outstanding features of the Project. From the very first it is important to realise that the Project embraces considerably more than just the Market, important and vital as that is. Included is a new General Lorry Park to replace the existing one which we all know is of very poor standard and often quite unusable in the rains. The new park will be of reinforced concrete construction and will accommodate upwards of 400 vehicles and is to be provided with amenities such as stores, stalls, shelters, toilets and security lighting. It is to be situated on the large area at the rear of *Tradev* in Aliu Jode Road facing the new Market. To provide for the traffic wishing to reach the new Park and the new Market from all directions, there will be a major road development in the area including a dual-carriageway perimeter road around the new Market, all with modern drainage and street lighting. This aspect of the Project should now be looked upon as progress in urbanisation which is rapidly taking place throughout the whole country and particularly in the Capitals and other major cities. The cost of these works will be N6 million and a substantial grant in aid is confidently expected from the State Government.

The objective and purpose of the new Market has been to give Sokoto a permanent Central Market preserving the long standing tradition of stalls for individual traders but incorporating all modern amenities plus special features to render the whole concept one which should ensure pride of place for Sokoto in National Development Programmes.

The site is the open space of over 50 acres behind these offices. It is, perhaps, not too easy to envisage that, within the space of two years, all the structures and other details which may be seen on the drawings exhibited today will have acquired substance on this land. Almost the whole area will be surfaced with a lightly reinforced concrete. To keep this drained, there will be a system of open lined drains protected by railing and top grillage. The whole will be surrounded by a high security wall. At the main (south) entrance will be situated the large Market Lorry Park to accommodate upwards of 150 vehicles and provided with grain stores, food hotels, shelters, toilet and security lighting. Adjacent will be parks for private cars and taxis. Nearby will be a Police Station, Area Court and Information Bureau. Each of the other three entrances will have private car and taxi parks with shelters. Inside the Market area, 5,000 stalls of varying designs and types will be provided to accommodate both wet and dry trades. Special provision is being made for meat, fish, oils and yam sellers. Within a Works Yard will be a Fire Station on 24-hour duty with trained personnel and a Landrover Fire Tender, sleeping quarters, workshops for maintenance staff, and garage space for plant and equipment such as septic tank emptiers, refuse collection vehicles and so on. Water supply including fire hydrants will cover the whole of the Market and storage is provided by a 100,000-gallon elevated tank. 12 cubicle toilet blocks will be appropriately spaced in the Market area. Full-scale security lighting will be installed over the entire complex and all key points will be connected by intercom. The Administrative Building, to house the managerial and accounting staff and a Clinic, will be a two-storey special feature in traditional style at the heart of the Market. Elsewhere will be other features such as a Mosque and open recreational areas with play facilities. The cost of the new Market with all these amenities will be N23½ million. The Authority is grateful for the assistance of the State Government with a loan of N10 million and it has already made arrangements with commercial banks for the remaining finance so that the total of N23½ million is assured.

The task is an onerous one but I feel sure that *Messrs. Kueppers (Nigeria) Ltd.* the Firm of Contractors who have won the Contract, have the capacity and capability of executing and completing the whole Project by June 1979.

SUDA, with our Consulting Engineers, *Scott Wilson Kirkpatrick (Nigeria) and Partners*, look forward to two years of very hard work in a spirit of understanding and co-operation culminating in the fulfilment by *Messrs. Kueppers* of this outstanding and splendid Project, the new Sokoto Central Market and its supporting works.

It will be for me a moment of great pleasure and pride to sign this Contract Agreement today for, and on behalf of, the Sokoto Urban Development Authority. In doing so, I wish to place on record my greatest appreciation and thanks to all those who have contributed towards making this possible, especially His Excellency the Military Governor of Sokoto State and Members of his Government, and other Government Officials who have actively participated in all the preliminary arrangements. Last, but not least, to the Management of SUDA and, of course, our Consultants, *Scott Wilson Kirkpatrick*. I look forward to the day when we all gather together again for the Opening Ceremony of the completed Project. Thank you.

* * * * *

The response given by Mr Siegfried Winkel, Managing Director, *Messrs. Kueppers (Nigeria) Ltd.*

Mr Chairman, Honourable Commissioners, Distinguished Guests, Ladies and Gentlemen,

Messrs. Kueppers (Nigeria) Ltd., the Company which I represent, is most honoured to have been awarded this very important Project of the New Sokoto Central Market and the supporting works. We are fully conscious of the mighty task which is now before us and which we are determined to bring to completion by the target date of 30th June 1979.

To keep this target date for the completion of all the works involved, as just explained by the Chairman in detail, you will agree with me that, with the usual way of construction, this will not be possible.

A detailed planning of the whole programme will be prepared, checked and controlled by a computer. Modern construction equipment, special formwork for reinforced concrete works, prefabrication of different elements of the construction will be provided. Such a preparation of the work based on industrial production experience is the only way for a successful completion of such a project in time, and not to forget the quality of the work required.

To organise all these things in time it is very important for us to have the full support and co-operation of all Authorities concerned. What we really need are quick and unbureaucratic decisions and I request all officers in charge to give us this support.

Ladies and Gentlemen, as I sign this Contract Agreement on behalf of *Kueppers (Nigeria) Ltd*, may I express our sincere thanks to the Sokoto State Government, the Chairman, Members and Management of the Sokoto Urban Development Authority for the opportunity to execute all these works which we will do to the utmost of our capability and capacity during the coming months and I am confident that we will give every satisfaction.

* * * * *

255

To: Permanent Secretary Federal Capital Development Authority Suleja
From: J.R. Muggeridge Consultant FCDA

Introductory Submission, Observations and Appraisal Concerning the New Federal Capital of Nigeria at Abuja, Niger State

1. Personal, Appointment, Arrival

(a) Personal

My previous public service in Nigeria covered the period April 1958 to September 1978. Initially appointed as an Executive (Civil) Engineer in the then Northern Nigeria Ministry of Works, I progressed from September 1959 to July 1971 in the ranks of Assistant Senior/Senior/Principal Executive Engineer occupying successively the duty posts of Provincial Engineer in Kabba, Benue, Niger (two tours), Kabba again (during the Civil War), Zaria culminating as Divisional Engineer in Kaduna. Before taking UK leave from July 1971, I was appointed Chief Engineer to the Kaduna Capital Development Board (KCDB) and took up the post in November 1971, remaining until November 1975. KCDB was legally constituted from 1st January 1972, and I played a principal role in its setting up and the early implementation of some important development projects of which the new Kaduna Central Market, opened in February 1975, may be regarded as an outstanding achievement.

KCDB also had the parallel but separate responsibility as the Town Planning Authority for an area of 25 miles radius from Kaduna, this also being an aspect of my duties in collaboration with a Town Planning Officer. About to retire in November 1975, however, I was asked by the newly appointed Military Governor of the then North Western State (Colonel Umaru Mohammed) to move to Sokoto where it was his intention to establish a Development Authority for that Capital on the lines of KCDB and, in particular, to design and implement a new Central Market for Sokoto. I was pleased and honoured to accept the move to Sokoto where for the first six months I occupied the post of Chief Civil Engineer in the Ministry of Works under the Permanent Secretary, Alhaji Shehu Kangiwa, during the preparation and passing into law of the Edict to establish Sokoto Urban Development Authority (SUDA), largely modelled on that of KCDB. Also during this period, and knowing that I was to become the General Manager and Chief Executive of SUDA (as from 1st July 1976), as an extra-mural activity I prepared the basic design for the new Sokoto Central Market which was to be the first major project to be undertaken by SUDA. The Military Governor appointed Alhaji Shehu Shagari as the Chairman of the Authority and, although at that time I knew of him by name only, the significance and immeasurable value of having him in that position was quickly apparent. His consistent encouragement, support, with advice and friendship - the last of which I treasured most during those first two years following the establishment of SUDA – will never be forgotten. It is fair to say that, but for his and the Military Governor's support, the new Sokoto Central Market would not be there to this day, receiving I believe, nationwide commendation. The eagerness with which I responded to the call to return to Nigeria will, therefore, be understood and, I fervently hope that I may be granted the opportunity to serve to the fullest capacity deriving from my professional experience during over 50 years, 20 of which have been in Nigeria, which, without question, is second only in affection to my own Country.

(b) Appointment and Arrival

In response to your letter of appointment of 9th February 1982, I left UK by air on 11th March 1982, reaching Lagos by 20.45hrs where I was received with every courtesy and privilege by State Protocol and accommodated in the Federal Government Special Guest House. I reported to State House and FCDA during the morning of Friday 12th March, at the former being asked to see the President at 19.30hrs. The following evening, Saturday 13th March, I had the great pleasure of spending almost two hours with him. On Monday 15th March, after travelling to Suleja via Kaduna you gave me a most kindly welcome. May I say how much I appreciated the reception given me here in FCDA and Suleja by everyone.

Acting on your initial instruction, I spent the next two days touring the City etc., Mr F.C. Obinani kindly acting as guide, and on the third day made myself known to as many of the Directors and Advisers etc. as possible. I was delighted also to renew contact with Mr Buhari Dikko, Chief Engineer, who had served under me in his first appointment as Executive Engineer at KCDB, and many others whom I had known in the course of my previous 20 years service. It was an experience not without emotion, as all were so sincere in their pleasurable greeting.

I am most grateful to you for giving me so much time in the late evening of Thursday 18th March, if only that by so doing you gave me confidence that you expect, and will be demanding from me, a dedicated contribution to this most crucial project of the new Capital of Nigeria. As a start, you agreed that I should set down some introductory observations, and an appraisal deriving from this initial and obviously cursory involvement in the Project. You accepted, too, that I might do so completely frankly, despite knowing that I must inevitably be far from conversant with the innumerable facts of such a project. Nonetheless, it is not unusual to find value in a new objective point of view. May I also mention that my long experience has taught me that, despite the great variation in the nature and magnitude which occurs in Project work, the approach, conduct and implementation should emerge as broadly similar if effective progress and ultimate success are to be realised.

2. Observations

(a) Over-riding political considerations

After the President had concluded his State Visit to the UK in 1981 he requested that I should see him. His strong determination to push ahead with the new Capital so that it could be the operational base of the Federal Government before the election of 1985, was quite evident then. It is, therefore, no surprise to find that that aspect is as powerful as ever, if not more so, if, as seems probable, progress is uneven or lagging. Without exception, everyone involved to whom I have spoken, accepted the dominance of the political consideration, although it might be that their efforts were not determined by it. However, its influence is inescapable, crucially up to September 1982, and certainly up to say July 1983. For that reason, it would be assumed that Government has, long since, laid down its minimum requirements/provisions in the way of buildings, services, amenities, communications, roads etc. etc. as near consistent as possible with the ultimate overall requirements/provisions of the completed Project, otherwise there is every possibility that the latter will be irreversibly and detrimentally affected. The rolling and cumulative effect on cost too must be mentioned in passing. Directors I have seen seemed somewhat uncertain or unaware of a specific, defined written schedule of minimum requirements to meet the political considerations, although in general terms each had fairly clear ideas. They were, however, much concerned about this aspect. As it is, during our discussion on Thursday evening you did outline minimum requirements for June 1982 (by which time the President intends to make his presence known in the City) and for September 1982, and also gave a general projection to say July 1983.

As you instructed, an indication only deriving from my notes at the time is attached and must be subject to preparation in the fullest detail if it is to form the basis for frequent and accurate monitoring. You will no doubt direct in the light of what follows later in this submission.

(b) General implementation
Ignoring the requirements demanded by the over-riding political considerations, it seems evident that works in progress fall into two main categories, viz. roads and buildings (mostly housing). I have yet to see the Airport, Jabi Dam etc. and, no doubt, there are other elements of Civil Engineering works of which I am still ignorant – in a few days it is not possible to assimilate all such activities, whether under active construction yet let off to contract awaiting a start, but to a seasoned eye a quick appraisal is still possible and can be useful. During touring, of course, I have seen the road and drainage works in progress but have not considered them in any detail. In fact, I have yet to identify clearly which actual roads are under construction on the sites. I have concentrated on the building construction works for the immediate purpose knowing that they are vital to meeting the requirements of Government.

Apart from special buildings such as the Conference Centre, Presidential Lodge, Presidential Guest House etc., the main concentration of building works is in the Accelerated District Construction Programme (ACDP). Related to the present nomenclature on the ACDP map, development in Area A predominates, although it is understood that Areas B,C,D,E, and P will now be progressively active. Figures of housing units of the various types under construction are given in progress reports and it is advisable to rely on these for the moment. Broadly, it seems that about 1,000 units are of panel (System) construction and about 2,000 of traditional blockwork construction. Some 200 of the latter are currently occupied by Police, FCDA site staff etc., on an improvised arrangement i.e. water is provided from water bowsers, electricity by generators. It seems that this arrangement is, or may have to be, used more generally in order to meet the requirements against September 1982 which appear to be uncertain. This may be due to my insufficient enquiries in the last few days but there is an impression of some lack of consultation and co-ordination amongst those concerned.

The Accelerated District was chosen to be experimental in relation to the development of other areas of the Capital. It is clear that, particularly in the case of the blocks of housing units, these are too close relative to land availability, and above all to tropical living conditions where air circulation is so vital. Architecturally, too, they are drab and uninteresting and much aggravated by repetition. Such design as they have is quite alien to a Nigerian setting, especially within the wonderful scenic opportunity and advantage of the location of the new Capital. One fervently hopes that the result of the experiment has been fully taken into consideration for the future, yet it is of much concern that no changes can be discerned in the start now under way in the NW area (two areas).

The sharply contrasting quality of construction work must be mentioned. The panel units by *SAE Ltd.*, are a pleasure to inspect but it is professionally impossible not to express much strong criticism of the very low standard seen at many of the traditional blockwork buildings of all types. I have not, as yet, seen the drawings and specifications, but I cannot believe that these are being observed to any validity. The Resident Director of the Consultants engaged for the supervision of the building contracts assured me that he had reported a number of the contractors for unacceptable workmanship, materials and general performance, but no action has resulted. The Project Controller confirmed that he too had reported likewise but without effect. May I instance one four-storey block (16 No.1 bedroom units) which I inspected with the Project Controller which, without doubt, should be condemned. I have earlier mentioned the NW area where, in essence, the known shortcomings demonstrated at ADCP are not being avoided. About 2,000 panel (system) blocks are scheduled and a considerable number are in progress. Also about 1,000 traditional blockwork units are to be provided and, again, those in progress are little better, if at all, than those at ADCP.

I could detail cases where roofing sheets and timbers are clearly well below specification and acceptability, and many instances where roof construction is too sub-standard to withstand the strong winds which are bound to be experienced later on in the high and exposed terrain of the City. The Capital is to stand for all time and therefore the highest standards of materials and workmanship are essential and should be insisted upon. Otherwise in the future there may well be grave problems of replacements, rehabilitation, expensive maintenance, for which the originators of the new Capital will be severely censured. I have to say that immediate correctives need to be applied to so much of the building work now in progress. It is a situation which demands priority attention. The newcomer who is acutely conscious of, but not involved with, the political consideration, perhaps sees this pressure to demonstrate the apparent significant progress being made at Abuja, albeit at the sacrifice of the lasting quality of the product, as, in the result,

THE LATERITE ROAD

producing the very opposite political outcome. It would be unfortunate indeed if that were to be the fruits of all the efforts being made to further this great imaginative concept.

3. Appraisal

As an appraisal of the practical/physical situation regarding the Project, the observations under 2(b) above may be adequate bearing in mind the very limited time for gathering information for an assessment. Despite its sheer magnitude, the creation of the new Capital Abuja, probably extending over 20 or more years, is nonetheless a finite Project in the meaning of that term. The FCDA has been created to carry it through to completion.

In that context, experience has shown that a Ministry structure is not wholly suitable as the most effective and efficient instrument for the implementing Authority. There will, of course, be provision for a Board with a Chairman (who may or may not be a Minister within Government) and Members drawn from various appropriate sources, whose primary function will be to determine and approve policy proposals, deal with major tenders and so on, but otherwise would leave the overall organisation and control to the officers appointed to the Authority, on account of their expertise and experience appropriate to the nature of the Project entrusted to the Board. Some of the officers may well be from Government on secondment although there are known to be those who are not agreeable to this, fearing that they may be overlooked for promotion in their parent Department. Also, such officers are subject to recall, posting etc., at any time which could deprive the Authority of an officer who has become conversant with the functions and methods within the Authority.

When what are now called Parastatals, such as KCDB and SUDA, came into being it was with the definite intention that their closely knit structure would be more dynamic and effective than a Ministry in carrying out Projects. Moreover, as the Projects would be creative and constructional it would be essential for the Authority's Chief Executive to be supported by a strong and experienced professional team of engineers, architects etc., under its own team leader. This team, in turn, would be supported by technicians, supervisors, draughtsmen etc., as necessary. Overall control, general administration and finance would be the responsibility of the Chief Executive and he would maintain constant contact with the leader of the professional team. A Ministry structure, with its long-established pattern of Departments and Divisions, tends to lead to Heads of Departments etc., going it alone rather than regarding themselves as members of a team. There is no recognisable team head outside the Permanent Secretary of the Ministry who brings together effectively the operations of the Heads of the professional Departments or Divisions. Allowing for my very brief association with FCDA, from my discussions with Directors I have sensed the absence of the feeling of a team and of a leader within a professional context. This is in no way to imply that the Directors do not look to you as the Head of the Ministry, but it is at the professional/technical level, where decisions on technical and professional aspects have to be jointly taken, that there will be a gap. I would like to suggest that this gap should be filled immediately as it is clear that the Project is at a most critical stage when it must move forward dramatically if it is to be ready to meet the requirements of Government as already mentioned and as broadly outlined in the attachment.

Already I cannot but be aware that, amongst the Directors, you have sensitive questions of relationship. I believe that, to a large degree, the Directors have been chosen to provide some balance of origin and relationship. If the need for a team leader is accepted then some difficulty may arise in the selection of a team leader from amongst the Directors, each of whom on professional grounds alone may be more than suitable. I may say that I believe the Directors would not look amiss at the appointment of a team leader from outside their number who should, by virtue of his detachment, be more able to bring them together professionally in determined pursuit of their undoubted desire to contribute to the Project to their fullest effect. Moreover, their leader would assume overall responsibility to the Chief Executive (Permanent Secretary) and the Board for their joint operations which, again, should make for general efficiency. I have not seen the Establishment for FCDA but an appropriate title for the team leader might be Chief Project Director, avoiding the use of a term such as 'General Manager' which, though customary with Development Authorities, implies that he is also the Chief Executive. No conflict could possibly arise, therefore, concerning your own status as Permanent Secretary/Chief Executive. It will be no easy task to establish the position and authority of the Chief Project Director (if appointed) since he will have to win the co-operation and understanding of the Directors, particularly the professional ones, but with open appeal and discussion I believe their confidence would soon be forthcoming and that they would come to see the overall advantage to be gained from having a leader at their level with a professional background and experience. I believe you to be much concerned about the urgent need to knit together all the material and practical requirements to satisfy the Government's political considerations.

4. Strategy for the coming months

In simple – perhaps military – terms, this means the deployment of resources – material, manpower, financial – to achieve the requirements of Government against June 1982, September 1982 and an initial projection to say July 1983. The attachment I referred to earlier may cover just an outline strategy which has to be drawn up, of course, in full and adequate detail including timing. Such a strategy may well be in existence, but its need is so vital that this exercise herein may not be without some value and interest. The merit of a strategy, when confronted with specific demands to a timetable, is that the limits of operations must be defined. Activities and operations which do not fall within the laid-down limits of the strategy must be ruthlessly rejected or set aside. As there are almost always financial strictures regarding any Project, invariably its estimate is overtaken by rising costs etc., the limits imposed by the strategy also producing closer financial control or restraint, which can only be budgetarily advantageous.

Any agreed strategy should be made known widely throughout the Authority concerned so that all those involved, at whatever level, may be conversant with the objectives to be achieved and may know the reason and purpose for works they are being called upon to perform.

For the successful preparation and prosecution of the strategy for these very crucial months ahead it is absolutely essential to know the extent to which Government and its various arms (Executive, Legislative, Administrative etc.) intends to function at Abuja from September 1982 and onwards to say July 1983. Even a phased movement of personnel, equipment etc. is an intricate operation which has to be thoroughly prepared and executed at both ends if chaos is to be avoided. From even the vague indications which I have gathered about Government's requirements – elements of six Ministries, for example – it is clear that FCDA is concerned with a highly complex exercise involving many practical and physical matters, not least of which are the basic needs for accommodation, offices, furnishings, services, road and other communications. Many hundreds from the President downwards will be concentrating on Abuja, and as the rainy season will not have finished this may well aggravate the problems and difficulties.

Reverting to the Ministry structure as against the more closely knit one of a Development Authority, the much greater freedom of decision-taking and implementation (up to prescribed, but still wide, limits) normally ruling in the latter, is essential to the effective conduct of a strategy, particularly one as crucial and short-timed as that now facing FCDA. The professional team with its Chief, as suggested earlier, would need this greater freedom and discretion if it is to produce the results demanded by the strategy. Since overall responsibility would rest with the Chief Project Director, it must be imperative to establish guidelines for his freedom of decision-taking and implementation, bearing in mind, of course, that he has constant access to the Chief Executive in cases of doubt.

As an aside, I must be allowed to point out how difficult, almost impossible it must be for FCDA to conduct its business while the offices in Suleja are so open to access by all and sundry. Many of those who fill the narrow corridors and crowd the ante-rooms of the Directors etc., surely cannot have legitimate business there. Such perpetual disturbance can only be detrimental to the efficiency of the staff who would conscientiously try to carry out their work. I mention this aspect only because such conditions which cause distraction could be one of several factors which would adversely effect the conduct of the strategy and ought, therefore, to be eliminated if at all possible.

5. Summary

Paragraph 1 above – Personal, appointment, arrival. No summary.

Paragraph 2 above – Observations

(a) Over-riding political considerations. Emphasises the political considerations and the minimum requirements for June 1982, for September 1982 and an initial projection to say July 1983 which must be achieved by FCDA.

(b) General implementation. Notes first impressions of activities etc. in Accelerated District A and two areas of NW District. Comments critically on the low standard of much of the building works particularly of the houses of traditional blockwork construction. Expresses disappointment with the experimental layout etc., of ACDP and points out that changes are not being reflected as yet in NW District. Senses a lack of professional consultation and co-ordination amongst those concerned with aspects of implementation in ACDP. Suggests that there is a danger that the demand for progress, which is seen to be taking place at the sacrifice of the lasting quality of the product, may produce the very opposite of the political outcome intended.

Paragraph 3 above – Appraisal
Questions whether the Ministry structure for FCDA, being a Development Authority charged with responsibility for a specific Project, is really the most effective instrument for implementation. The more closely knit structure associated with a Development Authority may be preferable particularly as the actual operations revolve round a team of experienced professionals such as engineers, architects and so on but which needs a leader answerable to the Chief Executive. Immediate consideration should be given to the selection of a team leader from outside the present Directors in FCDA, thus avoiding sensitive questions of relationship amongst the Directors. Leader could be designated Chief Project Director to preserve the status of the Permanent Secretary as Chief Executive of the whole of FCDA. Not easy to establish the position and authority of the Chief Project Director (if appointed) but with the co-operation and understanding of the Directors such an appointment should be beneficial to progress and implementation.

Paragraph 4 above – Strategy for the coming months.

Imperative to prepare, if not already done, a strategy to meet the requirements of Government against June 1982, September 1982 and an initial projection to say July 1983. Its merit lies in its definition of specific demands to conform to a timetable justifying the ruthless rejection, or setting aside, of all or any operations and activities which do not fall within the strategy. Also assists to control or restrain finance. Agreed strategy must be made known widely throughout FCDA so that those concerned at all levels may be conversant with the objective and purpose of their work being their contribution to the general achievement. The extent to which Government and its various arms intends to function at Abuja with the timetable must be ascertained, so that the strategy can be matched to it. Even phased movement of personnel etc., will be an intricate operation calling for thorough preparation and execution at both ends to avoid chaos. The exercise will be a highly complex one involving many hundreds from the President down-wards. Essential to grant greater freedom of decision-taking and implementation up to prescribed, but still wide, levels to the Chief Project Director, to ensure achieving the agreed strategy. Makes comment on the FCDA offices in Suleja which allows access to all and sundry, many of whom cannot have legitimate business to conduct. Such disturbance cannot be conducive to the efforts of the staff trying conscientiously to perform their work. Conditions could adversely affect the conduct of the strategy and should be eliminated.

5. Conclusion

Already this submission is much longer than I envisaged when I started its preparation, and I trust will not put you off reading it. I am fully conscious of the sketchy (and possibly inaccurate)nature of some of its contents. This is inevitable after only a few days' involvement in the massive affairs of FCDA and it may be presumptuous of me to write any comment at all. However, I can claim over the years to have acquired some capability for 'getting the feel' of an organisation in which one is to become associated. One's antennae become sensitive at picking up signals, small details which may be significant, conversations and so on. I have been so fortunate in finding those with whom I have made contact more than ready to talk, explain and point out what is taking place or is in course of preparation, although, inevitably, there must be some large areas of ignorance as yet on my part. In all probability, much of what I have written has already been committed to paper and, maybe, more than once. I am bold enough, however, to ask you urgently to consider – or if they have been made before, to re-consider – one or two of the suggestions made herein.

Finally, perhaps, the submission in itself, allowing for its probable errors and omissions, will be sincere evidence of why I was so delighted and honoured to be called to serve FCDA at what is certainly a most crucial stage in its life. I do hope you will accept that I am only waiting to take up any challenge and to be fully stretched.

J.R. Muggeridge 21st March 1982

* * * * *

Attachment – New Federal Capital of Nigeria at Abuja

Outline requirements on which the strategy to meet the requirements of Government has been provisionally assessed against the prescribed timetable shown. To be elaborated and fully detailed as soon as possible.

1. By June 1982

It is thought this primarily relates to the movement of the President and does not involve Government except marginally. It is the intention of the President as Head of State to be seen to have a presence, from time to time, in the new Capital, Abuja, as a lead-up to an actual physical Government presence and intermittent operation at Abuja from September 1982. Forecast of necessary provisions.

(a) International Airport equipped, staffed, and operational. Accommodation for airport staff to be provided at ADCP. Numbers to be ascertained.

(b) Airport Access Expressway

(c) Outer Ring Road

(d) Link Road to ADCP

(e) Presidential Lodge to include access, security lighting, parking, compound amenity, fencing etc.

(f) Flats for Presidential Staff, equipped with services, access, parking etc.,

(g) 200 housing units of which some are already in use by Police etc., in ADCP equipped with services, access, parking etc., for miscellaneous staff and other personnel.

2. By September 1982

By this time there is to be a noticeable movement to Abuja. It is to be expected that the President and the National Assembly will begin to hold some sessions in Abuja from time to time, and up to the beginning of the Election period of 1983. It is believed that the President has every intention of making his Independence Day (lst October 1982) Address from Abuja. If so, then it must be presumed that a Parade will take place.

NB Should there be provision of a Parade Ground etc., in Abuja in readiness?

Forecast of necessary provisions.

(a) Conference Centre fully equipped, furnished, access, parking, security lighting etc., etc.,

(b) 500 units provided by *SAE* within ADCP are earmarked to be fully equipped furnished, access, parking, security lighting etc., etc.,

(c) Remaining housing units as available in ADCP not being required by FCDA staff, Police etc., or having to be adapted as temporary offices for Ministries

others. Thought that 1,500-2,000 would be available, but a closer assessment will be have to be made without delay. All will require equipping, access, parking, security lighting etc.,

(d) NW District is expected to have available about 1,000 units, *SAE*, *Gamstac* and Roger Renaud plus a substantial number of block-work units. What is to be available will have to be equipped with services, access, parking, security lighting and so on.

(e) Presidential Guest House. But it is thought that it will be better for the President to continue to use the Presidential Lodge as there will be much noise and disturbance around the Guest House if building work is continuing at or near the area,

(f) Flats for Security personnel, thought to be about 200 families, to be equipped with services, access, parking etc.,

(g) One or two neighbourhood units (shops, clinic etc.) within ADCP may be available. If so, will require equipping , staffing etc.

Queries

(h) Offices.

(i) Mosque and/or Church

(j) Buildings for Maintenance Services including mechanical and electrical. Essential provision. Personnel, vehicles and equipment for refuse collection and disposal, emptying of septic tanks, distribution of water if mains supply not available or fails, clearing of blocked drains, replacement of taps, sanitary ware etc., etc., accommodation for personnel to be considered.

(k) Fire Station. Essential to have 24 hour Fire Service on site particularly when Government is in session. Tenders, personnel, specialist equipment, fire extinguishers, stand-by water-tankers for fire emergency. Staff quarters essential. NB No provision seen for fire escapes at four-storey blocks (one staircase only for a number of units).

(l) If schools are brought into use, housing accommodation for teaching staff,

(m) Possibly a bus service,

(n) Use of workers camp at Nyanyan. etc., etc.,

It is obvious that a great deal of information and reliable statistical data is required before this part of the strategy can be worked out. An exercise may already have taken place on these matters, but if not then it should be undertaken at once.

3. Initial Projection to say 2nd July 1983.

It may be safe to assume that the present Government will continue to use Abuja intermittently from September 1982 forward to the time approaching the 1983 elections. During this period (depending on availability of finance), it is likely that there will be steady progression towards greater permanence of Government at Abuja including the provision of the House of Assembly, Ministers' housing, Government offices and a matching increase in the provision of staff housing. Private development in the areas allocated for such purposes may well be seen once those with plots come to realise that the supporting services are available and that the movement of Government to Abuja is steadily taking place. At this moment, any projection to July 1983 must be largely speculative until it can be more clearly observed if the strategy up to September 1982 is progressing effectively and in the required direction.

21st March 1982

* * * * *

J.R. Muggeridge
Chief Project Engineer
FCDA
PMB 24
Suleja
Niger State
Nigeria

12th April 1982.

Dear Mr President,

Having just seen the piece in the NN about the ethical revolution you announced at Gboko, I felt I must write to you as a loving and admiring friend and tell you how fervently I wish you success. I recall how deeply worried you were about the canker worm of corruption in Nigeria during, for me, the memorable occasion when I came to State House soon after arriving back in the country.

First about FCDA. Being here now, my loyalty, of course, must be to FCDA but I cannot help but let you know how very disappointed I am, and there is no absence of the worm either. I must say no more. But I sat down to write to you from my heart and mind in support of the campaign against corruption. I remember soon after you became Chairman of SUDA you told me "...when I am given an assignment I have every intention of making a success of it." This was a good warning to me, but it was enough for me to know you would be behind me in my efforts to make SUDA succeed! Now I pray that if your presidency succeeds in nothing else but ridding Nigerian society of this degrading, squalid and destructive scourge for good and all, it will be a magnificent achievement.

You know I have been away from Nigeria for about three years. When you called me to come back, friends and others who had maintained regular contact here warned me about the changes which had taken place, for the worse they said, since I left. Be these as they may, corruption can permeate at all levels, rot the very fabric of society, is degrading and is destructive of every facet of society and renders spiritual values and attitudes of faith hypocritical and meaningless. I know you will well realise that corruption is destroying Nigeria and could take it into chaos again. While it persists and continues to grow I fear for the elections of 1983, the second of this Republic. I pray they may not be like the second of the First Republic in December 1964. I was Returning Officer in Minna, not far from here, and as I opened the ballot boxes and saw the wads of ballot papers I knew the attempt at a real democracy had failed, and so it turned out in January 1966 – something had to give.

Nigeria, of course, is not alone in this scourge but it is more blatant and deep seated. While mankind, worldwide, continues to pursue materialism thinking that that alone will bring happiness, prosperity and peace when all the signs point the other way, it is destined for failure, chaos, and ultimately destruction. Your faith, Islam, and mine, Christianity and all others, have told, for centuries, that that way lies failure, misery, oppression, all the evils, but still, like the Gadarene swine, mankind rushes on towards the abyss. Now nearing the end of my life, I am no longer uncertain. Humility and love, as God always has shown, are the guiding light of the world and are all that matter.

Despite all else, however, I think there is a stirring, a doubt, a feeling in the world, that there is something wrong, that man is moving in the wrong direction towards a cul-de-sac. May I hope that you will seize on this feeling, and capture its mood for your campaign. The Christian churches are faintly aware of this feeling of doubt and can still play a potent role in your efforts. I am sure you could win much support and encouragement from all the different religious leaders in the country if you called them to you and spoke openly to them about your own feelings and that corruption is destroying Nigeria. Perhaps this letter will reach you after Archbishop Runcie has left, but the aftermath of his visit should still be there and could be exploited.

I had to write to you about all this, and I know you will understand that I feel so much for you over this question, and how you will have kept your own integrity in order to fulfil your destiny for Nigeria.

I do so hope I will be able to see you when you come early in June. I know it will be difficult for me to arrange to see you privately but please, if you can, send for me when it is possible and then there will be no difficulty. It will be better if you do that.

As always my heartfelt greetings,

Jack Muggeridge

* * * * *

Federal Capital Development Authority
PMB24
Suleja
Niger State.

22nd May 1982

My Dearest Friend – I cannot address you otherwise for this letter.

I have now been in FCDA Suleja since 13th March. I was received with every courtesy but, naturally, there was some suspicion and apprehension, particularly amongst the professional Directors and staff as to what would be my duties and responsibilities. I think that atmosphere has been largely dispelled and, workwise, my niche as Chief Project Engineer with overall responsibility for the two operational Divisions of Development and Engineering and the Project Controller, Central Area, has been well accepted and is being of some use in so far as that is possible in the prevailing conditions here. The purpose is to divert technical matters and problems from the Permanent Secretary to me and I am authorised to give decisions but, of course, if policy or finance are involved then I must make a recommendation to him. This arrangement still has to settle down and it is rather disconcerting at times to find that the Permanent Secretary has already made or directed a decision!

From the start I was determined, to the best of my ability, to take part in what I then confidently believed was to be your greatest achievement for posterity and your Beloved Country, and indeed for the whole of Africa. You had called me to come back for that purpose knowing that to serve you again had continued to be my great wish.

You know that always I have told you the truth as I see it – our relationship has rested on that from the start. Admiring and loving you as I do, I cannot now do other than tell you the truth about FCDA. You expect – and can, in fact, demand – only the truth from me.

So with infinite sorrow and deep regret I have to tell you that this place, this FCDA, is rotten right through. I thought I would wait until you came in June but during your visit you will not be told the truth – no-one is who comes here, only what it is thought they want to be told. Now you will have been prepared to make your own judgement – if only you can find me wrong. Set aside what I am writing now and, in your wisdom, judge for yourself. What I am now doing may have to be regarded as an act of disloyalty but that cannot be helped. I cannot face you until I have unburdened myself and, at least, know that my conscience is clear.

Both of your Ministers here know of my great disappointment. As with you as Chairman of SUDA I still maintain that I must be frank and open, particularly when speaking to those in authority regarding my professional work and responsibilities. I think both Ministers here have come to expect such response from me whenever they call me. The Senior Minister knows that many things are wrong here but is lost as to how to take courage and to try to put them right, or to stop them continuing. The Junior Minister, young and inexperienced as yet, is also much concerned but is daunted by the terrible mess he finds within FCDA. He is aware that the present structure of FCDA is wholly wrong for its role. Recently, he instructed me to prepare a Report for – to use his own words – "…a format for FCDA." This I did, but at the time he instructed me I warned him that, inevitably, it would have to be prefaced by an unrestrained assessment of FCDA as it is, or as it appears to me. He recognises that his future political career will be judged, for good or ill, against his involvement in the new Capital City Project and that any failure could be laid, at least partly, at his door which could seriously, if not, irretrievably, wreck his political career which he seems set to pursue.

As for the Permanent Secretary, his position as Permanent Secretary to the Ministry of the Capital Territory, Chief Executive of the Federal Capital Development Authority (FCDA) with, in essence, responsibility for the Federal Capital Territory Authority (FCDA) – a body of doubtful legality in any case so far as I can ascertain – is quite impossible and is just one of the many factors which act against the effectiveness of FCDA. The malaise, of course, goes very much deeper (and is destructive) than just one or two administrative anomalies, bad as they are. Nonetheless, his operational position relative to the prime purpose of FCDA is quite wrong. There is no doubt that he has considerable administrative experience and, personally, I like him, and so far our relationship has been cordial and with mutual confidence. But what FCDA is all about, the scope and magnitude of what it is supposed to be doing and creating, is really outside his range of experience within Government. Like the Senior Minister, he is rather lost and is groping along most of the time to decide what to do and, of course, is under tremendous pressure all day and every day from so many quarters.

That there is a fundamental flaw in the structure of FCDA is serious and frustrating but that is virtually nothing by comparison with other deep-rooted ills. FCDA as an Organisation is at present, and probably has been for some time, completely out of control. No one person can be blamed, possibly those who have held responsibility for it in the past did not realise that it was losing its identity, its validity, and, above all, its integrity, dedication and independence, and it must be assumed that, at least, at some stage, there was a sense of dedication. Then when 1986 became 1982, such operational plan as it had, became distorted and a new strategy to meet the change seems never to have been devised. Now there is no control or balance, and proper planning, designing, letting of contracts, supervision and so on are all excused against 1982.

I wish you could visit these offices incognito. By 10.00am there is a ceaseless noisy pushing mass of youths, men and women, up and down the narrow staircases and along the corridors, constantly entering and leaving the small offices which are already overcrowded with staff whose occupations are difficult to discern and which they would have difficulty in performing if they had any. It

271

seems that the establishment of FCDA has endless vacancies which somehow must be filled, since everyone seems to be carrying an application form. Otherwise these people must just be paying social calls on their friends and relations in the offices. Others join them in the corridors etc. to jam the doorway to the Ministers' offices. In addition, there are always contractors, consultants' representatives scurrying around from one block to the other – you have to see it to believe the daily *mêlée* and noise. Bedlam is the only word to use. Most of the junior staff are completely undisciplined, come late and leave early, and are openly indifferent to their duties. Overall, I am sure there is gross overstaffing.

The surrounds of the offices, the whole of the Field Base, is squalid and a disgrace to the status of a Development Authority. The drains are full of refuse and rubbish, broken WC pans, drums, pipes, broker concrete, timber and overgrown grass, and now that the rains are here, the road verges are being washed away and the tarred edges deeply exposed. Most roads are potholed, with a number of cross trenches which have not been properly reinstated. Wrecked vehicles are lying around and FCDA vehicles are always around late at night and during the weekends – the Permanent Secretary has spoken of seeing them far afield. As you know, there are many visitors coming here now. Adjacent to the kitchen and dining room at the FCDA Guest House there is an area of filth, rubbish, builders' debris, presumably left by the contractor who built an extension at some time. It is distressing and makes one feel ashamed that visitors to FCDA should see these conditions of squalor, neglect and indifference in the place where this great Project is being created and directed – will the new City be the same?

There is little evidence of real dedication amongst the professional staff. I doubt if many really appreciate or comprehend the scope and magnitude of what it is they are having the opportunity to participate in. The attitude, particularly with the younger ones, is one of casual indifference mixed with cynicism that, in reality, it is all to do with politics, vote-catching, favours, contracts, corruption and certainly not with the creation of the splendid lasting new Capital City for posterity, for the Nation which is being constantly talked about and so lauded in the Press. They know and talk about it and they know too that many of the buildings being erected are of very low standard of construction, and that their reports to that effect go unheeded and why they go unheeded. I too have reported to the Ministers and the Permanent Secretary in the same way, and I believe that in one or two instances only have contracts been terminated because the work was so blatantly unacceptable.

Contracts have been let, started and never finished. The Junior Minister told me recently that out of 60 six-bed-roomed houses supposed to have been built at Gwagwalada in FCT, during a recent visit only ten could be located as having been completed. Once having been rendered outside, of course, much poor quality workmanship and materials is covered up but, even so, the signs of a poor standard can still be detected in badly fitting window and door frames, cracks, peeling decorations and, internally, cupboards and wardrobes which are so poor in finish and material that they should have been condemned outright. I keep saying that what is being constructed now is the new Capital City to stand as a lasting symbol in its beautiful setting of the greatness of the Nigerian Nation for hundreds of years. Every single building, flat, house, shop, health centre and all the roads, bridges etc. etc. must be to the highest standard, being that all are for posterity. Yet much of the building work is below any acceptable standard. It is a tragedy which grows every day it is allowed to continue.

The Accelerated District Construction Programme (ADCP) based on the original concept was selected to be the great experiment, so that any shortcomings could be corrected as other areas were being developed. The blocks are too close to each other and to the roads (of which there are too many in any case) sited without care and regard for the preservation of the amenity (trees were ruthlessly cut down), the architecture is drab and made worse by over-repetition. Coupled with the poor standard of construction, these areas will become slums in a few years, some perhaps collapsing – I am not given to exaggeration – yet no changes, so far as I know, are being made to remedy these drawbacks in the NW District where, too, the standard of building is little better.

The buildings are the very essence of the new Capital. Every care and thought should be given to their design and to introduce variety and interest – this is a Capital City not a Council Housing Estate – and their good construction should be of paramount concern. There is no feeling of imaginative expression of Nigeria and its culture and artistry, nothing but drabness and repetition. The multiplicity of consultants, on which there has been heavy and often unnecessary expenditure (as will be mentioned later), has produced a hotch-potch of styles (if any) and elevations, and nowhere can be detected any overall theme or common sympathy of approach to design. There is now only one building in the City which expresses Africa and Nigeria in particular – the guest house which I am trying desperately to have ready for you by mid-August. It is the only building worth looking at twice and has the most magnificent site in the whole City. I hope you will be pleased. These are personal views, but for a new Capital one looks for an imaginative, intellectual, cultural approach for anything to do with its creation and development. I see a 'grid-iron layout' of massive concrete combined with flamboyant vulgarity, all alien to Nigeria and, above all, to the soul of Abuja.

Earlier I said that FCDA was rotten throughout. Incompetence, indiscipline, lack of dedication and understanding of what a Project of this vastness means in terms of creativity and imagination, are contributory to that rottenness but the deeper rottenness is the recklessness – the Senior Minister's own words to me – of giving out contracts without proper documents and drawings at untendered prices and to contractors who cannot carry out the work properly (and may even never carry it out at all), receiving payment for work which should be condemned, the extravagance of consultancy for quite small projects bringing about confusion and delay. Inevitably, with this rottenness there must be deeply rooted corruption – in fact, it will be the corruption which causes the rottenness since to get a bribe integrity is sacrificed, and degradation sets in. You know how corruption is destroying this Nation, compounded with incompetence and indifference, FCDA, as it is now, should no longer be entrusted with the prosecution of the new Capital City Project. My mind is quite clear in saying that. It is the truth and others know it too, and you must be told.

I know that one strong element in your determination to establish the new Capital Abuja is a political one. I am, however, absolutely certain and convinced that you would not sacrifice the creation of the new Capital to the highest standard of design and quality of construction for all time, to political expediency. By no means is the political factor solely responsible for the present situation within FCDA, but sub-consciously it is a powerful influence on the attitude of many of those who should be carrying their responsibilities conscientiously and objectively and with full regard to their professional standards. To those without strong self-discipline it induces, at its best, indifference and cynicism, at its worst, corruption. Even if all were well within FCDA and the buildings of the new Capital were all that one wants them to be, Abuja has become a political football. If, in fact, it is as I have described it and this becomes known later on, would it not become a political boomerang?

Earlier, I mentioned the fundamental flaw in the structure of FCDA. With the establishment of the Ministry for the Capital Territory in 1979, FCDA's independence became blurred and then, with the further passage of time and other factors, it is now indistinguishable from the Ministry. Of course, you were the most wonderful Chairman of SUDA that anyone could have hoped for, but I always knew that I could rely on you so much to guard the independence of SUDA (at least from being under a Ministry) despite the military regime. You know how precious, how essential in terms of effectiveness, its independence was if it was to succeed. Did you not say to me shortly after we met, "You know, Mr Muggeridge, I do not take on an assignment without seeing that it succeeds." What a superb guideline to give anyone!

The Senior Minister realises that FCDA is too closely involved with the Ministry, particularly in regard to the position of the Permanent Secretary as Permanent Secretary of the Ministry and Chief Executive of FCDA, to say nothing of his responsibility for FCDA. He also appreciates that, despite the current political considerations, FCDA must retrieve and guard its independence and that the Project itself within FCDA should be in the hands of an experienced, dedicated professional team matched by a parallel supporting administrative and financial team. What must be supreme, insulated as much as possible from political considerations, is the quality in all aspects of the new Capital because it is for all time, not just for the furtherance of a particular set of political circumstances. A new Capital for Nigeria is bound to come sooner or later irrespective of politics. The inspiration, dedication, and the strong guidance towards the ultimate goal must be present all the time with sure confidence of what has to be achieved, however long may be the road to fulfilment. By and large, the right calibre of professional is not now in FCDA. They might well be encouraged to become so, if their potential was developed and brought out under the inspiration and dedication to the new Capital Project as such, free of other influences.

At present they operate within the Ministry structure, its style and influence, their staffing and administration are ministerial, their attitude and outlook are that of day-to-day work within a ministry except that there is constant confusion brought about by hasty instructions, decisions, and so on. Their thoughts and eyes are certainly not on the ultimate achievement. Perhaps, to be concerned with, to have to concentrate, on a Project of this magnitude and to work with inspiration and dedication, is outside the experience of many who now find themselves with FCDA. Leadership and direction are vital to the successful prosecution of the Project and to obtain the right response from those involved, but irrelevant pressures and destructive influences such as corruption, and connivance at poor quality work, must not be allowed to penetrate into the heart of those concerned who will then simply become time-servers, indifferent to any standards.

To return to the Ministry. The Minister appreciates that the FCDA Board should be independent of the Ministry (of which he is the Minister) with a part-time Chairman and Members, non-executive, to deal with policy, finance and tenders, as SUDA did under your leadership. The Minister having direct access to the President, is the person through whom FCDA passes those aspects of its business which have to go to the President/Government for decision – conversely, the Minister passes any directive from the President to FCDA. The Minister, in any case, has responsibility for the general overseeing of FCDA but in no way interferes with or directs its operations and decisions. He can, of course, be an ex-officio member of the Board. So far as FCDA is concerned, the intention seems to be that it should form the basis of a Local Authority for the Capital territory but excluding the City, which will arrange its own Body eventually. Also, as you will remember from SUDA, there ought to be a Town Planning Authority (set up under the Town and Country Planning Act of 1947, still extant so far as I know) for the whole of the Capital Territory to safeguard all development within the Territory. Its Town Planning Scheme will be the fully inclusive Scheme which will supersede that of SUDA when it is phased out, having completed its work.

I ought not to say all that because you will know it all only too well, but I had to put it in if only to emphasise that before even starting to make these changes (if it is decided to do so and I pray that will happen) a clean-up rescue operation at Suleja has to take place and that can only happen through you. I know you have the courage and stature needed for that – painful as the surgery will be – but I beg you to believe me that it must be done and now, otherwise the new Capital will not be just a failure but a disaster.

I will be dead and gone long before the real Capital emerges but it is at a desperately crucial stage at this moment and you will not shrink from applying the drastic corrective.

I must continue. As part of the overall financial review, I have been given an assignment to review all Consultancies to see whether their costs can be substantially reduced by cancellation, postponement etc. – I had already suggested this should be done when the crisis about finance arose nationally. I found that, as at 31st December 1981 there were 236 Consultancy Agreements extant distributed amongst 160 Firms with a fees commitment of N265 million, N102 million having been paid out against these up to 31st December 1981 – a pretty formidable commitment, and I have yet to see whether all the engagements are justified, which I doubt from what I have seen outside. During the last few weeks, it has become clear that FCDA has a very serious financial situation which has gone on increasing in severity due to the issuing out to contracts for building works in particular without regard to the availability of finance. Some have since been cancelled but I am sure no-one here maintains a record of commitments being entered into or which have been entered into over the years. I surmise that FCDA is well over-extended financially and this will get worse unless some firm action is taken. Several Firms have told me during the last few days that the cheques they were given were returned several times by their banks, and when this was told to the Finance Division it was admitted that this would happen, but the cheques were given out just to get rid of the contractors. Hardly in keeping with the status and reputation of a Statutory Authority dealing with the most prestigious Project of Nigeria. Even if the financial situation is eased here and more funds are made available to FCDA, because of the back-log much of any new money will, in fact, only go towards paying for works already carried out, not to further new works in the Project. I know there is a grave financial problem at FCTA too which is dependent on FCDA for money.

Again I appeal: I believe you are raising a loan of N600 million expressly for Abuja. I beg you not to let a koko of it come here until it can be used with probity and until you have decided about action in relation to the whole future structure of FCDA – the money would just go or be committed within days. You may, of course, be reserving the N600 million for the National Assembly Building which I understand is about to be let to contract. I saw the elevations on Friday here. I do not believe you can like them. This is to be the pinnacle, the ultimate expression of National greatness – I am sorry but I called it a monstrosity – so utterly wrong for Nigeria in any case.

I have said that, in general, the new Capital Project is failing because of the poor quality of most of the building works. Also that in my view, the whole concept needs to be deeply re-appraised in all aspects – amenity, aesthetically, spacing, design of major buildings, layout of the Central Area (that terrible grid-iron) etc. etc. No Master Plan is inviolate and particularly one associated with a new Capital which is to be the heart of the Nation. There must be regular reviews of the Plan against changing social, economic and even political changes – after all, its completion will span two decades at least and therefore changes are inevitable and must always be taken into full consideration. There are buildings now in progress, such as the Presidential Complex and the Conference Centre – two concepts which I personally dislike but at least they are being well built and should continue – but otherwise all building works should be halted and proper inspections and assessments made regarding standard and even design, to check the state of the work and to decide whether they should be continued and if so, on what basis. To be effective, this must be a ruthless, objective exercise and should be carried out independently of FCDA by reputable experienced professionals who, I am sure, would do this as a gesture to the Project without charge. I am sure it could be arranged. They would expect, however, to be given the fullest support and to know that their recommendations would be implemented. Road works in general are being well executed, but again the programme needs to be comprehensively reviewed bearing in mind the actual need for roads (their design, capacity, and number of carriageways) to match the pace decided upon for other aspects of the Project. Balance in all matters must be considered at all times and has been left out of consideration a great deal, particularly when funds are very restricted. Again, the road programme should be constantly under review and this could also be arranged independently at present. Now that the rains are increasing, the contractors will, in any case, be slowing down so that the moment will be propitious for the review.

My pleas:

1. You will know now that, because of the state of FCDA, I am appealing to you virtually to bring the Project to a halt, particularly the building work which is where irretrievable damage to the whole credibility of the new Capital City is taking place and should be stopped despite all other considerations.

2. At the same time, the whole concept desperately needs to be re-appraised with the object of injecting into it real imagination, greater regard for the amenity, variety, architectural interest and excitement and, above all, a consistent theme and expression of Nigeria with its culture, strength, traditions, colour and beauty, all conspicuously lacking at present. We do not want a new Town but a splendid new Capital City set in one of the most beautiful sites you could find anywhere. The possibilities are infinite and little if any advantage has been taken of them.

3. While the Project is virtually halted, FCDA needs to be urgently extracted from the Ministry and completely restructured to create an independent highly professional Organisation composed of really motivated and dedicated staff. Its first task would be to determine a strategy to enable the Project, or at least the most vital parts of it, to be put in full motion again but without prejudicing the re-appraisal of the whole concept and what changes or decisions may emerge from that for the future prosecution of the Project.

4. With FCDA as such extracted, and physically separated from the Ministry, the Ministry itself will have a great deal to do as a proper Ministry with its own Departments etc. Its business will include the important matters of preparing the framework for a Local Authority for the Capital Territory with all supporting elements, provision of public services for that Authority, determining the type of Body to be responsible eventually for the City and its services, preparing for the

Town Planning Authority for the whole of the Capital Territory, and it is not too early to embark upon the comprehensive Planning Scheme which will govern the development of all the area in the years to come, when FCDA is phased out having completed its work. All these are vital matters for the future control of the Capital Territory and should be prepared for now so that, as time catches up on events, hurried and perhaps ill-conceived arrangements have to be introduced as so often occurs with bad results which are difficult to correct later. Before many years the Territory will fill up and then all the problems of control and public administration will arise and yet again will the amenity suffer.

This you may not like. Refer to 3 above. I have said earlier that, in my view and without any reflection on them as individuals since I like them and on the whole we get on well, the present professional staff within FCDA are not of the right calibre professionally and, perhaps, temperamentally, to understand the true nature and immensity and complexity of what it is in which they are involved. Moreover, that their attitude has become indifferent and even cynical – this perhaps applies more to the middle grade professional than to the Directors – because of what they know is going on in FCDA regarding contracts, corruption, acceptance of poor quality work etc. etc., I need not spell them out. Frankly, I think the high hopes they may have had when they joined the FCDA for the new Capital have been dashed by these circumstances which is very dispiriting for them – they can say "…the same old story again." Many, of course, would welcome the restructured FCDA in the belief that it would operate effectively, with interest and vitality. They would feel a greater sense of participation in the actual professional achievement. But the first 6-12 months of the new FCDA will not be easy and will be crucial to its ultimate success and to its becoming a really dynamic Board bent on fulfilling its role. Careful guidance and planning and preparation will be essential at the start. Frankly, my assessment is that there has been more than enough of the involvement of 'Consultants' in FCDA and the new FCDA should keep them out at much as possible.

There are people like myself who spent years in Nigeria on professional work and loved it as I do, who I am sure would welcome the chance to return specifically for this Project to make up a really experienced, qualified dedicated team (they would not come if they were not) to constitute the nucleus of the new FCDA. They would form the leaders in their respective disciplines and would have with them chosen engineers, architects, planners etc., drawn from the best of those now in FCDA – even in my short time here, the small team of men who are working with me on your house are more interested now and appreciate more what they are doing and why, because they feel a sense of purpose. I believe that these key people – perhaps six in all – could be recruited and that they could be sent through UKTA (which means that their salaries would be paid by the UK Government) for say 6-12 months entirely for the new Capital. I would join them, say, as Manager/Secretary or similar to make sure that they could settle down quickly and get going on the work. I would work with them as well, of course, on the Project. At the top of the new FCDA there should be a really fine

Nigerian professional and you would have to persuade Tukur Usman to take the post! Frankly, I expect all who would come would know him and he them. I do, and to me he is another you – but not you – no-one could be. I have always like and admired him. You see, this Project needs people who know and love Nigeria irrespective of nationality. In fact, they are the best people to be involved because it is both an emotional and professional involvement. In a way, such people often think more of a country than do the indigenous people!

I must finish. I know I will have distressed you and upset you too, I expect. I took that risk but I had to write all this. If by so doing, I have made my position impossible in FCDA, then, naturally, I must go, and you will decide. I should understand. It's all poured out now. I know there are those – and some are here – who would want to see you go down on this vulnerable Project, more so now with the financial situation and restrictions. Do not give them the chance. Remember, Dearest Friend, that it is of you I am thinking in this matter.

With all my affection

Jack Muggeridge

23rd May 1982

* * * * *

Record of Meeting called by The President on 6th June 1982 at the (temporary) Presidential Lodge at Lower Usman Dam, Abuja Capital Territory, attended by all Ministers in the Entourage, the Head of the Civil Service and the Permanent Secretary Ministry for Federal Capital Territory

Mr President held a meeting in the Presidential Lodge at Lower Usman Dam on 6th June 1982 at which all Ministers in the entourage, the Head of the Civil Service and myself were present.

At the meeting various issues were discussed and directives were issued by Mr President with a view to achieving smooth commencement of movement from September 1982, as follows:

(i) CENTRAL AREA ROAD B1   The contract for this road was awarded to Messrs. Julius Berger by the President in Council. This contract could not be executed because of lack of funds. Mr President was informed that Messrs. Julius Berger indicated their willingness to provide funds for this project, or in the alternative to commence work on the project and start taking payments later in the year when the financial position of the Government improves. Mr President directed the Minister for Federal Capital to explore means of getting Messrs. Julius Berger to start work without having to sign contract at the moment, and that payment could be considered when financial situation improves.

(ii) THE AIRPORT EXPRESSWAY   The contract for this project was awarded to Messrs. Dumez and similarly, because of lack of funds, the work could not be commenced. Mr President was informed that Messrs. Dumez have offered to accept payment by oil instead of money. The Minister for Federal Capital was directed to consider the proposals with a view to make some suitable arrangement so that they can commence work on some understanding, including deferred payment.

(iii) OFFICE BLOCKS   Mr President observed that to make September movement a reality some concerted effort will have to be made to get the office blocks finished in time. He felt that the project was moving too slowly. It was explained to Mr President that actually only two of the blocks were initially awarded and to be made available by July 1982. The remaining six were awarded later. However, the contractor had undertaken to deliver the two first blocks in July and thereafter other two blocks every two weeks. It was agreed that this speed was still inadequate and as such the Minister for Federal Capital was directed to get the contractors to provide stronger labour teams under very intensive supervision to ensure that these projects are completed in time. Mr President further directed that these office blocks should be adequately furnished and external works provided on schedule.

(iv) HOUSES   Mr President observed that even though a lot of work had been done in the City on all projects, it was very clear that the FCDA was not able to show a large number of completed houses fully furnished and provided with facilities for people to move in. In this regard, he directed that the Minister for Federal Capital should ensure that adequate number of houses are fully finished and furnished and well equipped for people to move in.

(v) DESIGNS Mr President observed that generally the design of houses in both ADCP and the North West District (NWD) were not good. He was aware that FCDA was spending a lot of money on Consultancy. He directed that all future designs must be compatible with the Nigerian social set-up. Mr President was given assurance that the subsequent Districts were designed in such a way that they fit the social set-up of the Country. Mr President directed that all designs must bear our social set-up in mind making adequate provision for Boys' Quarters as opposed to the earlier philosophy of planning the City.

(vi) Mr President asked for the arrangements being made to take care of the situation of the early settlers of the City. He was informed that this issue was discussed at the Seminar on movement to Abuja and arrangements were being made to provide sufficient classrooms to cater for children that were coming. Furthermore, families of officers moving to Abuja who are teachers are going to be considered for recruitment to ensure that they have employment and also that the children do not suffer lowering of standard. Mr President directed that a specific Education Officer be assigned the task of providing the educational requirement. He also directed that there should be at least one Secondary School organised in the City to cater for any day school children that come with their parents.

(vii) MEDICAL FACILITIES On answering Mr President's enquiry on this subject, he was informed that a Medical Officer had been assigned to ensure adequate medical facilities in the City to take care of the people moving in. This was noted. Mr President emphasised that the people moving in should be made as comfortable as possible and they should have adequate medical facilities.

(viii) NATIONAL WOMEN SOCIETY – CHILD DAY CARE The Minister for National Planning informed Mr President that the National Women Society are requesting to get land and develop it in Abuja for Child Day Care. It was agreed that for September movement, even if land was allocated, there was no way they can finish their building in Abuja, and as such Mr President directed that the Minister for FCT should provide facility for them to start operating on temporary basis in Abuja, until they are able to develop their own, for which the Ministry must give them land immediately.

(ix) PRIVATE SCHOOLS Mr President directed that Private Schools should be allowed to grow and that the Ministry should consider allocating land to applicants. In particular, CORONA SCHOOL was known to have applied for land and the MFCT was directed to consider their application immediately. In general, Mr President directed that it is the policy of his administration to encourage Private Schools and Hospitals, and as such he urged the MFCT to consider such applications speedily.

(x) 1982 INDEPENDENCE DAY CELEBRATIONS Mr President observed that the ground for the 1982 Independence Day Celebrations was not ready, as such he directed that consideration should be given on what site to use out of the various alternatives suggested such as the Airstrip, the Airport, Middle of a chosen street outside the Presidential Complex, or the Festival Ground which had been suggested by the Inter-Ministerial Committee on this subject. Mr President directed that he will celebrate the 1982 Independence in Abuja, and in order to make movement easier for people who may wish to leave Abuja the same day, instead of the Garden Party, he will give lunch to about 1,000 guests including representatives of all the States of the Federation. For hosting the lunch he directed that MFCT should discuss with the contractor for the Presidential Complex, Messrs. G. Cappa, and work out the possibility of having the lunch in that premises. Furthermore, he directed that adequate accommodation should be reserved for all Guests including State Contingents, Police and the Army. Blocks of flats should be earmarked for the contingents.

(xi) THE PRESIDENCY Mr President observed that people never appreciated the size of staff in the Presidency, as a result provisions have not been made for them. He observed that if he was to come and stay in Abuja, certain minimum facilities must be provided. He cited facilities like Family Quarters, Servants Quarters i.e. cooks and stewards, house for ADC (military) which must be close to Mr President, house for ADC (Police), accommodation for guards that must sleep in the premises of the Presidential Lodge - (in Ribadu Road they number about 120), house for NSO that number about 25 in Ribadu Road, accommodation for maintenance staff such as: drivers, mechanics, electricians, telephone repairers, air-conditioner repairers, family servants. He directed that Minister for FCT must immediately sort these out with the Chief of Personal Staff to ensure that adequate provisions are made by September 1982.

(xii) THE VICE PRESIDENT In replying to the question on Mr Vice President's accommodation, Mr President was informed that the Ministry did not anticipate that Mr Vice President would move in by September. A house is being designed for Mr Vice President but that would not be ready this year. It was anticipated that as soon as Mr President moves into the Presidential Complex then the small Guest House can be available to Mr Vice President until his house is available. Mr President directed that a house should be arranged for Mr Vice President where he can be put up whenever he comes for meetings etc. in Abuja.

(xiii) EXECUTIVE OFFICE OF THE PRESIDENT Mr President was informed that the Executive Office of the President was anticipated to be accommodated within the eight blocks of the offices until the permanent office is built in the Central Area. Mr President directed that the Minister for FCT should discuss this further with the Secretary to the Federal Government with a view to reaching mutually acceptable arrangements.

(xiv) THE NATIONAL ASSEMBLY The design of the National Assembly was condemned by Mr President in the sense that it did not show Nigerian architecture. Mr President was informed that the designers of the National Assembly were Messrs. Kenzo Tange and they were made to have 3 Nigerian experienced architects – Messrs. Oluwole Olumuyiwa, Nsegbe and Benna – to work with them to ensure that Nigerian input was made. Mr President observed that even under that arrangement the designs were not Nigerian in outlook as such. Minister for FCT was directed to have a look at the designs again and see what improvement could be made at least in the outlook to show some Nigerian architecture on this building.

(xv) HEIGHT OF BUILDINGS It was generally observed that height of Ministry Buildings would pose problems of maintenance. Mr President was informed that during the planning of these buildings the Government took decisions on the height ranging up to 30 floors but the Presidential Committee on Abuja had recently recommended a review on which decisions were awaited. Mr President confirmed that he had approved the recommendations of the Committee on Abuja as such the Minister for FCT will review the height of buildings. It was observed that generally, 15 floors are normal and anything beyond that can be considered for scaling down.

(xii) CONSULTANCY Mr President observed that the Ministry for FCT had engaged far too many Consultants at great cost to the extent that the bulk of the money being spent on Abuja is going to Consultants. He directed that all projects that are not considered very urgent should not be embarked upon even on Consultancy basis. He cited the example of the Monumental Tower which he felt was not very urgent, nor is the gas supply consultancy. The FCT was directed immediately to review commissions of Consultants and ensure that only urgent projects are taken care of at the moment.

(xvii) OTHER FACILITIES

(a) FIRE STATION Mr President was informed that Fire Stations are being built in the ADCP and North West Districts but as these may not be ready by September the Fire Fighting Unit already established by the FCDA will be used initially.

(b) POLICE FACILITIES Mr President was informed that Police Stations and some accommodation were being provided by the FCDA, and the Ministry of Police Affairs will provide the bulk of their requirement as land is allocated to them in various locations.

(c) AIRPORT Mr President observed that unless landing aids were fully installed landing cannot start, as such he directed that Ministry of Aviation must take urgent steps to fully equip the International Airport. He also directed that Minister for FCT should continue pressurising the Minister of Aviation in this regard.

(d) APPROACH ROADS It was observed that all approach roads to the Federal Territory are in bad shape, as such Federal Ministry of Works to take urgent steps to improve the situation, in particular the contract for Keffi-Abuja Road was to be reported upon, as to whether any progress was being made or not.

3. GENERAL   Mr President informed the meeting that in view of scarce resources it was necessary that concerted effort should be made on specific projects to ensure that people moving in September are provided with reasonable comfort. He directed that for Ministers and Permanent Secretaries and other Top Government functionaries, flats were not suitable for their accommodation, as such, Ministry for FCT should provide four bedroomed bungalows for them.

4. Mr President finally directed that towards minimum movement MFCT should ensure organising task masters for each vital project so that this project can be finished and made ready before movement commences.

5. Mr President finally indicated that he will make another visit to Abuja before September 1982 to inspect progress on specific vital projects.

Signed Mohammed (Alhaji Aliyu Mohammed)
Permanent Secretary
Ministry for Federal Capital Territory.
(Not dated)

* * * * *

Report to the Permanent Secretary

The New Capital City of Abuja and Immediate Strategy

1. Even before being involved with the Ad Hoc Committee to review the National Assembly Building, I had, naturally, devoted some time to studying the whole concept of the New Capital City of Abuja as illustrated by the Master Plan and as I found it being physically expressed on site. The Plan was not entirely new to me as I had seen it in 1979/80 when I was invited to discussions at Milton Keynes Development Corporation in the UK because of my long association with Nigeria. Even then I had some misgivings about the general concept for Nigeria, particularly in regard to the residential layouts and the design of the buildings which were the particular concerns of the Corporation at that time. I do now regret that I was not more forthright and persistent with the Officers of the Corporation, even at the risk of making myself thoroughly unpopular with them. In fact, I obviously did do that since it was mooted that I might possibly be offered engagement with the Corporation to be stationed at Abuja as their liaison officer or such like post, but after my sessions with the staff there, silence followed!

2. May I now offer you some rather crucial extracts from the Master Plan.
Page 65: "NIGERIAN TRADITIONS. In addition to functional and site-related factors, the varied ways in which Nigerian cities have evolved and related cannot be ignored in developing a plan for the New Capital City which is for all the people. A major shortcoming in past planning for Nigerian Cities has been the failure to recognise and accommodate the indigenous patterns of urban organisation and adaptation present in the country. Yet Nigeria has an important urban tradition. The tradition includes how people have lived both in cities with ancient roots dating back centuries, and in new towns created during the colonial period. The New Capital City of Nigeria must preserve and build on that which is unique and valuable in Nigeria's urban tradition. Whether new or old, cities in Nigeria have also developed in different areas of the country with different economies and cultural traditions, indeed, the cultural pluralism of Nigeria suggests that the City Plan must simultaneously permit the different segments of the Nigerian population to maintain an important degree of continuity with their social and cultural traditions, while encouraging, where appropriate, amalgamation of the various streams of urban tradition and lifestyle into a new and modern Nigerian urban context."

Comment. A great deal of verbiage characteristic of much of the Master Plan and typical of its source but, at present, one looks in vain for signs that "...the New Capital City of Nigeria preserves... that which is unique and valuable in Nigeria's urban tradition" or evidence of "...the cultural pluralism of Nigeria..."

Page 79. "THE CENTRAL AREA PLAN The Central Area of the New Capital is the hub of both the City as well as the Nation itself. This is true not only in a symbolic sense but in physical actuality as well. All affairs in the City and the Nation will focus on it. It will also be the centre to which representatives of other nations will come. Therefore, it will symbolise Nigeria to the world, thus reaching beyond national concerns alone. The importance of this symbolic role cannot be underestimated in the design and organisation of the Central Area. The location of the Central Area within the City, its definition as a place, its relation to its natural and man-made surroundings, its internal organisation, and its arrangement of symbolic elements are matters of supreme importance. The way in which these abstract considerations are manifest in the form of a physical plan will determine the plan's success. Since these matters can have a great effect in the future on the national self-image, and even on the role of Government itself in the future of Nigeria, they have been given careful consideration and detailed review by FCDA prior to selection of the Central Area Plan.

Comment. It may well be true, of course, that FCDA did give "...careful consideration..." but all the signs are that it is high time that a further very careful consideration and detailed review should be undertaken and by FCDA on its own, without interference from or direction by the ombudsman-type consultant architects who, so it seems to me, are dominant at present. Moreover, they seem, to have scant regard for the very cultural and traditional elements so often emphasised in the Master Plan.

Page 83. GRID STREET PATTERN "Several design purposes are achieved by use of a grid street pattern in the Central Area, in contrast to the curving pattern which characterises the development sectors. This approach has been conscientiously selected for a number of reasons: continuity of views; the combination of rolling terrain in the Central Area site and the imposing backdrop of Aso Hill and the adjoining escarpment of lower hills requires a street pattern in which views are continuous rather than interrupted."

This is, in my view, an utter *non-sequitur*. Views will be "...interrupted" in any case, by the buildings to be erected in the Central Area and now more so than ever by the 28-33 storey buildings which it now seems are threatened amongst the Ministry buildings in this area – see later. 'Unexpected' views which occur in built-up areas due to 'interruptions' create interest and encourage people to visit spots set aside for the very purpose of providing 'uninterrupted' views.

Continuing the extract: "Flexibility and predictability of Movement and Land Use – The characteristics of simplicity, flexibility, and predictability are appropriate to the Central Area where changes in land-use patterns are likely to occur with greater frequency than elsewhere in the City. Furthermore, the Central Area will be the most highly accessible place in the New City. Possible additions to and changes in routing of public transit lines is a matter of greatest importance in maintaining maximum accessibility in the Central Area. The grid pattern accomplishes this best. It allows one-way streets; the easy re-routing of traffic, eliminates peculiar intersections; and allows greatest flexibility in the location and aggregation of building sites."

Comment. Not one of these points is an argument in favour of the grid pattern which cannot be met by a more imaginative and interesting use of the terrain –

the 'flexibility' already mentioned. In fact, the grid pattern will impose a restraint on the whole layout. The very rigidity of the grid pattern will, inevitably, cause much interference with and possible destruction of the existing natural environment (which is God's gift to the Capital one could say), but to what extent cannot be determined with any precision at this stage but, at least, there should be no ineluctable commitment to the grid pattern as of now.

Continuing further with this extract: "Juxtaposition of contrasts, the imposition of order. The character of rolling terrain lends interest to the Central Area site but it does not impose either a constraint on straight streets nor produce a sense of natural order. The contrast of natural order and the man-made orderliness of a grid street pattern produces a unique juxtaposition of qualities in which disorder has been overcome."

Comment. This last sentence is just a meaningless 'juxtaposition' of words – yet again characteristic of so much of this Master Plan – and defies interpretation. It would be interesting to ask for an explanation.

Finally: "Under these circumstances, the picturesqueness of curved or non-geometric street patterns would be out of place and inappropriate."

Comment. The very use of the word 'picturesqueness', normally associated with 'old-worldiness' or carefully preserved Elizabethan villages and the like, is just an attempt to dismiss any idea that "…curved or non-geometric street patterns", being old fashioned, out of place or inappropriate, could be preferable and even more interesting than the grid pattern. The various statements under the heading 'Grid Street Pattern' are wholly unconvincing.

Page 86. THE SPATIAL TREATMENT OF MAJOR BUILDING TYPES

"Three distinctly different types of buildings are associated with three different types of the space defining requirements in the Central Area. Buildings that are objects in space. The Parliament Building and the cluster of buildings associated with it are conceived of as building surrounded by space. Therefore, their treatment will be monumental in character.

Buildings that make space. The Ministry Buildings lining each side of the Mall define its spatial limits rather than occurring in space. This is equally true of buildings surrounding other squares in the Central Area. Buildings making spaces should be relatively low in order to perform that function. Buildings that identify places from a distance. In modern cities encompassing vast distances, the visual identification of important places is difficult to accomplish without tall buildings. Office towers often serve this identification function. The commercial /business core with its tall buildings serves this function in the Master Plan."

Comment. Although of the view that 'tall buildings' (meaning, perhaps, any building over say twelve storeys) should be avoided, and ought not to be necessary in the new Capital with its large area, it can be conceded that their use for commercial/business buildings may be justified or, at least, accepted. Now, however, I understand from the Consultants engaged for the structural design, that the Ministry of Works building has to be partly 28 storeys. (Others are said to be contemplating above this height, 33 or 34 storeys, but I cannot confirm this in relation to Ministry buildings). Is 28 storeys 'relatively low' as mentioned under Buildings that make space above? Moreover, for this building, site investigations so far carried out are not considered adequate and probings to bedrock will be essential. The Consultants have already written to DES on this aspect.

Now let me refer to 'Communications/Monumental Tower Abuja' which has just come to my notice. Consultants in Toronto, Canada, were commissioned in September 1981 (by letter) to prepare a Preliminary Design for this Tower. Incidentally, its proposed site has been changed to the 'cultural axis'. Why the commission was given at such an early stage is not recorded but, possibly at the instigation of the various Media who need some such tower for their functions. On 10th June 1982, I was invited to an in-house review of the Consultants' submission prior to a more formal presentation on 16th June 1982. In addition to an elaborate booklet in which the proposed tower was shown to be the third highest extant (372 metres) a cost estimate prepared by QU-ESS Partnership of Kaduna was available, which showed an estimate of N88 million for the Tower complete, including all essential components at ground level, and N23 million for ancillary facilities such as cinema, carpark, revolving restaurant platform etc. etc., a total of N111 million, but note that there is no estimate for foundations which, as with the MOW building, will require detailed investigation and will be a major item of cost, bearing in mind the nature of the structure. The Consultants' fees (architectural, QS etc.) presumably will be based on the estimate of N111 million (if, by any chance, the Project goes to final design stage, then there will be other fees for structural, mechanical etc., consultants – hardly less than N2 million I would say). When this commission was given out, was it seriously considered that this Project could be implemented in the foreseeable future, and was it envisaged that such a grandiose scheme would emerge – in fact, did the terms of reference lay down what has now been produced? Perhaps this is yet another example of Consultants seemingly being given *carte blanche* to produce any fantasy they like. I doubt if you have yet seen another Project which is due for presentation soon, namely the building for the National Universities Commission, the estimated cost being N50 million. It was produced by the architects who designed, and saw through to completion, a new office building for the Commission in Lagos only a few years ago, and the cost of that was N600,000!

Returning to the general concept. In the Master Plan text there are repeated references to "...the symbolic quality of the seat of Government." Is this quality being expressed in the Presidential Complex and the National Assembly Building, to mention two buildings essentially 'Government'?

3. Conclusion

I feel certain there are other aspects of the concept which should be the cause of disquiet as to the manner and style in which it is now being implemented. Conversely, some changes in regard to the points I have mentioned, may already have taken place, of which I am unaware. There is no real reason why I should be kept informed. In any case, however, where does the responsibility for the Project really rest? For example, how has the apparently significant departure from 'relatively low' to '28 storeys' for the MOW building come about? Is FCDA the decision-making authority in such crucial matters? Apparently, the need for this change arose because of the demand of MOW for office space which could only be met by going up. Maybe I have been mis-informed, but I understand that the problem was referred to Kenzo Tange who decided on the 28-storey building as a means of solving the requirement. Surely, such a fundamental change requires the fullest consultation within FCDA, to say nothing of reference to the Board or even Government? Possibly, all such consultations have taken place – I would not know but the Consultants for the structural design have certainly been asked to design for 28 storeys.

I am finding that I am being invited to in-house discussions and reviews on submissions which precede actual presentations by the Consultants concerned. Also, you instructed me to undertake with others the review of the National Assembly Building but, always, I sense that we are being presented with a *fait accompli*. I am open to correction but I must say quite bluntly that, in my view, FCDA is being dominated by Consultants - and by one or two at that – yet it is FCDA, which must ultimately take the criticisms (and already these are by no means insignificant) if the new Capital City fails to express the spirit of Nigeria – "…the hopes and aspirations of its people" is the oft-used phrase. Posterity can only blame those who are responsible today.

I am a non-Nigerian but I feel very sadly and deeply that there is much which is fundamentally wrong in the concept of the new Capital City, and that there is a dire need now for a complete and thorough review before it is too late. If others in FCDA were asked, I think you would find that I am not alone in this view and appeal. May I hope that you will accept that, in preparing this paper, I am solely concerned that the new Capital City should succeed in the best possible way and I will be very happy to devote myself to any greater involvement in its prosecution which you may think suitable.

J.P. Muggeridge

Chief Project Engineer

13th June 1982

Note   The original of this was returned to me with the following hand-written comment by the Permanent Secretary:

CPE

Indeed consultants have dominated FCDA and apparently FCDA has lacked experienced people. Fortunately our meeting with Mr President has given us some lee-way to effect corrections. In fact, I have already directed you to propose possible changes in the National Assembly. Please develop this your minute into a paper which EMC can take urgently.

Initialled by PS.

15th June 1982

Note by JM (CPE).

'The meeting with Mr President' is that of 6th June 1982 during his visit and inspection at Abuja – see detailed minutes taken at the meeting by the Permanent Secretary. I was not present.

* * * * *

Immediate Strategy

Absolutely vital to get control of contracts, expenditure etc.,

1. Advise all building contractors who have not started work not to do so pending further instructions. Contractors on major projects such as Cappa, Presidential Complex, Conference Centre, Government Guest House, some of the system buildings etc., to be allowed to continue but inform them that all contracts (Civil Engineering etc.) are now to be reviewed. Order no more contracts to be let.

2. Order a complete schedule of all works contracts (buildings, roads, drainage etc.) including those completed but still not fully paid for (remember to include those still having some retention money to be paid) with details of value of contract payments made to date and other relevant details. Object is to assess total commitment and to review position and determine action to bring it down. Concurrently freeze all payments except salaries etc.

NB Review of Consultancies already in hand.

3. Set up a panel, preferably of outsiders if possible, to prepare schedules of all staff in all Divisions including FCT – I believe it is not really known who are employed here, and I have heard it said that there are some who only come occasionally to work but go elsewhere to work say in Kaduna for part of the time – these schedules would then be ready for use as and when the future style and needs of each of the three (or possibly only two) Organisations, Ministry/FCTA and FCDA are determined. It is essential to have these schedules so that deployment of staff between the Organisations can take place without confusion. Stop all recruiting at once.

4. Urgently prepare and implement a scheme for extracting FCDA from the Ministry and setting it up as a separate independent Authority including its own finance and finance Department away frown the Finance Division. It should have its base in the City right from its beginning in one or two of the *SAE* blocks of flats which are well built and services inside seem good. These could be used quite well as offices for FCDA and also for living accommodation, but the whole place must be properly furnished and given facilities from the start. All this could be done quite quickly while the other operations are in hand. Management and professional staff and others to be carefully selected. All work to do with Projects to be transferred to FCDA as quickly as possible.

5. Concurrently, the Ministry would be sorting itself out regarding staff etc., and would undertake work to do with resettlement, compensation, a scheme for setting up the Local Authority for the Capital Territory including services required. For these duties, of course, the Ministry would retain the Divisions of Engineering etc., with their staffs after the transfer of some to FCDA. Directors would probably remain and be given titles similar to those in Ministries, Chief Civil Engineer and so on.

The whole Project is out of control and out of balance.

Examples:

Contracts let for building Ministers' houses and for others but plots can hardly be identified and there are no roads and other services as yet.

National Universities Commission building. Architects have been engaged but no agreement. Have produced a preliminary scheme to be presented to FCDA soon. I asked the estimated cost and was told N50 million. Fees for preliminary work will be at least Nl.5 million. What chance of building this for some years?

Large shopping centre has been designed for the Central Area, just like the one at Milton Keynes, which is terrible in any case. What is the need for this for some years? Fees again.

Central Market. Quite unsuitable. Mostly luxury shops. Cost again is N140 million. To build in sections will not be satisfactory as sections will not be an entity. Remember that was one of the points against the Dar El Handash scheme for the Sokoto Market. Need to build a market as an entity now to cope with a population of about 200,000 but so planned that it can be expanded as the need arises but still remain an entity. In any case, this way it can take account of social and economic changes as the years go by.

Central Area. This grid-iron layout. No regard for the terrain and as now set out is bound to call for the clearance of most of the trees and natural features so as to establish the awful regularity of the grid-iron layout. Also now it seems that the central area is too small to provide for all the Ministries and so building will have to go up! MOW building has to be designed for 28 storeys! Can you imagine what that will be like after about six months when all the services break down?

In any case such high-rise buildings are utterly out of keeping with the terrain. No imagination at all.

Now, because of the roads, the area is boxed in. Here we have a new capital with 500 sq. miles and yet all the buildings have to be crowded into a central area! Moreover, the intersections are too close as plots are 200 x 200 metres. In due course, the congestion on the grid-iron will be terrible with intersections so near each other. No good saying all will be well with traffic lights! Do they always work?

Monumental communications tower. This is just a piece of fantasy, yet consultants - and many of them – have produced a proposal – again no fees settled and no agreement so far as I know. Cost will be? Fees will be based on this. What chance of this being built? Many things should come before this.

Many other illustrations of schemes being let off which cannot possibly be implemented for years – and should not be in any case.

The Ministry for the time being would remain in Suleja but would begin to prepare for complete removal to Gwagwalada which will be its HQ and that of the Local Authority to be established. Field Base as such would close down.

Now these are just the initial immediate actions, the vital exercise is to get control of contractors, expenditure etc., in a ruthless directive and at the same time to separate FCDA from the Ministry. Then FCDA must establish its Board, decide how best to re-appraise the whole Project and this must be done by FCDA itself: those outside who are now taking decisions, making plans for the development of the Project, should not be allowed to continue. FCDA must get hold of this Project and ensure that it is done imaginatively, with regard to the lovely amenity etc. This is not being done at present. The first operations are drastic and ruthless, but if not done, then the effect will not be adequate to rescue the whole Project from the way it is going now. Above all, there must be a halt to low standard work.

13th June 1982

* * * * *

Federal Capital Development Authority
Suleja

25th July 1982

As always, My Dearest Friend,

I have to write to you again. I am not being dramatic but this place is yet nearer to disaster or collapse. I am told you intend to come for a visit at early September. Could you not possibly come sooner in August if only for a day on a Saturday or Sunday without any formality or others. I do so beg you to do so.

I know what I am enclosing will tire you to read but I must send them to you. The Security system is a death blow – I simply refuse to believe that you would countenance the expenditure of £4 million for the Guest House if you knew about the scheme. This will put the total cost of this house nearly up to £10 million I can assure you. What will the Security System be for the other place? As you will see the Minister intends to come to Lagos about it.

Please believe the Consultancy Report. I have the supporting details. It reveals utter profligacy over the last year or so. You have given your directive but will the Board take the drastic action which is so obviously called for.

Dearest Friend, you have so many burdens and responsibilities but, at this very moment, there can be none more critical and crucial in every way than Abuja if it is to be saved from disaster. Only you can do that.

My fondest love and respect as always,

Jack Muggeridge.

* * * * *

In the Jungle with the other Muggeridge

As published in the *Sunday Sketch (Nigeria)*
8th August 1982
From Richard Hall in Abuja, Nigeria.

We now learn that President Shagari's overseer in Abuja is not the Minister, Federal Capital Territory but a retired 72-year-old Englishman, Jack Muggeridge. We further learn that it was not the late Alhaji Aliyu, Makaman Bida nor the NPN that persuaded our President to return to politics but Jack. Headline, by-line and story culled from the London Observer 18th July 1982.

Jack Muggeridge is not such a God-botherer as his brother Malcolm, but like him he has a strong sense of what is right and proper. That is why he finds himself, at 72, supervising the world's biggest construction job in the heart of Nigeria.

Abuja is the Brasilia of Africa. Gigantic cranes rear above the jungle, contractors from a dozen countries fight against time and geography, nearly £1,000 million has been committed and the work has scarcely begun.

"I think that Abuja is the most exciting site for Nigeria's new capital," says Muggeridge in that precise, slightly clerical family voice. "Look at those hills." He waves towards the middle distance, where huge domes of rock rise like black breasts out of the greenery.

Muggeridge came back to Nigeria from his retirement cottage near Leighton Buzzard, at the invitation of Alhaji Shehu Shagari, the country's President. The two are old friends: Shagari says that Jack (they are on first name terms) persuaded him to return to politics a few years ago.

When Muggeridge ended his 20-year stint as a public service engineer in Nigeria, he told Shagari – in slightly rueful jest – that he would gladly come back just to clear out the drains around the presidential palace.

He arrived in March to be the chief project engineer for Abuja, a vision so colossal that nobody can name the ultimate cost. Four main government buildings in the heart of the new capital have been designed on such a scale that they will use up £800 million. Merely the air-conditioning for an official guest house is down at £12 million, and the elaborate wall around the house is costing £4 million.

Although mesmerised contractors throw such figures around, Muggeridge is more concerned with being the presidential watchdog. He also lives with a deadline – since Shagari is intent upon starting to live in Abuja in September. It will be the makeshift venue for national Independence celebrations on 1st October. Work is being forced ahead day and night, on a modest (but of course temporary) presidential lodge; it will ultimately serve as a minor guest house. Nigeria's politicians will foregather symbolically in a still unfinished conference hall.

Then everyone will hurry back in some relief to Lagos, the present capital, but Shagari hopes his political point will have been driven home, a year ahead of Nigeria's next general elections. "God forbid that someone else should come into power in October 1983 and scrap Abuja," says Shagari. By 1985, he believes, it will be a functioning reality.

The anxiety to develop a new capital began 12 years ago, after the Biafran war. The Muslim northerners were dominant then (and still are), so they were understandably eager to wrest the power from Lagos on the coast.

Abuja, 300 miles inland, is in the very centre of the country, but the coastal peoples complain that it is embedded in Muslim territory. You might imagine that the top brass in Lagos, a noisome hellish spot, could hardly wait to get to the sylvan delights of Abuja, but civil servants view the move with alarm since many of them have what might gently be termed commercial interests tied up in Lagos.

It is the Brasilia story all over again. Shagari is pitted against both inertia and hostility. Yet beneath his self-effacing ways, he is tough and adroit enough to be the favourite for next year's elections, to win another term to push Abuja forward.

His man on the spot, Jack Muggeridge, is non-committal about the overall design, dreamed up by American consultants and interpreted by a Japanese architect, Kenzo Tange. You soon start to feel bewildered, even unnerved, by Abuja, into which Nigeria is pouring 12 per cent of its gross national product. System-built blocks of flats rise in jungle clearings, while armies of contractors' signboards flank newly built highways leading everywhere and nowhere.

But already there are alarm bells, because Nigeria is in financial crisis. Its reserves derived from oil exports, are nil today. At the start of last year they were £4,500 million. Shagari's critics lay a lot of the blame on Abuja. Contractors claim they are not being paid and 40,000 workers have been laid off. The starting of some of Abuja's most grandiose buildings has been postponed – although there is frenzy enough without them.

At the centre of the vortex, Muggeridge stays calm. After all, he will be 73 next month. "I should just like to keel over," he says, then adds, "I do not fear death – I look forward to it." The sentiment sounds familiar.

From a corner of his office, I watched Muggeridge coping with a highly excited civil servant, complaining of some intricate trouble with a firm of foreign consultants. He was calmly magisterial. "Do allow me to speak first," he said. Finally he accepted a mound of documents. "I shall read them this evening," he promised. Instead of tending his garden in Leighton Buzzard, Muggeridge is working 15 hours a day, seven days a week.

I parted from him in the jungle. His white hair glistening, he was staring at the plan held open by an intent Japanese. "Tell my brother you saw me," he called as I left.

* * * * *

295

To the Permanent Secretary

Report on the Review of Consultancy

1. At its meeting on 27th July 1982, the Board received the Review of Consultancy which you had instructed me to prepare in May 1982. As you were not present at that meeting, a copy of the Report is attached hereto.

2. The deliberations of the Board are summarised in (v) on page 14 of the Minutes of the Board meeting, the main decision being that a small Committee should be appointed with a view to studying the report further so as to identify the priority and urgent commissioning of consultancy that henceforth could be allowed. The Board appointed Alhaji Wudi and myself to that Committee with the Hon. Minister as Chairman.

3. Although the Board did not formally adopt the suggestions under paragraph 9 FOR CONSIDERATION page 9 of the Review Report, it was understood that, in general, the proposed procedures were acceptable. Taking these in turn:

(a) and (b) on page 9. As it happened that the 7th Co-ordination Meeting of FCDA Consultants was due on the 12th and 13th August in Suleja, it was considered to be convenient and expeditious to take advantage of this occasion to speak *en masse*, by way of explanation, to those who would be attending and also obtain up-to-date details as to the position of their respective assignments. So that the Minister for FCT could address the gathering and make the initial announcement concerning the need for the review, the meeting was postponed until the 17th and 18th August – copy of his Address attached. Members of about 90 Consulting Firms attended which represented a wide range of Project Assignments. Each was given a Form 'A' (copy attached) to complete, if possible, at the meeting, otherwise to send in within seven days. To date, the response has been good. After the Minister's address, I explained in some detail the necessity for the review and that, inevitably, a substantial reduction in consultancy would have to take place, particularly in regard to buildings such as those for Ministries, Parastatals and so on. I stated that the Board would now be determining its possible development strategy for the next year or so and this would govern the extent to which outside consultancy would be required. Consultants should now, therefore, in the light of these explanations make their own interim decisions as to proceeding with their assignments pending hearing from the Authority, probably within six weeks or so. With the Forms 'A' were some guide notes showing how it was intended to classify assignments into five general groups to facilitate the review procedure and make subsequent decisions.

As will be seen, Group 1 covers actively on-going projects and I explained that, in general, it was unlikely that the related Consultancies could or should be affected but that, even so, each would have to be assessed as part of the overall review. Group 3 Consultancies would certainly need to be scrutinised since it is clear that not all the Projects concerned were likely to be implemented during 1983 and 1984. Those Consultancies in Group 3 specially concerned with the design of houses for Ministers, Advisers, Legislators etc., of which a considerable number are already under contract, more than likely, had already completed their assignments except, perhaps, for occasional supervision, although it was expected that the structural consultants would be invited to provide resident (full-time) supervision in the near future because experience elsewhere in Abuja had shown this to be essential if contractors are to be properly guided in the carrying out of this particularly vital part of their contract work. Those Consultants in Groups 4 and 5 will be the most drastically affected by the review. Members of the Board frankly accepted that in the case of Ministries and Parastatals etc., there had been untimely and excessive engagements of consultants which, in fees alone, had created a heavy financial commitment for the Authority about which there must be substantial relief and without delay. That, in fact, construction of any of the Ministries can be started is virtually out of the question unless, massive internal funds or external loans are made available to the Authority in 1983 and 1984. In simple hard terms, this issue can only be resolved by initiating a complete halt to all consultancy in Groups 4 and 5 particularly as the situation is further complicated on account of the Presidential/Government Directive regarding height of buildings limitation to 15 storeys in the Central Area. Some of the more forward designs already prepared involve 28 and 32 storeys and others at an early stage may well have decided upon heights in excess of 15 storeys in order to meet the requirements of the users. This issue is referred to later but is one which has to be faced and some decision taken by the Authority as soon as possible. Those Consultancies which were not represented at the meeting on 17th/18th August must be sent Forms 'A' for completion and return if the review is to be comprehensive. Necessary action is in hand to send out the forms but may take a little time. Although 9(a) and (b)are not actually being implemented entirely as envisaged in the Report, there is little doubt that being able to explain the position in person to those consultants who attended the meeting was of considerable value for the future.

(c) on page 11 of the Review Report.

Since embarking upon the review of consultancy and the later preparation of the Report to the Board, it has become increasingly obvious that there is little or no scope for a forward development strategy for 1983 and 1984 unless the Authority can be assured of a massive injection of funds with which first to cover considerably overdue and running payments for construction projects already in hand or committed, including much of the consultancy which has been carried out and, therefore, must be paid for even if curtailment/postponement/ cancellation can be arranged. In other words, 1983 (and probably 1984) will be a year in which progress can be seen only in the completion (it is hoped) of projects now under construction.

No doubt this situation will not be acceptable and will be inexpedient in the prevailing political circumstances. At least, a minimum forward strategy has to be devised in the hope that the necessary funds will be forthcoming. It is here then that it would be expected that FCDA Annual Estimates (Budget) for 1983 would have to be closely related to continuing commitments and forward strategy possibilities, these two being, in themselves, heavily interdependent. I have no knowledge of, and neither have I been called upon in relation to the consultancy review to be involved in, the FCDA Annual Estimates for 1983 which, presumably, by now have been prepared or are in course of preparation. It will be understood, therefore, that even when all the consultancy returns are in, it will not be possible to go further by way of proposals for curtailment/postponement etc., without information as to the forward strategy of the Authority which should be determined by the Annual Estimates. Apart from other factors, finance is all important to the outcome of a review of this nature.

To return to the question of height restriction in the Central Area. Because of its importance, it was one of the items intentionally included for discussion at the meeting on 17th/18th August. Naturally, speakers referred to its effect beyond just the question of physical height e.g. space allocation. The issue is one which has many repercussions and I am sure you will agree that it cannot be ignored. It is surprising if the Director of Architecture has not yet discussed this with you since it must be resolved, as already there are some few Ministries' buildings which have reached an advanced stage of design and beyond.

4. In relation to the Review of Consultancy which is in progress, may I ask you to consider:

(a) That there is urgent need for active consideration to be given to the Directive from the President and Government regarding the height limitation of 15 storeys in the Central Area because of its repercussions upon many other aspects of the whole Project.

(b) The need for the Authority to prepare a forward development strategy for 1983 and 1984 against which the consultancy requirements can be determined bearing in mind the expected allocation of funds for the ensuing year(s).

(c) That this Report should be brought to the early attention of the Hon. Minister for FCT so that he may be aware that all relevant data etc., is being assembled for presentation to the Consultancy Review Committee set up by the Board at its meeting on 27th July 1982.

5. As this is a subject which is of concern to all Directors etc., it is suggested that you may decide that this Report should be circulated for inclusion in the agenda of a forthcoming Directors EMC meeting with you. In any event, it is hoped that you will find time to study it and indicate your comments and decided action.

6. Proposal for Consultancy Unit Within FCDA

Now may not be the most propitious moment to consider setting up a consultancy unit within FCDA – office accommodation alone would present a problem – but as this was part of the instruction when you sought the consultancy review it is re-submitted now. It was originally submitted on 20th June 1982 but may have been overlooked.

JRM

CPE 2nd September 1982.

Note. Items not attached – not now available to me.

(a) Copy of the Review of Consultancy.

(b) Minutes of the Board Meeting on 27th July 1982.

(c) Minister's Address to Meeting on 17th/18th August 1982.

(d) Copy of Form 'A' with guide notes.

JM

31st May 1998

* * * * *

To the Director of Architecture

Report on the Review of Consultancy

1. In your capacity as a staff member of the Committee appointed by the Board to deal with action required concerning the Consultancy Review, it is right that you should now assume responsibility for its continuance. As you know, I have been unable to give any time to this matter due to preoccupation with the Government Guest House and now I am taking some leave.

2. At present, you have all the Forms 'A' returned by those Consultants who attended the meeting in August in Suleja. You also have blank Forms 'A' with other relevant papers to send out to Consultants who were not at the meeting but who should be required to provide completed Forms 'A' as soon as possible otherwise the records will not be comprehensive. I had intended to identify these from various sources including the attached papers, but I am sure you will be able to do so from records in your own Department. It is important, if possible, that all should be contacted particularly those concerned with buildings and quickly.

3. We have already discussed the area of consultancy in which the real potential financial commitment is very heavy – namely architecture – and agreed that those concerned with Ministries, Parastatals, facilities such as Health Centres, Neighbourhood Centres etc., in the various areas such as BCDEF, IJKL, MNOP, must be thoroughly and, perhaps, ruthlessly, reviewed so as to bring about a significant reduction in the drain on limited financial resources. Moreover, I must remind you that, particularly in the Central Area, the situation is complicated by the Directive regarding height restriction to 15 floors which cannot be ignored. In these cases, however, where postponement of consultancy may be decided upon, the question of revision (if applicable) to comply with the Directive can also be postponed and will only arise if and when the consultancy concerned is revived.

4. We have agreed that, by and large, present engineering and planning Consultancies should continue but these should be discussed with the Directors concerned to ensure that any which can be postponed or cancelled are dealt with in that way as soon as possible. Clearly, no new ones should be necessary particularly in regard to soils investigations for Ministries and Parastatals which are, in effect, being halted.

5. It seems likely that the coming financial year will be one of 'consolidation' in the sense that the financial restraints will be such as to preclude progress with projects. Nonetheless, it is still essential for the Board to determine its development strategy for the next two years so that you have that in mind when preparing recommendations for postponing etc., present Consultancies. Otherwise you will be unable to put forward proposals in that regard to the Consultancy Review Committee. You may wish to discuss these aspects with the Hon. Minister in his capacity as Chairman of the Committee – also, of course, with the Permanent Secretary.

6. Associated with this Consultancy Review is the proposal I made some time ago (under direction from the Permanent Secretary) for setting up a Consultancy Unit within FCDA. I am still of the view that this is feasible and should be initiated. You should have a copy of my proposals in this matter. The Permanent Secretary has had a copy for a long time but, so far, has not commented to me.

7. I would strongly urge that this Review of Consultancy should be carried through with all seriousness otherwise the Authority cannot avoid its cumulative burden.

8. This Memo, copied to the Permanent Secretary

J.R.M.

CPE

17th October 1982

* * * * *

Alhaji Aliyu Mohammed
Permanent Secretary
Federal Capital Development Authority
PMB 24
Suleja
Niger State
Nigeria

11th November 1982

Dear Alhaji Aliyu Mohammed

I promised I would let you know my position once I was at home.

For family and personal reasons I have to tell you that it is not possible for me to return to Nigeria certainly by the 19th November. As you know too, I became increasingly out of sympathy with the whole concept of the new Capital and I remain utterly convinced that the Project must be completely re-appraised if it is to succeed and avoid being a disastrous failure.

I will write again soon and, of course, I must tell the President my position.

Yours sincerely

Jack Muggeridge

* * * * *

Alhaji Shehu Shagari
President of the Federal Republic of Nigeria
State House
Ribadu Road
Lagos

2nd December 1982

Dear Mr President,

I wrote to the Permanent Secretary of FCDA on the 11th November to explain why for family and personal reasons I found I could not return to Nigeria at the end of my leave on 18th November 1982.

However, you are aware of the deeper – and for me, very sad – reasons for my non-return, certainly at present. How glad I am that I was able to keep my promise to you about the Guest House at Abuja despite all the difficulties. Once I became personally responsible for it, I realised why you called on me to return as I had said I always would if you wished it. It was God's will that thereby I was able to show my love and respect for the Alhaji Shehu Shagari I served with all devotion in Sokoto. Would that it were possible for that personal service to embrace the whole concept of the new Capital about which I remain utterly convinced that it must be completely re-appraised if it is to succeed and avoid being a disastrous failure. I just cannot work for FCDA as now constituted with its gross incompetence, widespread corruption, complete indiscipline and lack of all dedication. I do grieve so much that I am unable to make sure of the creation of the splendid new Capital of which you should be so proud and for which you should be remembered for evermore by your countrymen.

I know you will understand my feelings about not returning to Nigeria as of now.

With deepest affection and respect

Jack Muggeridge

* * * * *

Mr J.R. Muggeridge
Darnley Lodge
Maidenhead
Berks

29th December 1982

My Dear Jack,

I thank you most sincerely for your letter dated 2nd December 1982 which I received on Christmas day. While wishing Merry Christmas and Happy New Year, I feel rather sad that you have decided not to come back to us for reasons which, of course, I fully understand. I do appreciate your feelings of disappointment in regard to Abuja and you know that I share these views with you. The only difference is that you are an Engineer while I am a Politician and we tackle our problems from different angles. I assure you that I am dealing with the matter in my own slow but sure manner.

I like to express my sincere thanks to you for your kindness and respect to me personally and for your interest and devotion to Nigeria. You have certainly honourably fulfilled your promise to me and did a wonderful job in preparing the beautiful Guest House at Abuja in record time. It will join the Kaduna and Sokoto Markets as monuments of your untiring efforts, dedication to duty and love for Nigeria. Words will not be adequate to thank you for your contributions to the development of Nigeria which you have served so loyally the best part of your life. It is still my hope and prayer that you will again one day decide to add more to your laurels by returning to continue with your good work.

Thank you and Happy New Year to you and all the members of your family.

Yours very sincerely

Alhaji Shehu Shagari
President of the Federal Republic of Nigeria

* * * * *

Eng. Jack Muggeridge MBE   *Hotel Nassauer Hof*
Flat 39 Mander Court   Wiesbaden
8 Derby Road
Caversham
Reading RG4 5EY
United Kingdom

9th July 1997

My Dear Jack,

I was delighted to meet and talk to you once again in London last week. I felt rather flattered by the generous remarks about me in your draft memories which has given me more than fair share in a whole chapter of your very busy and useful life. But I know that you have been speaking with your heart and I thank you immensely.

I have carefully gone through the papers which you handed over to me. I have decided to pass them back to you from here in Germany with my Comments simply because I wanted to make up for the time that I have wasted before responding to your letter dated 20th July 1997.

I believe the best approach to these matters is for me to make side remarks where appropriate so as to attempt to answer your questions. I strongly suggest that in future you should send me direct questions rather than a draft and I will try to quickly answer them as best as I can.

This approach could also, in my opinion, reduce to the minimum the problem of your having to go through the arduous task of reading a series of books and magazines.

I have completed my medical check-up today and happily the reports have been rather encouraging. I intend to return home over the week-end and look forward to receiving your questionnaires as soon as possible. If however you prefer the first approach I will gladly accept and try to comply. Thank you.

With great admiration and affection
Yours always

Shehu U.A. Shagari
Turakin Sokoto

* * * * *

20th July 1997

Dearest Friend,

Thank you so much for your letter and papers of 9th July 1997 which reached me three days ago. So very typical of your genuine interest and help towards what I have set out to do.

I agree at once to your direct question and answer suggestion for the future. I will now feel freer to pose questions of a Nigeria-wide basis regarding the content of the earlier Chapters still to be attempted.

The Chapter on FCDA has still to be completed, of course. Questions are bound to arise.

I shall relish the recollection of our meeting in London until we meet again in July 1998.

My warmest greetings to your family
For you, abiding affection and every good wish,

Jack Muggeridge.

* * * * *

Jack Muggeridge MBE CEng FICE FIHT Retired
Full Member of The Institution of Royal Engineers
Flat 39 Mander Court,
8 Derby Road,
Caversham,
Reading RG4 5EY
Revised Tel. 0118 9473819

12th March 1998.

Dearest Friend,

Am I right to be looking forward to seeing you in London in July this year? I long to see you.

Towards the end of 1997 I had to put aside the Memoir when, unexpectedly, more papers, cuttings etc., of my brother Malcolm came to light which should have been included in the great mass I sent to the USA soon after his death for the Special Collections at the Buswell Library of Wheaton College Illinois. Under an Agreement he had made with the College all his papers, memorabilia, were to go there and be available to accredited researchers and other interested parties. I had spent four delightful days at the Collection in November 1994 helping the staff over queries, deciphering manuscripts and so on. These later papers were not in good order and a number of manuscripts required transcribing – his handwriting was always very difficult for those not familiar with it – and, in any case, many explanatory notes were necessary. Eventually, I was able to get everything away just before Christmas.

Now I must concentrate on the Memoir with special attention to the concluding Chapters dealing with Sokoto State (SUDA) and Federal Capital Development Authority (FCDA). You have seen the draft of the SUDA Chapter which, however, on re-reading, requires some editing to give it a 'sharper' effect. This can be done later.

Also you have seen the draft introductory pages of the FCDA Chapter which, for me, is certainly the most sensitive and significant Chapter of the Memoir.

Despite the intrusion of the Malcolm papers, I have made time to gather together documents (reports, letters etc.) relevant to my time – short as it was – with FCDA. While doing this, I found my concern increasing as to how this time should be written up as a record of public service but bearing much in mind that it took place in an atmosphere charged with strong personal feelings within a quasi-political situation.

My letter to you dated 12th April 1982, written only a few weeks after joining FCDA, although expressing strong support for your ethical revolution, included 'how very disappointed' I was about FCDA. Then followed my long unrestrained personal letter of 22nd May 1982 sent in the knowledge that you would be visiting Abuja early in June.

In the event, you came, you inspected and held a meeting with the Permanent Secretary, Ministers and officials. The Minutes of that meeting – I was given a copy – clearly indicated your own growing concern. Before you left, you called for me and I was able to 'open up' to you. Thenceforward, I had to decide that my personal regard for you must override other considerations and that you must receive copies of my reports, past and present, while I remained with FCDA in addition to personal letters in which I could be unrestrained. I intend, therefore, to build the rest of the FCDA Chapter around my reports and letters. Only in this way can I adequately account for my period with FCDA.

One difficulty is that I do not have a copy of my crucial report on Consultancy which, in fact, set in train all that followed. It is this, perhaps, which is the most revealing of the canker within FCDA. My report was presented to the Board at its meeting on 27th July 1982. Is it possible that you have kept a copy? If so, please do not take the trouble to send it to be but be kind enough to have it with you in July. I will then photostat and return to you by post.

Of course, you will see every word that I produce and give me your advice as to inclusiveness or exclusiveness of copy documents.

Away now from FCDA! My record of our meeting in London on 8th July 1995 shows that you told me you had completed your autobiography and that it would be published by *Heinemann* in Nigeria. Has it come out? I could order a copy through *Heinemann* UK.

With abiding affection and every good wish

Jack

PS I include a photostat copy of this letter because it is easier to read. Cotton ribbons – needed for elderly portable typewriters like this one – are no longer available and the modern nylon ribbon does not suit. We oldies are the forgotten people today!

* * * * *

Eng. Jack Muggeridge MBE
Flat 39 Mander Court
8 Derby Road
Caversham
Reading RG4 5EY
England

22 Shehu Crescent
Adarawa
PO Box 162
Sokoto
Nigeria

17th May 1998

My Dear Jack,

I thought it will be useful to respond to your letter dated 12th March, 1998 before I arrive in London on 28th July 1998 for my usual annual vacation. I know that you expect me to reply perhaps in as much detail as you have recalled events during your short but memorable period at the FCDA. Unfortunately however the episode of 31st December 1983 has caused the tragic loss of all my records which explains why it has taken so long for me to complete my autobiography. On that occasion the ADC to General Buhari (who incidentally is now the Emir of Gwandu) seized all the papers in my private Library in the State House, Ribadu Road, Lagos and up to this day they cannot be traced! I therefore envy you and your late brother Malcolm for being so fortunate with your personal records of service to humanity. Congratulations.

I will not, however, ever forget your kindness and devotion to me as a friend for everything you did in SUDA and FCDA to make my work easy. With your valuable advice I have been able to check the menacing situation in Abuja and bring it to a reasonably manageable situation before I was forced out of the scene. You are perhaps aware that on my brief second term in office I made drastic changes in work and staff at the FCDA, that things had already started to move in the right direction by the end of 1983. A lot of water has passed under the bridge since then. Nevertheless it is gratifying to observe that the pessimism expressed in your letter from Suleja dated 22nd May 1982 has now been happily debunked. The real Capital City of Abuja has at last emerged and Jack Muggeridge is still alive and kicking! It might not be the Abuja of your dreams but it is still beautiful and modern, at least on African standards. The cankerworm of corruption and graft still persists here as elsewhere in this filthy world of ours, but our consolation must lie in the Wisdom and Justice of the Almighty Allah who oversees whatever is happening in this Universe. I have strong faith that He will never let us down.

Looking forward to meeting you once again in London. Thank you.
Sincerely yours

Shehu U.A. Shagari
Turakin Sokoto.

NB Note by Jack to Gerrit Jan: Shehu Shagari usually visited London at the end of June or in early July so '28th July' must be a mistake by his secretary. He arrived on 28th June and tried to contact me by telephone, but failed to notice the change of number on one of my letters. He eventually reached me on Friday and I was able to see him on Saturday just before he left for Germany.

* * * * *

Jack Muggeridge MBE CEng FICE FIHT Retired

6th June 1998

Dearest Friend

I was delighted to receive your letter of 17th May and to know that I must be patient until the end of July when I will have the joy of seeing you in London. I will be agog for your call.

How cruel that all your personal papers were seized. Yet so typical. Those who usurp power by force become haunted by the fear that someone will do likewise to them, and are obsessed by a sense of insecurity, ever suspicious and watchful for plots against them to be found in such sources as personal papers, telephone calls and the like.

I knew I had only to tell you the truth about FCDA for you to take necessary action and it is sad that, in December 1983, you were unjustly denied further progress.

Herewith, in draft, are the last pages of the Chapter of the Memoir headed 'Federal Capital Development Authority' so that when we meet you will be able to suggest any changes. Please, you will do so freely.

With abiding love and Best Wishes,

Jack

* * * * *

Obituary Published in *The Royal Engineers Journal* August 2001

J.R. Muggeridge MBE

Born 15th August 1909, died 30th March 2001, aged 91

Whilst Jack Muggeridge was a fervent admirer and erstwhile supporter of his elder brother, the journalist and broadcaster Malcolm Muggeridge, he enjoyed a successful and long career in his own right as a Civil Engineer. Born in Croydon, he was the youngest son of Henry Thomas Muggeridge, later to become Labour MP for Romford, and his wife Annie. Jack started his career in Civil Engineering as Engineering Assistant to the County Borough of Croydon, and later to the Borough of Margate, and appointed Senior Assistant in Southgate, North London in 1936.

Captain Jack Muggeridge Royal Engineers

At the outbreak of the Second World War he initially joined the Civil Defence Service being in a reserved occupation within a local authority but was eventually able to secure his release and be commissioned into the Royal Engineers in 1942. After spending some time training officers in Bailey Bridge construction, he was selected to work with Donald Bailey, superintendent and senior designer at the Experimental Bridging Establishment in Christchurch. By the time of Captain

Muggeridge's arrival in Christchurch, the first production bridges were already in service in Europe and the Far East and over 600 firms became involved in the mass production of bridge components and during the last three years of the war some 500,000 tonnes were manufactured, representing over 200 miles of bridging. Jack Muggeridge, already expert on Bailey Bridge construction and launching techniques, became part of a small team of technical officers working closely with Donald Bailey involved in further developing and stretching the capabilities of the revolutionary bridging system, testing the strength of new materials and components and solving the practical problems fed back to EBE from experiences in the field.

After the war he resumed peacetime occupation as Deputy Borough Engineer for the Borough of Southgate from 1946. In 1958 Jack left the UK to work as Provincial Engineer for the Ministry of Works in Northern Nigeria. He used his war service bridging experience to good effect carrying out many special bridging assignments in Nigeria, often replacing weak wooden bridges carried away by floods with Bailey Bridges, or else providing temporary crossings during the demolition and replacement of inadequate road bridges. He was awarded the MBE in 1969. On independence in 1971 Jack was appointed Chief Engineer to the new Kaduna Capital Development Board with the challenging task of helping to develop the new State capital, Sokoto. He was for many years a close advisor and friend to Dr Alhaji Shehu Shagari, former President of Nigeria until deposed by a military coup in 1984.

Leaving Nigeria in 1980, and already well past the normal retirement age for overseas work, Jack later spent six months in Malaysia with Oxfam where he worked with the Malaysian Red Crescent Society supervising the maintenance and improvement of refugee camps set up there to care for the many thousands of Vietnamese boat people. He said that this particular period was 'an unforgettable experience' and crystallised for him the desperate need for qualified engineers in such places, providing the expertise in laying on basic services such as clean drinking water and sanitation.

Returning to the UK, he became Secretary to the newly formed Register of Engineers for Disaster Relief (RedR), the charity aimed at overcoming the difficulties experienced by relief organisations such as Oxfam and Save the Children Fund in recruiting professional engineers to join disaster relief teams.

Further brief consultancy spells in Nigeria followed in 1982 and 1984 before he again returned to his REDR work. He finally retired in 1990 at the age of 81, still very fit and active. Jack spent his last years in Berkshire, visited regularly as a point of reference by many friends and associates of Malcolm. It had fallen to Jack to also care for Malcolm and Kitty during his brother and sister-in-law's final years in Robertsbridge. At a stage when Malcolm felt no longer able to leave the house, interviewers would turn up at Park Cottage with their outside broadcast equipment and record their sound bites under Jack's direction. After Malcolm's death in November 1990, Jack's small apartment in Reading held a number of significant and interesting photographs of his brother's life and times, along with a full collection of published works, and he became a vital point of reference in the preparation of biographies and articles on Malcolm. Jack would send many a letter to those who wrote and reflected on various aspects of his brother's often controversial career and any perceived slights, errors and omissions in their recollections were firmly 'corrected' and, perhaps, more than occasionally sanitized.

In the past year in which he celebrated his 91st birthday with a trip on the London Eye, Jack took a keen Civil Engineer's interest in the problems surrounding the Millennium Bridge, the design and execution of which he greatly admired. No doubt influenced by his long experience in Nigeria, he maintained that all bridges needed to have considerable natural movement and this feature should in his view have been exploited as an interesting attribute rather than a problem to eliminate.

Jack married Sylvia (née Jenkins) in 1943 and leaves four sons, one daughter, eleven grandchildren and a great-grandson.

* * * * *

Obituary as published in *The Independent*

by Nicholas Flynn
10th April 2001

John Raymond Muggeridge, Civil Engineer: born Sanderstead, Surrey 15th August 1909; MBE 1969; Secretary, RedR (Registered Engineers for Disaster Relief) 1979-89: married 1943 Sylvia Jenkins (four sons, one daughter; marriage dissolved 1962); died Reading 30th March 2001.

In 1982 Richard Hall of *The Observer* travelled to Abuja, in the heart of Nigeria, to visit the world's largest construction site – the building of the new state capital – "a vision so colossal that no-one could name the ultimate cost."

It was a chaotic scene where cranes rose above a jungle in which contractors battled against time, political uncertainty, and the exotic location. "At the centre of the vortex," Hall found a calm, white-haired 72-year-old man working 15 hours a day, who had been persuaded by the Nigerian President, Shehu Shagari, to leave his retirement home in Britain to come and oversee the project. The man was Jack Muggeridge.

I met Muggeridge myself for the first time a year or so later at the house of his brother Malcolm, the writer and broadcaster. He hardly mentioned his adventures in Abuja, nor did he give any indication of his work helping Vietnamese boat people in Malaysia, or the extent of his involvement with the charity RedR (Registered Engineers for Disaster Relief) which he had co-founded in 1979. He was content merely to chat about his brother's work and was a meticulously well-mannered and charming companion. It was impossible not to realise, though, that you were in the presence of a remarkable person who had lived, and was continuing to live, his long life to the full.

John Raymond Muggeridge was born in Sanderstead, Surrey, in 1909, the youngest of five sons born to H.T. Muggeridge, the pioneer socialist and Labour MP, and his wife Annie. Soon after Jack's birth the family moved to 17 Birdhurst Gardens, a semi-detached house in South Croydon, designed by H.T. and built by a co-operative. In this more prosperous setting the Fabian activities of the family and the exuberance of the Muggeridge boys – Douglas, Stanley, Malcolm, Eric and Jack – were viewed askance by their more sedate and conservatively minded neighbours. Certainly it was an unusual household, one in which such concepts as the overthrow of capitalism and the inevitable triumph of a virtuous and downtrodden proletariat formed the backdrop of family life.

The boys' situation was further complicated by the fact that their father had singled out Malcolm (in whom he felt he had discerned a special brilliance that would outshine the others) to fulfil vicariously all that he himself had, through poverty and circumstance, been denied. This favoured role involved Malcolm in a special relationship with his father, as well as a Cambridge University education, from which the four other brothers were excluded.

Understandably, Douglas and Eric seem to have felt some resentment at this situation – Stanley's reaction remains unrecorded, as he died in a motorcycle accident in 1922. Jack, however, seems to have been completely unconcerned.

After attending a small junior school near his home, Jack joined his brothers in 1918 at the Croydon Borough Secondary School at the early age of nine. On completing his education he decided on Civil Engineering as a career and got a job with the Borough of Croydon. He later moved on to Margate and then to Southgate in north London.

Muggeridge's abilities stood him in good stead during the Second World War when, despite his reserved occupation status, he managed to leave the Civil Defence Service and join the Royal Engineers in 1942. He rose to the rank of captain, and eventually joined Donald Bailey in Christchurch, Hampshire, as part of an élite team developing and refining Bailey's design for a modular bridging system, the great advantage of this method being that the components were readily transportable, could be assembled in the field and could take far heavier loads than previous constructions. In 1943 Muggeridge married Sylvia Jenkins.

Resuming civilian life after the war, Muggeridge returned to Southgate as Deputy Engineer. By 1956 however, the financial strain of supporting a growing family prompted him to look for more lucrative employment abroad and he accepted the position of Provincial Engineer in the Zaria Province for the Ministry of Works in Nigeria. He was later to describe it as "…the best of jobs".

Spartan living conditions in the intense heat and long hours of fruitful work suited Muggeridge, and while other Europeans weakened their constitutions with the temptations of club life, he was content to exist on a meagre diet and a simple routine. Perhaps inevitably, the long periods away from home that the job entailed eventually took their toll and in 1962 he and Sylvia were divorced.

Jack Muggeridge had become a close friend of Shehu Shagari, who was the first President of Nigeria after the declaration of Independence in 1971. Shagari recruited Muggeridge for the monumental task of supervising the development of a new state capital at Abuja, a task that would occupy him up to and beyond his retirement.

In 1979 Muggeridge and a friend, Peter Guthrie, with the help of £1,000 donated by Oxfam, set up RedR, a charity devoted to bringing relief in disasters by selecting and training personnel to be supplied to humanitarian aid agencies worldwide. After his retirement, apart from six months spent with Oxfam in Malaysia improving refugee camps for the Vietnamese boat people, and two more stints in Abuja in 1982 and 1984, Muggeridge spent the next 10 years working as Voluntary Secretary to RedR.

Throughout the 1980s Muggeridge combined his work with RedR with a self-appointed role of general factotum to his brother Malcolm and Malcolm's wife Kitty. As they became increasingly frail he tried to provide a buffer between them and the demands laid on them by Malcolm's fame. After Malcolm's death in 1990, Jack took on the massive task of sorting and collating all of his papers before their transportation to Wheaton College in Chicago where they are now held. He went through thousands of items, deciphered and typed illegible letters, and finally he visited Wheaton in 1994 to lecture on his brother's work.

Jack's flat in Reading, in which he spent his last years, became a sort of HQ in the battle to protect his brother's name from his many detractors. Willing as he was to help anyone who was genuinely interested (Richard Ingrams has acknowledged the extensive help he received when working on his 1995 book Muggeridge), Jack was indefatigable when he thought Malcolm's name was being unjustly used.

When Gregory Wolfe brought out a biography the same year, Jack Muggeridge was surprised to find his own name placed among those whom Wolfe claimed had helped him. As it happened, he had only learnt of the book's existence through a bookseller's advance list and had received one letter from the author in the year before its publication. He produced a 53-page document detailing what he thought to be the book's inaccuracies and intentional slurs. This was then deposited at Wheaton College for the use of future scholars.

Anyone visiting Muggeridge in this last decade could not but have been aware of the innate goodness of the man and of the serenity stemming from his deep Christian faith. If they had been invited to visit around midday, a meal would have been prepared and covered with a tablecloth. After a chat and a cup of tea Muggeridge would spring up and say, "How about some lunch?" whipping off the cloth with great panache to reveal a few tomatoes, a small dish of pickled beetroot and some bread and cheese. If you ventured at his insistence to take a second tomato, you could tell that he was marvelling at the extraordinary appetite of the younger generation.

That he lost none of his courage and independence right up to the end of his life was shown during his 87th year when he discovered, on two separate occasions, that his car had been stolen from outside his flat. When the police proved unable to help, Muggeridge started walking around Reading and its environs until he found the car, the first time parked in a residential street, the second in a supermarket car park. He then took the keys from his pocket, got in and drove it home.

* * * * *

Obituary as published in the *RedR Newsletter* No. 55 Autumn 2001
by Peter Guthrie, RedR founder

RedR member Jack Muggeridge who died aged 91 was a cornerstone of RedR from early in its development until it came of age in the later '80s.

On seeing an announcement in the technical press that RedR had been formed to assist the frontline agencies to respond more effectively to disaster relief, Jack immediately volunteered. I had worked for Jack in 1974 as a fresh graduate on VSO in Kaduna, Nigeria where Jack was the Chief Engineer of the Kaduna Capital Development Board. Recognising my name in the press report, Jack felt he could be of use and was very quickly assigned to become one of the first RedR volunteers, working with Vietnamese Boat People in Malaysia. On his return after three months, Jack became the almost unpaid Secretary of RedR, working out of Scott Wilson's office (and living in our house) in Basingstoke for several years until the ICE kindly agreed to make space available, initially in Eccleston Square and later in Gt George Street. When Jack went on his assignment he was 72 and he only left RedR when the President of Nigeria personally beseeched him to return to Abuja to sort out a major construction project.

Jack loved RedR (he insisted on calling it R.E.D.R.) and was in turn held in the greatest affection by every member. It was widely accepted that experience in Nigeria counted heavily in one's favour when being selected for an assignment, and the register, although computerised very early on, was held in its entirety in Jack's head, along with an awesome amount of detail.

Earlier this year, my wife Lorna and I attended Jack's funeral where the many facets of Jack's fascinating life were revealed always showing a man of compassion, of principle, of integrity and a deep commitment to helping others. Many members of his family were largely unaware of the enormous contribution Jack made to a small, new, unfashionable organisation, which simply would not have survived its early years without his tireless efforts and profound commitment. As a result of my year working under his direction in Nigeria, I was honestly able to say that Jack had had a deep and lasting effect on my professional life and I am privileged to have known him. RedR is fortunate indeed to have had Jack as its first Secretary, and we all owe him much.

Note: RedR - Engineers for Disaster Relief - relieves suffering in disasters by selecting, training and providing competent and effective personnel to humanitarian aid agencies worldwide. Its President is HRH The Princess Royal. Website: www.redr.org

* * * * *

Obituary as published in *The Daily Telegraph*

4th May 2001

JACK MUGGERIDGE, who has died aged 91, put his wartime experience in the construction of Bailey bridges to good use in post-war overseas disaster relief.

A Civil Engineer, Muggeridge left Britain in 1958 to work for the Ministry of Works in Northern Nigeria. There, he used his bridging experience to good effect, replacing weak wooden bridges carried away by floods with Bailey bridges, and organising temporary crossings while inadequate road bridges were being replaced.

Subsequently, after Nigeria had gained Independence from Britain, Muggeridge became chief engineer to the Kaduna Capital Development Board, charged with the challenging task of helping to develop the new state capital, Kaduna, and the surrounding area.

He later served a similar role in the development of the city of Sokoto, also in Northern Nigeria; and he was for many years a friend and adviser to Dr Alhaji Shehu Shagari, the President of Nigeria until he was deposed by a military coup.

Muggeridge left Nigeria in 1980 and spent six months with Oxfam in Malaysia, where he worked with the Malaysian Red Crescent Society, supervising the maintenance and improvement of refugee camps set up to care for the Vietnamese boat people. The experience left a deep impression on him, and reinforced his belief in the pressing need for qualified engineers in such situations to provide the essential services of clean drinking water and sanitation.

On his return to Britain, he became founder secretary to the Register of Engineers for Disaster Relief (RedR), a charity set up to help such organisations as Oxfam and the Save the Children Fund to recruit qualified engineers to disaster relief teams.

John Raymond Muggeridge, always known as Jack, was born at Croydon on 15th August 1909, the youngest son of Henry Muggeridge, who later became Labour MP for Romford. Jack's elder brother was the journalist and broadcaster Malcolm Muggeridge.

After school, Muggeridge became an engineering assistant to the County Borough of Croydon, and later to the Borough of Margate, Kent. In 1936, he was appointed Senior Engineering Assistant to the Borough of Southgate, north London. With the outbreak of the Second World War in 1939, Muggeridge remained with his local authority in a reserved occupation until 1942, when he was commissioned into the Royal Engineers.

After spending some time training officers in the construction of Bailey bridges – prefabricated bridges that could be speedily built for emergency use – Muggeridge was selected to work with Donald Bailey himself, then superintendent and senior designer at the Experimental Bridging Establishment at Christchurch, Dorset.

By this time, the first Bailey bridges were already in service in Europe and the Far East, and more than 600 Firms were involved in the production of bridge components. Muggeridge became part of a small team of technical officers involved in developing the bridge's capabilities, testing the strength of new materials and components and solving practical problems that arose in the field.

After the war, Muggeridge returned to the Borough of Southgate as Chief Engineering Assistant. He was Deputy Borough Engineer of Southgate from 1946 until 1955. Before leaving for Nigeria in 1958, he worked as a Manager of a building and Civil Engineering Firm in north London.

On his return to Britain, Muggeridge continued to work for RedR until his retirement in 1990. He returned to Nigeria on two occasions, in 1982 and 1984, to consult on the development of the country's new federal capital, Abuja. Jack Muggeridge was appointed MBE in 1969.

He married, in 1943, Sylvia Jenkins; they had four sons and a daughter.

* * * * *

318

Family

Photographs

Jack and Sally at a Buckingham Palace Garden Party
19th July 1990

Jack with Malcolm and Kitty at *Park Cottage*

Park Cottage with *The Ark* on the right where Jack lived for some time

Jack at *Park Cottage* with his son John and nephew Leonard

On the canals with grandson Jonathan

Jack with his great-grandson Oliver

Jack and Sally on the London Eye in August 2000,
91st birthday treat

On his 90th birthday with Sylvia and his eldest son Robert

Family and friends gathering on his 90th birthday

The Church at Whatlington in East Sussex
final resting place for Jack and other family members

Sally tending her father's grave wearing his favourite cardigan

Sally with Shehu Shagari on a visit to London in June 2004

Bibliography

Wakar Nijeriya (Verse, written in Hausa) by Alhaji Shehu Shagari
Northern Nigerian Publishing Company Ltd. 1973, Reprinted 1978

The Story of Nigeria by Michael Crowder
Faber and Faber 1962, 1966

President and Power in Nigeria – The Life of Shehu Shagari
by David Williams *Frank Cass & Co. Ltd.* 1982 ISBN 0-7146-3182-5

Democratic Heroes of Northern Nigeria by M.I. Aliyu
Baraka Press and Publishers Ltd 2004 ISBN 978-135-117-9

Shehu Shagari – The Biography of Nigeria's First Executive President
by Okion Ojigbo *Tokion (Nigeria) Company* 1982 ISBN 978-30008-0-2

Shehu Shagari – An Autobiography by Shehu Shagari
Heinemann Educational Books (Nigeria) Plc 2001 ISBN 978 129 940 1

Shehu Shagari: My Vision of Nigeria by Aminu Tijjani & David Williams
Frank Cass & Co. Ltd 1981 ISBN 0 7146 31817

Meet Mr President
Federal Government of Nigeria Publication

Beckoned to Serve by Alhaji Shehu Shagari
Heinemann Educational Books (Nigeria) plc. 2001

My Life by Alhaji Sir Ahmadu Bello (Sardauna of Sokoto)
Cambridge University Press 1962

My Command – An Account of the Nigerian Civil War 1967-1970 by General Olusegun Obasanjo *Heinemann Educational Books* 1980 ISBN 978-129-784-0 (Nigeria) 0-435-96533-6 (UK)

Soldiers and Oil – The Political Transformation of Nigeria Edited by Keith Panter-Brick *Frank Cass & Co. Ltd* 1978 ISBN 0 7146 3098 5

The Biafra Story: The Making of an African Legend by Frederick Forsyth *Penguin* 1969

Yakabu Gowon: Faith in a United Nigeria by John D. Clarke *Frank Cass & Co. Ltd* 1986 ISBN 07146 32864

Four Guineas – A Journey Through West Africa by Elspeth Huxley The Reprint Society, London 1955

The First Dance of Freedom – Black Africa in the Post War Era by Martin Meredith *Hamish Hamilton* 1984